SLOUCHING TOWARD TYRANNY

Slouching Toward Tyranny

Mass Incarceration, Death Sentences and Racism

Joseph B. Ingle

Algora Publishing
New York

Library of Congress Cataloging-in-Publication Data —

Ingle, Joseph B. (Joseph Burton), 1946-
    Slouching toward tyranny: Mass Incarceration, Death Sentences and Racism / Joseph
B. Ingle.
        pages cm
    Includes bibliographical references and index.
    ISBN 978-1-62894-120-3 (soft cover: alk. paper) — ISBN 978-1-62894-121-0 (hard
cover: alk. paper) — ISBN 978-1-62894-122-7 (ebook) 1. Discrimination in criminal justice
administration—United States—History. 2. Discrimination in capital punishment—
United States—History. 3. Race discrimination—United States—History. 4. United
States—Race relations—History. I. Title.
    HV8699.U5I54 2015
    364.3'400973—dc23
                                    2014049136

Cover image: Prison fence razor ribbon wire. Creative Commons.

Printed in the United States

For the way makers:
  Bill Alexander,
  Will Campbell,
  John Egerton,
  John Ensign,
  Emile Joffrion,
  Andy Lipscomb,
  Charles Merrill,
  and Bill Webber,
                and
                Becca

Acknowledgments

When a work takes two decades to complete due to execution crises and the vicissitudes of life, the writer draws upon a number of people for assistance.

The first draft of *Tyranny* received careful review by Mary Egerton Higgs and the benefit of her editorial skills. She came my way through the recommendation of her brother John Egerton, a friend and fine writer who encouraged me and many others in the writing life.

Tony Dunbar also looked at an early draft and provided helpful comments. Tony's friendship since our days with Southern Prison Ministry in the early 1970s and his writing continue to be a blessing in my life.

Art Gatewood, Bob Pryor and Bob Brewbaker have been encouraging of my writing for many years. Their friendship has sustained me through this and my other works. Together, we comprise the four "amigos" who kayak together each spring, celebrating our friendship of forty years.

John Vile gave the manuscript a careful read after it was completed and made helpful grammatical suggestions which had escaped me.

My students in the Osher class I taught at Vanderbilt University gave me a forum for sharing these ideas. I am grateful for their receptivity and dialogue.

Ken Penegar is the one person who has seen this work through for me, from beginning to end. Not only did we spend months going over it in detail, his honest appraisal and our ongoing discussions reaffirmed my commitment to seeing the work published. And it was Ken who brought Algora Publishing to my attention; I appreciate their diligence and support in bringing this project to completion.

Finally, to my brothers and sisters, some dead and others still alive, who have allowed me into their lives while condemned by the State, I owe a debt that can never be paid. They have graced me with their presence and honesty, their failings and their humanity, their friendship and their love. It was by being with them in their suffering that I learned something was terribly wrong in this country. Witnessing the cruelty to which they were subjected through the entire machinery of state killing almost drove me mad. But it also compelled me to grapple and seek to understand how this could be happening. They are the midwives of this book.

Sole gratia,
Joe Ingle

"There is no document of civilization that is not at the same time a document of barbarism."

— Walter Benjamin

Table of Contents

Introduction

When I went to Harvard University on a Merrill Fellowship in the spring of 1991, I did so for two reasons: 1) To leave the killing ground of the South where I had lost over twenty people to the executioner since 1979, and 2) To try to begin to comprehend what I had experienced through the killing machinery in the various Southern states. The time at Harvard commenced a twenty-year process of reading, writing (*The Inferno: A Southern Morality Tale*, 2012) and continued work with the condemned. I wrote the present book as a result of the reflection and work begun at Harvard which continued with my return to the South.

I realize that for those of us born, reared and educated in the United States of America, it is difficult to consider the government of the country in terms of tyranny. We have been inculcated with the notion that America is a democracy, indeed, the foremost advocate of democratic government and a champion of human rights throughout the world. In a very real sense, this belief in the government of the United States is as authentic as it is profound. From our beginnings with the founders of the country and the framers of the Constitution, we have aimed for lofty democratic aspirations. The Pilgrims spoke of building "a city on a hill" that would be a beacon for all to see. In the Declaration of Independence, Thomas Jefferson wrote: "We hold these truths to be self-evident, that all men are created equal, that they are endowed with certain unalienable Rights, that among them are Life, Liberty and the pursuit of Happiness."

It is this very history from which I took a deep draught through my education growing up in North Carolina. I was in Boys State in high school studying how government worked at the University of North Carolina School of Government, shook John F. Kennedy's hand when he came to Raleigh campaigning for the office of President and became a student leader in college. I helped organize major changes in the student life at St. Andrews Presbyterian College as well as actively oppose the war in Vietnam. I was the embodiment of an engaged, active citizen through my coming of age in North Carolina.

My pursuit of democratic rights led me to fight against the death penalty via Union Theological Seminary in New York and living in East Harlem. It was there I visited my first jail, and that experience led me to prison ministry when I returned to the South after graduation. And to be engaged in prison ministry in the South in 1974 meant dealing with the death penalty.

I became Director of the Southern Coalition on Jails and Prisons in the spring of 1976, the year the U.S. Supreme Court gave the country its peculiar 200th anniversary present by permitting the reinstatement of the death penalty on the July 4th weekend (*Gregg* v. *Georgia, Proffitt* v. *Florida* and *Jurek* v. *Texas*).

My colleagues and I fought against the death penalty and excessive prison incarceration across the South right through 1990. I came to know and love death-row prisoners, met with governors, bishops, U.S. and state senators and representatives, worked with victims' families, did civil disobedience and went to jail, fasted, and did simply anything and everything one could to halt the killing machinery wherever possible and make a witness against it. Yet the body count rose and my experience in the corridors of power and the death houses of the South led me to think that perhaps what I had been taught about democracy was not quite right. Maybe the government, like a runaway train, had run off the track.

Acute melancholia came in the autumns of 1988, 89 and 90. I was profoundly sad, beyond sad, really enervated. Maybe it was my emotional state, not the government, that had leapt the track. I sought counseling and with the help of a good therapist and medication began to combat the overwhelming weariness that overcame my life. During this time, William Styron buoyed me when he told me: "You can get over this. I know you don't believe me when I tell you this but you can get over it and it will never come back." Bill had known the depths of melancholia (*Darkness Visible: A Memoir of Madness*) and was kind enough to write the introduction to my book *Last Rights: 13 Fatal Encounters with the State's Justice*. Our friendship developed through the fight against the death penalty, which he abhorred.

So, I came to Harvard a broken man. What I had been taught about democracy had been repeatedly shattered as the men and women I knew on death row were exterminated no matter what information we put before governors, judges or religious leaders. Clearly, "life, liberty and the pursuit of happiness" only applied to certain people. Rarely was there justice in this process. Rather, it was all about killing and winning the next election by posturing about being tough on crime.

My time at Harvard allowed me to delve into history, take a course in constitutional law, and begin to assemble some cognitive context to my wrecked emotional landscape. And the more I read, the more I began to rethink what I had been taught. I realized there was another aspect to the historical effort to establish a truly democratic form of government in the United States. It was the story of oppression established by the very people who founded the country and wrote the Constitution. In 1991 the study of such oppression had only recently begun to be incorporated into the public consciousness. But people were beginning to consider the facts of stealing Native American land and the near extermination of the native inhabitants in America, the yoking of Africans to slavery after forcefully removing them from their homes on another continent, and the relegating of white women to second-class citizenship.

This dialectic of slavery/freedom was difficult to understand. The shards of my own emotional life revealed how little I understood it. But perhaps the primary reason for Americans to feel problematical when confronted with such contradictory history was the unique sense of righteousness we Americans maintained. Indeed, in the 20th century alone, we began with a war "to keep the world safe for democracy," then fought a second world war twenty years later against German tyranny and Japanese aggression, only to plunge into a military conflict in Korea as part of a United Nations peacekeeping force to stem Communist expansion, and, finally, to let our ideals go astray in the forests of Vietnam during the last third of the century. And now, in the 21st century, the citizens were misled into war against Iraq and a war of revenge in Afghanistan.

T.S. Eliot, in "The Four Quartets," observed: "We had the experience but missed the meaning." It became my belief that Eliot's description applied to much of Western and American history. So, let us begin our journey by considering the concept which illuminates our interpretation of American history: The racial tyranny of the majority.

The perception of a majoritarian tyranny of whites over minorities in this country was initially articulated by a Frenchman, Alexis de Tocqueville. Tocqueville's classic analysis of 19th century America, *Democracy in America*, raised the concern of the tyranny of the white majority. Tocqueville observed and feared the power of the racial majority (whites), over and against the racial minorities (blacks and Indians). Although we will examine this insight in depth later in the book, it is the fundamental perspective which guides our interpretation of American history.

As members of the white, European majority, Western civilization experienced history primarily from the conquering, triumphant perspective. Just as Tocqueville noted, this American belief in democracy became imbued with a sense of manifest destiny. Although this history has been frequently recounted, the view from the bottom up, the racial minorities suffering from the oppression of the white majority has not often been considered and this is the first recounting of it from the beginning of American history to the present day. In order to understand its personal dimension, and how it manifests itself in modern history, we turn to the life of Warren McCleskey and the landmark U.S. Supreme Court case *McCleskey v. Kemp*.

It is reasonable to wonder why one would start a history of the United States with a story that takes place in the last decades of the twentieth century. After all, this is a history so surely we should start at the beginning, the coming of white people to the New World. And why begin with one man, a condemned one, and not the broad scope of understanding needed for a book about American history?

The answer is the angle of vision of Americans, especially white Americans, in the 21st century. As W.E.B. Du Bois pointed out long ago, our vision is obscured by a veil. It is the veil of racial discrimination that still warps our perspective and understanding even in this century.

Most white people who read the last sentence will instinctually say, "Whoa. Wait a minute. We have had a civil rights movement, we have elected an African American as President of the United States, segregation is a relic of the past." All of which is true but misses the underlying reality of modern day America because racism is more subtle and sophisticated, less obvious but hardly vanquished. Warren McCleskey and his case—*McCleskey v. Kemp*—provide a teaching moment to enable us to pierce the veil and see that the ugliness of racism is still with us and is exacting a terrible toll. Or to put it in the words of Alexis de Tocqueville, the racial "tyranny of the majority" of the whites over African Americans and Native Americans is still operative in American government.

Warren McCleskey was sentenced to death for the murder of police officer Frank Schlatt in the course of a robbery in Atlanta, Georgia. He was one of four involved in the robbery, which will be detailed later in the chapter. He was the only one of the four to receive the death penalty and sent to the Georgia Diagnostic and Classification Center in Jackson, Georgia, which houses death row. It is there I came to know him.

When Warren and I became friends in the 1980s, those of us working against the death penalty in the South realized that although the U.S. Supreme Court had upheld capital punishment once again in 1976 (*Proffitt v. Florida, Gregg v. Georgia* and *Jurek v. Texas*) after striking it down in 1972 (*Furman v. Georgia*), the same realities that led to abolishing it in 1972 still existed in the South. Our first hand experience of working with the condemned, finding them lawyers, working with their families, attending trials, clearly revealed the death penalty was still reserved for the poor and discriminatory against African Americans. The studies documenting our anecdotal experiences began appearing in the late 1970s (Gross-Mauro being among the first). It was clear to us that although the constitutional standards of the law had been changed, the administration of the law had not and it was an instrument of tyranny reserved for the poor and African American.

Warren McCleskey's lawyer, Jack Boger of the NAACP Legal Defense Fund, knew what the reality of the death penalty was in the South. Jack and I were natives of North Carolina. He procured the services of Professor David Baldus to see if our experiences of the racial discrimination in administering the law could be established scientifically and taken into a court of law for remedy. Warren McCleskey was Jack's case so the Baldus study would be filed in court under Warren's name.

David Baldus undertook the most sophisticated multi-regression analysis possible in reviewing all murders committed in the state of Georgia from the passing of the law until Warren McCleskey's crime. His results were definitive and no one to the date of this writing has contradicted them. To put it simply, David Baldus and his research remain uncontroverted.

What did Professor Baldus discover with his analysis of the administration of the death penalty law in the state of Georgia? The results determined there was extensive racial discrimination in the application of capital punishment in Georgia. The data was particularly revealing on race of victim. If a white person was killed the imposition of the death penalty was 4.3 times more likely than if a black person was slain; this is over twice the level of statistical proof that correlates smoking to lung cancer. Of course, if a black person kills a white person (the charge Warren McCleskey faced at trial) the rate goes up significantly, anywhere from 11 to 22 times more likely depending on the other variables.

Once the study was completed and the proof of racial discrimination was documented, Jack Boger went to federal district court and filed *McCleskey v. Kemp*. The case was heard in federal district court, reviewed by the 11th Circuit Court of Appeals and finally the U.S. Supreme Court. In the course of the *McCleskey* case journeying through the courts, I visited Warren McCleskey on death row in Georgia. It is important to know the man as well as the case to understand the import of the racial tyranny of the majority in this country.

Warren McCleskey: The Man

Warren McCleskey, the man with the dancing brown eyes and generous smile, provides us a keyhole through which we glimpse the reality of the South in all its beauty and horror. In order to come to know him, we go to the prison that housed him in Georgia—the Georgia Diagnostic and Classification Center (GDCC).

We park the car in the lot of GDCC and shout up to the guard in the tower outside the prison. He identifies us from the memo he has received and opens the barred gate so we may proceed. We pass through and the gate shuts behind us.

We walk through a tunnel, a passageway carved through the hill which separates the prison from the outside world. Our shoes echo off the shiny linoleum floor. We've made this walk many times before. The white interior of the tunnel reminds us of Stanley Kubrick's movie *A Clockwork Orange*, but with a slight difference. In Kubrick's futuristic vision, a gang moved through a tunnel, its violence progressing toward the audience. But here, we approach the violence, moving closer to the caging and killing machinery known as death row, the death house, the electric chair.

A stairwell awaits at the end of the tunnel. We climb the steps that lead into a foyer. There, another guard asks us to remove any metal which would set off the metal detector. Belt, shoes, rings, even glasses, are placed on the table before we pass through the machine.

Having passed inspection, we reassemble our possessions and a sliding barred gate opens. We proceed into a large waiting room where we sit to await the arrival of Warren McCleskey.

When Warren initially came to death row, he met Billy Moore, another death row prisoner. They became good friends with Billy easing the way for Warren in the strange environment. As their friendship grew, they established a fund to help the prisoners who did not have any money. Death row prisoners looking out for other less fortunate prisoners reveals the village character of death row.

A guard appears at the door. He opens it and Warren McCleskey strides through. We greet Warren with a hug, then sit down on the uncomfortable stools for our two-hour visit.

Warren is dressed in prison whites with a blue stripe down the pant leg. He is of slight build with a ready smile. His hair is closely cropped and he is about 5 feet 11 inches tall. He asks about our families and we bring him up to date. The current of friendship and love rocks gently here, like a boat in a slight swell as sea.

Warren is on top of his case and we discuss its progress through the courts. But mostly we just talk about the daily exigencies of our lives. The two hours are quickly gone.

We have a prayer before we part. As we hold hands firmly, each prays aloud. Warren prays for us, not himself.

We exchange farewell hugs and the guard allows us to depart through the wire mesh door. There is much to ponder as we return to the car.

The drive back to Atlanta takes an hour. Reviewing the visit with Warren is transforming. Visiting him reminds us of Dietrich Bonhoeffer's writings from prison. The humility, the truthfulness, the love, the reconciliation and grace that pour forth as he recounts the ordinary events of prison life. He detailed taking care of those less fortunate through the fund he and Billy Moore created. His powerful Christian faith somehow transcends the state's determination to exterminate him.

Visits with Warren, and others on death row across the South, leave a piece of ourselves with the condemned. We would not have it otherwise, but it creates anxiety as we watch the appeal proceedings wind down. The electric chair awaits. The reality is that the powers and principalities in this country do not acknowledge the humanity, the child-of-God status of Warren McCleskey and the other condemned. Rather, the law has condemned them, as it did Bonhoeffer and Jesus, and the law does not have room for grace.

In the summer of 1991, after a denial of his appeal, Warren's execution date was set for September 1991. A clemency hearing was scheduled for September 24, 1991, the morning of the scheduled execution. This was the routine of state killing in Georgia.

The Trial

The chain of events that led Warren to this execution date began on May 13, 1978, at the Dixie Furniture Store in Atlanta, Georgia. Four men robbed the store and it triggered a silent alarm. Frank Schlatt, a police officer who responded to the alarm, was shot and killed at the scene.

There were four men apprehended at the scene of the crime. Of the four, only one of them volunteered information as to who killed Officer Frank Schlatt. In exchange for this testimony, Ben Wright received a reduced sentence. David Burney and Bernard Dupree, who did not talk, received life sentences. Warren McCleskey, the man Wright stated had shot Officer Schlatt, confessed to the robbery but steadfastly denied shooting anyone.

Lesson One about the death penalty: The felony murder law, someone killed in the course of a robbery, is the most common reason for the death penalty. For the state, it matters little who actually committed the killing, just so someone is given the death penalty for doing it. It is a matter of winning a case, in this instance the obtaining of perjured testimony from a thief and the actual murderer, not concern for justice or truth.

The prosecution realized that even with Ben Wright's testimony there was insufficient evidence to assure McCleskey's conviction. Although they kept the deal with Wright a secret from the defense, jury and judge, his credibility was subject to cross examination. Hence the prosecution arranged for Offie Evans to also testify against McCleskey. Evans, an informant for the police and prosecution, testified that McCleskey had confessed to him in jail that he killed the police officer. The fact that Offie Evans was an informer who had struck a deal with the prosecution for relief in his case in exchange for the bogus testimony against McCleskey was withheld from defense counsel and the jury. Warren McCleskey had confessed to nothing because he had not shot Officer Schlatt.

On October 12, 1978, on the basis of the self-serving testimony of Ben Wright and the misleading testimony of Offie Evans, Warren McCleskey was convicted of murder and sentenced to death by electrocution.

Lesson Two about the death penalty: It matters not that you may not have committed the worst murder or even committed a murder at all. What matters is that you can afford a good lawyer. Ninety percent of capital cases are defended by court-appointed lawyers who are appointed to defense because the defendant is too poor to pay for a good lawyer. As Steve Bright, a veteran of capital case defense puts it: "It is not committing the worst murder that sends someone to death row. It is having the worst lawyer."

In the battle of resources, Warren McCleskey's court-appointed lawyers had little expertise or money to mount a defense. The state of Georgia, on the other hand, spent thousands of dollars to insure McCleskey was convicted and condemned.

The Appeals

However, Warren McCleskey did have a dedicated and determined appellate lawyer in Jack Boger, who was with the NAACP Legal Defense Fund. Jack had brought David Baldus to the case and the Baldus study established the existence of significant racial discrimination in the administration of the death penalty law in Georgia. A pattern of discrimination had been revealed that clearly indicated a black person charged with killing a white person was almost predetermined to be prosecuted for the death penalty. The appeal had reached the U.S. Supreme Court and its decision had been rendered on April 22, 1987.

The U.S. Supreme Court Chief Justice was William Rehnquist. A strong supporter of the death penalty, he had spent the previous year unsuccessfully imploring Congress to restrict death row appeals. With the *McCleskey* case, he faced a dilemma. On the one hand, the data revealed the existence of racial discrimination in the functioning of the death penalty in Georgia. If this was upheld, it would result in another decision like *Furman v. Georgia*, which struck down the death penalty in 1972. On the other hand, if there was a way to defeat the *McCleskey* case despite its overwhelming evidence of racial discrimination, Chief Justice Rehnquist would have delivered a mortal blow to those lengthy appeals and the issue of racial discrimination in the use of the death penalty.

Chief Justice Rehnquist found the deciding vote in Associate Justice Lewis Powell from Virginia. Justice Powell was President of the American Bar Association. He hailed from Richmond, Virginia, the former capital of the Confederacy. Although not determinative, it is indicative of what one might expect of a racial discrimination claim considered by someone from Richmond when the actions of the Fourth Circuit Court of Appeals, headquartered in Richmond, are examined. When this body of judges met for a conference or other judicial group gatherings they would sing "Dixie," the anthem of the Confederate States of America. Indeed, Chief Justice Rehnquist joined in singing "Dixie" when he attended those judicial conferences. It is in this environment and with these colleagues that Lewis Powell practiced law. So, it would come as no surprise that *McCleskey v. Kemp* would be decided by a 5–4 vote with Associate Justice Powell writing for the majority in denying relief to Warren McCleskey.

In order to circumvent the Baldus study, the Supreme Court resorted to an old legal trick. If there is no way to get around a case which promises results justices might not wish to see, simply change the constitutional standard on which the case was brought to the Court. The constitutional standard was that a plaintiff had to establish a pattern of racial discrimination, which the Baldus study convincingly did in *McCleskey*, in order to obtain relief. By changing the standard so that the plaintiff had to prove particular discrimination, the majority of the Court invented a new standard which had not been the law when the McCleskey case was filed. So, *McCleskey* was denied 5–4 but not because he failed to prove his case under the accepted constitutional standards. Rather, he was denied because five white justices on the Supreme Court did not wish to see the result of his winning on the existing constitutional grounds. As Justice Powell asked, did McCleskey expect the Court to declare the criminal justice system unconstitutional in Georgia? The answer to that question was obviously a declarative Yes! —If the system was racist, as it was so revealed by the Baldus study, then under the law it should be deemed unconstitutional.

In his dissent, Associate Justice William Brennan eloquently bespoke the terrible reality of *McCleskey v. Kemp*:

> It is tempting to pretend that minorities on death row share a fate
> in no way connected to our own, that our treatment of them sounds
> no echoes beyond the chambers in which they die. Such an illusion
> is ultimately corrosive, for the reverberations of injustice are not so

easily confined . . . And the way in which we choose those who will die reveals the depth of moral commitment among the living.

In summary, the U.S. Supreme Court could not tolerate granting relief to Warren McCleskey and thousands of other prisoners, most of whom were African American. By inventing a new constitutional standard of particular discrimination, a standard that must be proved without contacting jury members about their racial motivation, the Court effectively made the standard virtually impossible to meet. Although the Supreme Court ruled in another case that " justice was not a matter of administrative decree," the Rehnquist Court proved that its administrative decree was indeed the rule, even if it wasn't justice.

While *McCleskey v. Kemp* was winding its way up the judicial ladder of appeal, a list of informers had been released by the Atlanta police department that included Offie Evans' name. Evans was the informer in the cell next to Warren McCleskey who testified that Warren confessed the murder to him. This was the surfacing of the withheld information that in return for a deal for a lesser sentence, Evans would testify against McCleskey.

Jack Boger mounted another legal challenge based on the fact that the evidence of Offie Evans being an informant was withheld from the defense and jury thus leading to the impression Evans was a reliable witness rather than a man providing self-serving testimony. Boger brought this evidence before the federal district court in a hearing December 23, 1987. The judge granted McCleskey relief finding that the jurors should have known Offie Evan's status as an informant for the Atlanta police department, in order to evaluate the credibility of his testimony that Warren "confessed" to him. A new trial was ordered. But the state appealed.

Once again, the fate of Warren McCleskey would be decided by the U.S. Supreme Court. On April 16, 1991 a decision was rendered in *McCleskey v. Zant*. The Court, in a 6–3 vote, ruled against McCleskey. Associate Justice Marshall was outraged and issued, in part, the following scorching dissent:

> Ironically, the majority seeks to defend its doctrinal innovation on the ground that it will promote respect for 'the rule of law'. Obviously, respect for the rule of the law must start with those who are responsible for pronouncing the law. The majority's invocation of 'the orderly administration of justice' rings hollow when the majority itself tosses aside established precedent without explanation, disregards the will of Congress, fashions rules that defy the reasonable expectation of the person who must conform their conduct to the law's dictates, and applies those rules in a way that rewards state misconduct and deceit. Whatever 'abuse of the writ' today's decision is designed to avert pales in comparison with the majority's own abuse of the norms that inform the proper judicial function.

Execution Day

On the morning of September 24, 1991, Warren McCleskey was denied clemency by the Pardon Board. Jack Boger launched a final, desperate, appeal challenging the clemency proceeding. The chairman of the clemency board had stated prior to the hearing that nothing would change his mind about opposing clemency for Warren. Meanwhile, Warren remained on death watch as the legal challenge navigated the courts. He was in a cell with a view of the electric chair, waiting while the courts deliberated.

Billy Moore, Warren's best friend on death row who had received clemency previously and had been moved to another prison, was summoned to the chaplain's office. It was 5:00 p.m., September 24, 1991. Warren McCleskey's execution was set for 7:00 p.m. Chaplain Thomas dialed a telephone number that would enable Billy Moore and Warren McCleskey to talk one last time.

A voice on the other end of the line said: "Hello, is this William Moore?" Billy was blessed and overjoyed to hear his friend's voice. He responded: "How are you, my brother and friend?"

Billy recounted the conversation:

> We talked for thirty minutes. It was a wonderful blessing. I am very thankful to the Lord for providing me with the encouragement and support Warren gave me during the phone call. I thought it rather funny. Here I was, expecting and desiring to provide encouragement for my brother hours before his execution, and as it ended up, he provided the blessings. He provided the encouragement."

> It was truly an inspiration to see the Holy Spirit moving in Warren, as a river. It was very evident and reassuring that the Lord had done a fantastic work in Warren's life, especially while he was in the midst of this crisis. He was focused. This helped to comfort me. In that position, everything around you is so crazy. If you try to control it, it will just swallow you up, and you will not be able to help your loved ones and the many friends who come to see you for the last time.

> Warren expressed his love for me and his appreciation for all that we, as brothers in the Lord, shared over the years. He told me my help meant a lot to him, especially since he knew I was truly able to understand exactly how he felt. He was both surprised and overjoyed to see how the Lord was faithful in pouring out the Holy Spirit in the midst of such troubled and overwhelming times.

The events that followed Warren and Billy's conversation would test anyone's faith. Shortly before 7:00 p.m., a stay of execution was granted so the courts could consider the apparently predetermined nature of the clemency board's decision. The court hearing ended at 11:20 p.m., but the judge stayed the execution until 2:00 a.m. so higher courts could review the case. At 2:17 a.m. Warren McCleskey was strapped into the electric chair. He began his last statement only to be interrupted by the warden, who announced the U.S. Supreme Court was still deliberating.

Warren was removed from the electric chair and returned to the holding cell. At 2:53 he was once again taken to the death chamber and was buckled into the electric chair. The Supreme Court had ruled against him. He again gave his final statement, eloquently and completely. At 3:04 the electrocution began. Warren was pronounced dead at 3:13 a.m. September 25, 1991.

Lesson Four about the death penalty: It is an instrument of tyranny. Warren McCleskey was impaled on the proverbial sword of the racial tyranny of the majority. The three branches of government on the state level functioned to deprive him of his basic constitutional right to a fair trial. The federal level of judicial review of the state functions went out of its way to insure the state functions were upheld despite uncontroverted evidence that Warren McCleskey suffered from systematic racial discrimination. In each instance it was the white racial majority denying Warren and the others on death row, primarily African American and all poor, equal justice under the law. Instead, the white majority sought to guarantee their slaughter by the state.

T.S. Eliot wrote in his "Four Quartets":

> We had the experience and missed the meaning,
> And approach to the meaning restores the experience
> In a different form, beyond any meaning
> We can assign to happiness.

As we review the fate of Warren McCleskey and all the others executed as a result of *McCleskey v. Kemp*, we recall another line of Eliot's from the "Four Quartets":

> Go, go, go said the bird: humankind cannot bear very much reality.

Coda to *McCleskey v. Kemp*

The Baldus study of Georgia's discriminatory practices in administration of the death penalty has been replicated in eighteen other jurisdictions. The results have proven to be the same no matter whether a state or a city administration of the death penalty was considered. Racial bias lurks at the heart of criminal justice system in the United States of America.

In the spring of 1991, as Warren McCleskey's case was losing on appeal and spinning Warren toward extermination, I was studying constitutional law at Harvard. It was an excellent class taught by Professor Randall Kennedy. The class provided me valuable learning about the formal, legal incorporation of racism into the American system of government. Professor Kennedy was thorough and held a high opinion of meritocracy. As an African American, he clearly wanted everyone to succeed on their merits.

Of course, I was struck by the irony of this position since I had spent the last twenty years working with the many African Americans who, no matter their merits, had little chance to live much less succeed in the South. And it was not as if the condemned deserved to be there. Rather, as Warren's case demonstrated, it was racial discrimination and its evil twin, poverty, that inevitably led one to death row. In coming to know Warren and so many others, I had seen how a turn in the road due to those two factors could easily lead to death row. It was not a matter of how bright or able one might be. So, imagine my astonishment when I became aware that Professor Kennedy, the exponent of meritocracy, was also a proponent of the death penalty.

I had come to Harvard University on a Merrill Fellowship, retreated to the North for respite from the Southern killing ground, taken a course to learn about the development of racism in the framework of American law, and was being taught by an African American who believed in the death penalty. The irony of this experience left me flabbergasted and my new Canadian friend, Andrew Stirling, a pastor also on fellowship who took the constitutional law course with me, was kind enough to allow me to repeatedly share my incredulity at the ironies in the context of this course.

Randy Kennedy was espousing support for the death penalty despite the evidence in *McCleskey* v. *Kemp*, a case decided in April of 1987, and one that we studied toward the end of the semester. It was stunning for me to see an intelligent, articulate African American law professor elaborate his belief in the death penalty at Harvard University. He maintained this position despite the fact that *McCleskey v. Kemp* stood in the tradition of *Dred Scott*, *Plessy v. Ferguson* and *The Civil Rights cases of 1883*, all cases emanating racial bias. Of course, this was personal for me because Warren McCleskey was not a mere legal case but my good friend. Not only was he my friend, he was one of the finest human beings I knew in or outside of prison.

The class with Professor Kennedy taught me that it was not lack of intelligence or ignorance that led people astray in the matter of the death penalty. It was a fundamental misunderstanding of American history, one that I also shared. It was only by reconstructing history anew, from the bottom up, with the perspective of the minorities under the tyranny of the white majority, that we could comprehend aspects of our social policy such as the death penalty and our criminal justice system. It was Warren and my other friends on death row who taught me the truth of Dietrich Bonhoeffer's conclusion, that we must learn "to see the great events of world history from below, from the perspective of the outcast, the suspect, the maltreated, the powerless, the oppressed and reviled, in short from the perspective of suffering." Hence, the long arduous struggle of writing this work commenced.

A final irony rankled me in the *McCleskey* case. As a native of North Carolina, born in the tobacco market town of Greenville in 1946, my family thrived through the Golden Leaf as did much of eastern and piedmont North Carolina. My maternal uncles, Uncle Blue and Uncle Joe, bought and sold tobacco. Accompanying them to a tobacco auction and hearing the trill of the auctioneer was enchanting. My maternal grandfather, Granddaddy, made a living as a bookkeeper for the tobacco companies.

From my childhood until I left home for college, I seemed to be encased in wreaths of blue-grey cigarette smoke from my parents and my aunts and uncles. Tobacco was a way of life, second nature to most North Carolinians. The tobacco smoke was omnipresent, turning me completely off and I never so much as smoked a single cigarette.

Then when I became an adult, I observed a revolution in the habits of Americans, including North Carolinians. The U.S. Surgeon General, C. Everett Koop, published medical findings that cigarette smoking caused lung cancer. In time, the tobacco companies went from being perceived as benign employers to becoming Big Tobacco, the merchant of death. All this occurred in a matter of two decades.

The statistical proof that linked cancer to cigarette smoking carried the day in the public eye. Millions of Americans stopped smoking cigarettes, and the tobacco companies responded by targeting the youth and international markets for their deadly product. A dramatic drop in smoking in the United States resulted from the public education campaign.

1. *Electric chair console, Riverbend Maximum Security Institution, (RMSI) Nashville, Tennessee Photo by Gigi Cohen.*

The American public reversal on tobacco consumption was a remarkable turnaround as a result of an extensive public education campaign. Yet as I marveled at the changes in my native North Carolina on this issue, I became curious about the statistical data regarding smoking and lung cancer when I compared it to the statistical data on racial discrimination in the *McCleskey* case. A striking anomaly stood out. David Baldus uncontroverted study of all the murders in Georgia established racial discrimination definitively. It did so at a rate of statistical significance that was two and half times greater than the correlation between smoking and lung cancer. Although the U.S. Supreme Court decision was issued in 1987 against McCleskey, this data had been introduced in federal district court in 1982. As we discussed the *McCleskey* case in the Harvard law class on constitutional law, the fact of a pattern of racial discrimination in the administration of the death penalty had been established for almost a decade. Yet where was the public outcry? Where was the remedy? Where was the public education campaign that would change laws and protect the civil rights of people caught in a demonstrably racist system? There was none.

And why might that be the case? It was because the white majority, represented in the legislative, executive and judicial branches of government, were determined to maintain the death penalty as an instrument of tyranny against African Americans, by any means necessary.

Justice Lewis Powell in his majority opinion (5–4) in *McCleskey* wondered if he was expected to declare the system unconstitutional in light of the Baldus study? Obviously, the answer to that question was in the affirmative. But Justice Powell, from Richmond, Virginia, could not see his way to do so even though the Civil Rights Movement had left the criminal justice system untouched in its racial practices. This was a system rooted in slavery, black codes, segregation, the convict lease system and slavery by another name— peonage. But Justice Powell must be given his due, because in retirement he stated he wished he had voted for *McCleskey*. Just as we give the former Governor of Georgia and President of the United States Jimmy Carter his due for finally opposing the death penalty in 2012. This would be the same death penalty he signed into law as Governor of Georgia. Unfortunately for Warren McCleskey and others executed under racially discriminatory laws, these regrets sound somewhat hollow. Each of them, and all of us, are best served by once again considering Justice William Brennan's dissent in *McCleskey*:

> It is tempting to pretend that minorities on death row share a fate in no way linked to our own, that our treatment of them sounds no echoes beyond the chambers in which they die. Such an illusion is ultimately corrosive, for the reverberations of injustice are not so easily confined . . . And the way in which we choose those who will die reveals the depth of moral commitment among the living.

CHAPTER I. ARRIVAL AND BEGINNINGS (1619–1808)

Now that we have pierced the veil that obscures the reality of the racial tyranny of the majority, and examined how it works in one crucial aspect of society in the 21st century, we can resume our initial quest for understanding how it originally manifested itself. The why of the origin of this process of invidious discrimination we will leave to others but the how can be learned from examining the historical record. Given our own participation in the modern version of this racial tyranny, we examine the record with humility and with the understanding of our own complicity in this system. So we look back before there was this elaborate system of government that perpetuates what we deal with on a daily basis. We examine the development of the tyranny of the majority in hopes of learning how it began. Although the records are limited, they are revealing.

In 1619, one year before the arrival of the Mayflower in New England, a Dutch ship sailed into Jamestown, Virginia. This ship contained twenty African slaves, including Antony, Isabella and Pedro, who came ashore in August of 1619. Their Spanish names indicated the Dutch ship probably stole them from a Spanish slave expedition. The Dutch captain exchanged his human cargo for provisions. Despite the Africans status as slaves on the Dutch ship, their arrival in the English colony named for the Virgin Queen Elizabeth changed their status. They were no longer slaves. Rather, they became indentured servants just like 90% of the English settlers.

Antony and Isabella fell in love and were married. In 1623 or 1624 (the record is not clear), their son William was born. William was the first black child born in English America and he was baptized in the Church of England. This would also imply that Antony and Isabella worshiped in this church as well.

The newly arrived Africans found themselves in an agricultural environment. It was peopled by European settlers who labored as indentured servants and a few wealthy land owners. The elite class, men like John Carter, needed labor to grow the tobacco for export to England. Indentured servitude provided the labor pool as men and women sold their labor for a period of time in exchange for ultimate freedom, food and whatever the cost was of the transport from England to Virginia. For purchasing such indentured servants, the John Carters were rewarded with a fifty-acre headright for each servant. The planters utilized the fifty acres for each purchased servant to enlarge their already substantial land holdings. The indentured servants usually worked for a period of four to seven years.

As the seventeenth century unfurled, the planters experimented with Indians as slaves as well as trying to keep the indentured servants in a status of perpetual servitude. But neither proved satisfactory as a reliable labor pool. As the Native Americans increasingly resisted white encroachment, the English labor supply dwindled because of improved economic conditions in England. The kidnapping of poor Englishmen, "spiriting," could not keep up with the demand for labor on the fertile Virginia soil. By the 1660s, the shift toward slave labor was codified for the initial time. In 1662, the Virginia governing body enacted the following statute: "Whereas some doubts have arisen whether children got by an Englishman upon a Negro woman shall be slave or free, Be it therefore enacted and declared by the present grand Assembly, that all children born in this country shall be held, bond or free only according to the condition of the mother." This innocuous appearing statement actually reveals a revolution in understanding the status of offspring. As far back as one can note in English law, a child's parentage, hence inheritance, was determined by the father. Now with one sentence, the status of the child was determined by the mother.

Christianity, which had proved so successful against the Jews in Europe and natives of the Caribbean islands, as well as Central and South America, led the way in Virginia. In 1667, the Virginia Assembly enacted a statute that made it clear "the conferring of baptisme does not alter the condition of the person as to his bondage or freedom." The church allowed the state to define who was a human being and in so doing abandoned whatever authentic moral claim it once had from the gospel. By abandoning the teaching of Jesus and the apostle Paul about freedom, the church joined hands in creating an apartheid society with the state. Of course, this would eventually include separate religious buildings and denominations as white over black manifested itself throughout the country.

By 1700, there were between six and ten thousand black slaves in Virginia. Although Massachusetts passed the first slavery law, the institution exploded in the South as it solved the labor shortage. By 1776, Virginia had more than two hundred thousand blacks, over half of the entire black population in the colonies. From 1671 until 1775, over one million Africans were brought to America by British or American slave ships. There were over two thousand British or American ships transporting forty to fifty thousand Africans annually.

The impact throughout the Southern colonies was profound. From 1680 to 1750, the black population grew from 7% to 44% in Virginia. In South Carolina it jumped from 17% to 61%. Georgia changed from a colony founded on the principle of abolition to maintaining a 45% slave population by 1770.

How did this transformation from indentured servitude to slavery occur? England, a country that had slavery before the Norman conquest, utilized chattel slavery but abolished it in 1833. England began shipping Africans to the colonies by the thousands. Profit, of course, was a reason. Labor was a need, certainly. But how did this brutal and voluminous transatlantic passage emerge so prominently in such a relatively brief time?

From Massachusetts to Virginia, within a fifty-year period, the colonies embarked upon the enslavement of Africans as a legitimate course of action. One of the key roles was played by the Christian church. The church sanctioned the institution of slavery and worked with the state to enslave the Africans just as it cooperated in the vanquishing of the Native Americans.

Lerone Bennett describes in vivid detail what the church was blessing:

- [a] bishop sitting on an ivory chair on a wharf in the Congo and extending his fat hand in wholesale baptisms of slaves . . . rowed beneath him in chains to the slave ships.
- [a] greedy king raiding his own villages to get slaves to buy brandy.
- [a] pious captain holding prayer services twice a day on his slave ship and writing the famous hymn "How Sweet the Name of Jesus Sounds."

It was also deserted villages, Bennett goes on to write, bleached bones on slave trails and people with no last names, like Caesar negro, Angela negro . . . and people with some given distinctive names . . . Like Captain Tomba, who came to America, and Nealee, who did not. She was left to die along the trail, too exhausted to go on.

This was a very strong and therefore valuable slave, Captain Tomba, who was spared his life even after leading a ship-board slave revolt and killing three sailors. But he paid for that survival by being "whipped and scarified" and having to witness the cruel executions of those with less "stoutness and worth" . . . a process know in the trade as Rogues of Dignity.

Bennett provides this summary characterization:

Captain Tomba living, Nealee dying, John Newton praying, the King of Barsally stealing, the fat bishop baptizing, Captain Harding torturing these people and millions like them made the slave trade one of the cruelest chapters in the history of man.

In order to perpetrate cruelty of the dimensions demanded by the slave trade, it is helpful for the perpetrators to feel morally convinced of their rectitude. The Christian Church provided the *raison d'être* for a barbarous enterprise. The European Christian approach provided for the killing and enslavement of "heathen" Africans and "savage" Indians, just as it functioned to root out the heretical Jews on the continent. The Christian church in the colonies and in Europe facilitated the moral justification necessary to kidnap twenty-four million Africans into slavery via the transatlantic slave trade. It became the largest slave trading system in history.

In 1645, Emanuel Downing forwarded a letter to John Winthrop, his brother-in-law:

If upon a Just Warre the Lord shold deliver (Nargansett Indians] into our hands, wee might easily have men woemen and children enough to exchange for Moores, which wilbe more gaynefull pilladge for us than wee conceive, for I doe not see how wee can thrive until we get into a stock of slaves sufficient to doe all our business, for our children's children will hardly see this great Continent filled with people, soe that our servants will still desire freedome to plant for themselves, and not stay but for verie great wages. And I suppose you know verie well how wee shall maynetyne 20 Moores cheaper that one Englishe servant.

This was an exchange rate too great for a Puritan to ignore. For the cost of one English servant it would be possible to maintain twenty Africans. At about the same time in Virginia and Maryland in the 1640s, certain planters were holding on to their black indentured servants for longer periods of time, some even for life, although no law permitted them to do so. North and South the idea of slavery had germinated. African slavery was a cheap way of solving the labor problem.

In 1641, the Massachusetts Body of Liberties declared there "shall never be any bond slaverie, villinage or Captivitie amongst us, unless it be lawfull Captives taken in just warres, and such strangers as willingly sell themselves or are sold to us." The "unless" permitted African, Indian and European slavery. Connecticut had enslaved Indians since the Pequot war of the 1630s, Virginia in 1661, Maryland in 1663, New York and New Jersey in 1644, South Carolina in 1682, Pennsylvania and Rhode Island in 1700, North Carolina in 1715, and Georgia in 1755.

In order to separate slavery from indentured servitude, the question of heredity was addressed by Virginia in the statute previously quoted from 1662:

> Whereas some doubts have arisen whether children got by any Englishman upon a negro woman shall be slave or free, Be it therefore enacted and declared by the present grand Assembly, that all children borne in this country shall be held, bond or free only according to the condition of the mother.

This took care of the question which arose when white men fathered children from slaves. Would those slaves inherit the patrimony of the father, as done under English law? The answer to this had to be no, because white men having sex, forcibly and otherwise, with black women was common practice at this time, and those offspring could not be defined as slaves if they were accorded the lineage of the white father. By definition, the color of their skin had to constitute their condition of social death.

The churches, the planter elite, the white majority came to regard themselves as white, over and against the black Africans. Hence it was only a matter of time before personhood was taken out of the definition in slavery. The slave became property not person as the Virginia Assembly referred to them when discussing baptism (see prior quote). This psychological refurbishment was necessary for the wealthy class to bind the white journeyman class to them on the basis of race and overlook the class difference. Although the passage of laws paved the way, it took time because the white and black indentured servants had no concept of race and shared the same miserable living conditions. In order to overcome this obstacle the ideology of race was born.

> The idea developed by the Virginians (and Americans) was simple and profitable. The idea was that all whites were biologically superior to all blacks, who were infidels and heathens, a dangerous and accursed people who embodied an evil principle that made them dangerous to the moral and the politics of the community. The truth or falsity of this idea disturbed few men then (or now). The only thing that mattered was that this idea or something like it was necessary to justify, past, present and future aggression against blacks. (Lerone Bennett, *The Shaping of Black America*)

The white, land-owning merchant and planter class closed the door on any future for Antony, Isabella and William as well as the generations that would follow them who happened to have black skin. The whites became masters for life over the blacks in their midst. They went on to pass laws outlawing manumission of slaves. To be black in the colonies at the end of the seventeenth century was to be in a condition of social death.

CHAPTER 2. WILLIE WATSON, JR.

When Captain Tomba revolted and killed three white men, the Slave Regime responded. "Captain Harding, weighing the Stoutness and Worth of the two slaves, did as in other Countries they do by Rogues of Dignity, whip and scarify them only; while three others, Abettor but not Actors, nor of Strength for it, he sentenced to cruel deaths . . . " The white personification of power parsed out the responsibility in light of his own self interest. We may regard such a decision-making process as a brutal relic of a distant past. But before reaching that conclusion, let us turn to a modern reckoning of a black man who killed a white woman. Then we can determine if the tyranny of the white majority has been left in the 17th century with Captain Harding or perhaps it functions equally well under a different guise in modern American society.

On the night of July 23, 1987, five of us arrived about 9:15 p.m. at the steps of the lovely Governor's mansion in Baton Rouge, Louisiana. We were brought in a black limousine provided by the Governor from the airport. The occasion of our visit was to participate in a long-standing Southern tradition with the Governor, a tradition that has evolved over time from crude to sophisticated, from lynching to electrocution. We had arrived at the mansion to discuss with Governor Edwin Edwards the fate of Willie Watson, Jr., a man scheduled for electrocution at 12:01 a.m. on July 24th. The decision facing the Governor was how to respond to a black man who raped and murdered a white woman.

The members of our delegation were Congressman John Conyers, a Michigan Democrat and Chairman of the U.S. House of Representatives subcommittee on Criminal Justice; Dr. Jerome Miller, who authored a detailed and moving portrait of Willie Watson's life, which the trial judge had refused to allow at Watson's sentencing hearing; Jed Stone and Ralph Whalen, Watson's lawyers, and me. The meeting had been requested by Congressman Conyers, an African American opposed to the death penalty, who was concerned about Louisiana's accelerated execution rate and the considerable injustice he felt surrounded this case.

We were met at the mansion's tall entry doors by a courteous, sandy-haired young man who introduced himself as "Mr. Guidry." He escorted us through the foyer and into the parlor, a well-appointed room with comfortable furnishings. Immediately, a black man dressed in a red coat and dark pants asked to take our refreshment orders. He then disappeared, and Mr. Guidry explained that Governor Edwards was en route from a speaking engagement in Shreveport, where he had addressed 550 black preachers.

I was struck by the irony of the Governor's audience. Had a single minister in that gathering questioned Gov. Edwards, let alone challenged him, about the scheduled execution of Willie Watson shortly after midnight? I feared not. Edwin Edwards was running for reelection and needed the black vote to win. Consequently, he was playing the black religious community with the manipulative skill of a master politician, and that community enjoyed the attention. Watson was a disposable item on everyone's agenda.

As we settled in the parlor to await the Governor, the United States Supreme Court was deliberating on Watson's final appeal. Since the Court was in recess, the justices were reviewing the papers and participating in a conference telephone call in order to make a decision on the case. Jed Stone telephoned the clerk of the Supreme Court from one of the telephones in the parlor of the Governor's mansion. By keeping the clerk of the Court apprised of his whereabouts, he could receive a call from the Court as soon as a decision was reached on his client's case.

Congressman Conyers telephoned Jesse Jackson, who agreed to speak with Gov. Edwards about a reprieve for Watson. We then talked strategy and kept an anxious vigil, realizing that time was a slender and disappearing essence.

As we awaited the arrival of Edwards, the lovely environment and the gracious hospitality lent an eerie staging to the grim decision at hand. The mansion itself was charming. We were attended to as if we were royalty, and as we sipped iced tea from crystal glasses, I felt for a moment that it could just as easily have been one hundred years previous—1887—with the end of Reconstruction and the return to power of the white oligarchy.

The reality is that today we deal with precisely the same set of social dynamics, just a little more sophisticated, that would have swung Willie Watson from a tree 100 years ago. Race figures into it, but not in the way one might imagine. Of the 93 executions that had taken place in the United

States over the past decade (87 of which were conducted in the South), 50 of those executed were white, 56 were black and six Latino. The racism is not abundantly apparent, although the number of blacks executed was disproportionate to their makeup of the population, when considering who is executed. But racism comes into clear focus when we discover the race of the victim: 81 were white, nine were black, three were Latino. The fact is we are more likely to execute people who kill whites than those who kill people of color. It is simply because we value white life more than the life of people of color. Indeed, from 1608 through 1976, when the death penalty was reinstituted by the Supreme Court, approximately 18,500 people had been executed. Of that number, 31 were white people executed for killing a black person. In reality, it should count only as 21 because 10 of the executed whites were slave owners killed for destroying property, black slaves, rather than concern over black humanity.

At approximately 10:30 p.m. an aide appeared to inform Stone that the Supreme Court was calling. He arose from his seat and strode to the telephone to learn the final judicial decision about his client. Stone spoke briefly into the phone and hung up. He turned, his face pinched and ashen, "We lost. Four to four." Because of the resignation of Justice Lewis Powell, there were only eight justices on the Supreme Court. It was a tie you die decision.

After a brief explanation from Stone, Whalen called the court back to copy down the opinion of the dissenting justices. The scrawled words on Whalen's legal pad eloquently demonstrated the arbitrariness of the capital punishment lottery:

> Four members of this court consider the above issue sufficiently compelling to have voted to hold the case until *Lowenfeld* [a companion Louisiana case previously accepted by the Court] is decided. Three votes are sufficient to hold a case, but it takes five votes to stay an execution.

> The Court today thus permits Mr. Watson's legal claim to stay alive while condemning Watson himself to die under a sentencing scheme that within a matter of months the Court may conclude is unconstitutional. Half of the members of this Court believe that Watson's claim might be indistinguishable from Lowenfeld's, yet tonight Watson will be executed while Lowenfeld may prevail and be spared. This prospect is the ultimate derogation of the Court's duty to provide equal justice under law. We dissent.

The justices had split equally on the merits of the case, but, unlike baseball where the tie goes to the base runner, here the tie went against Willie Watson.

At 11:40 p.m., more than two hours late for his appointment with us, Edwards briskly entered the parlor, shaking hands and uttering a perfunctory greeting: "What can I do for you gentleman?" The governor was energetic, indeed, his well-coiffed hair and dapper appearance suggested vigor in spite of the late hour. One would have thought the Governor had just returned from a Sunday afternoon promenade. We were 20 minutes from an execution. (I had been with men facing electrocution at Angola and I knew the pressure Willie Watson was under as the Governor took his time.)

"Governor Edwards," I said, "I am sure you have been unavoidably delayed, but we have been waiting since shortly after 9 o'clock and there is no way we can make an adequate clemency presentation to you on behalf of Willie Watson in 20 minutes. We are requesting that you delay the execution so we can discuss this case with you." My words tumbled out as I tried to restrain myself and stay calm while the minutes counted down.

"What makes this case different than any of the others?" the Governor replied. Four justices of the Supreme Court had just provided an easy answer to that question. Stone and Whalen told Edwards about the Court's decision to review the legal claim even though they did not vote for a stay of execution. Conyers announced that Jesse Jackson was on the telephone to discuss the situation with the Governor.

Edwards told an aide to get the warden on the telephone line. Whether that was simply the traditional securing of an open line to prison or an indication that Edwards would inform the warden he wanted the execution stopped, we had no idea.

The aide called, but the warden wasn't there. As we tensely waited for the warden to be found, I reminded the Governor that Jackson was waiting on the phone line. "Oh, is he still on the line?" came the reply. Edwards arose and walked to a nearby telephone. After several minutes of tense conversation, he returned to the circle. It was almost midnight, and there was still no word from the warden.

Three minutes before the scheduled electrocution, an aide appeared and informed the Governor that the warden had finally been located and was on the telephone. Governor Edwards left the room for this call. Shortly after midnight, he reappeared. "I've ordered a stay of execution," he said. "Until you present your facts and his lawyers can visit him again."

Stone and Whalen made a few parting points and then left to make the 50-mile drive to Angola, where Willie Watson waited to be killed. The rest of us began an earnest presentation about Watson's life. As we talked, the feisty, combative attitude Edwards had greeted us with gave way to a more reflective mood.

Watson's story was a poignant one, making him worthy of clemency regardless of the Supreme Court decision.

Miller described the life of a black boy growing up in rural Louisiana under the care of his Aunt Tu. When Watson was 11, his aunt died. Despite the presence of other family in the area, Watson's mother insisted he return with her to the housing projects of New Orleans.

Suddenly uprooted from his known family and support, Watson ran away on four separate occasions, each time making his way more than 55 miles to his aunt's home. Despite his desperate unhappiness in the urban environment, his mother forced him to return to New Orleans.

In the city, a particularly potent combination of drugs known as "T's and Blues" was readily available. Although Watson held steady employment during his teenage years, he felt lost without the love of his family; eventually, he gave way to the escape provided by drugs. The result was a psychotic state induced by a massive overdose—and the awful rape and murder of a young woman.

If the death penalty law fashioned in the state capitol of Baton Rouge and upheld in the marble chambers of the Supreme Court in Washington, D.C. had truly functioned as it purported to function, Watson's story would have been told to the sentencing jury at trial. His psychiatric evaluation describing the psychotic state induced by the drugs would also have been admitted at trial. But this crucial information was ruled inadmissible by the judge, in spite of legal precedent to the contrary. Now we were reduced to this final plea for mercy.

As we shared Watson's life and reviewed the Supreme Court's decision, we asked Governor Edwards to be the ninth justice on the Court and to cast his vote with the four members of the Court who had voted to accept the case. This would allow Watson, the person, to survive while *Watson* the legal case was decided in court.

As the conversation progressed, it became clear that before this meeting the Governor had had no knowledge of the case beyond the initial execution time. When we concluded our 90-minute presentation, Edwards graciously offered to house us for the night, but I quickly and politely declined. Despite the optimism of my colleagues, I was filled with foreboding.

Conyers, Miller and I returned to our hotel to await the Governor's decision, which he promised to make within the hour. I had awaited similar decisions too many times before, but the factors under consideration in this case were extraordinary: a divided Court voting to review the legal claim but to kill the petitioner; Watson's personal history as a sweet-natured person who had committed a horrible crime because of a drug-induced psychosis; Watson's excellent prison record and the support of the guards on death row; and Jesse Jackson's and John Conyers requesting a stay of execution. I wanted to believe that surely this case merited at least a reprieve until the Supreme Court acted in *Lowenfeld*.

Nonetheless, I feared that all of that would not be enough to stop this electrocution. The politics of the death penalty always seemed to control such situations in the country; people on death row were placed in a category in which they were no longer considered to be human, and the courtesies shown us during the evening at the Governor's mansion could not mask that ugly truth. Willie Watson was no different than Captain Tomba. He only had a Potemkin display of due process and judicial review, and at bottom he was still a black man who killed a white person.

Shortly after 2 a.m., July 24th, Edwards' aide telephoned us at the hotel. He informed us that clemency had been denied and that the execution was scheduled to proceed immediately.

At the Louisiana State Penitentiary in Angola, Willie Watson, trying to fathom the machinations of the Supreme Court, wondered aloud to Jed Stone, "Why can't a tie be for me?"

And then toward the end of their visit, taking a final drag off his unfiltered cigarette, Watson rose to the occasion. "Let's get on with it, "he said politely.

CHAPTER 3. THE SLAVERY REGIME (1662–1865)

By 1662 the law white over black was drawn in the colonies. Later, slavery statutes were passed, slave codes introduced and refined, and the ideology of racism was underway. The idea of black people as property—needing permission to marry, to move or travel—was the implementation of a police state of total domination on the basis of race. Thus, since this action was taken and supported by all three branches of government, initially on the state and then also on the federal level, it makes this period the Slavery Regime.

For almost the next hundred years, the English colonies manifested a fundamental contradiction. On the one hand, chattel slavery for blacks was acceptable. Yet, for white colonists, an increasing demand for liberty was articulated. Dr. Samuel Johnson of England noted the irony: "How is it that we hear the loudest yelps for liberty among the drivers of negroes?"

The slave society that evolved before the American Revolution was characterized by the following elements: increasingly Southern based with slaves confined to relatively small holdings (great majority under fifty per holding), blacks were a minority of the total population (about 35% in 1790), slavery was agrarian based, especially so with the crops of tobacco and rice, and blacks increased in population upon settling on the land. The sugar plantations of the Caribbean offered a distinct contrast. The Caribbean slave mortality rate was high and reproduction rate low, slaves composed 90% or more of the majority population, owners were absentee, and slave holdings frequently reached five hundred or more.

Given the factors addressed above, as the American Revolution approached, only about one fifth of all slaves in the colonies were African born. In the

Caribbean and South America, the African importation was dramatically higher due to the high death rate and low reproductive rate of the slaves.

In the 1730s and 1740s, the Great Awakening swept America. The Protestant religious revival increased interest in religion among whites and also led to more proselytizing among blacks. When the religious revival of the 1770s and 1780s broke out, the slave population was accepted by Baptists and Methodists as Christians. Although this development did not last fifty years, and blacks were then forced to organize their own church and denominations. By the time of the Civil War, Protestant Christianity was a major part of the slave community.

The period of the Slave Regime prior to the American Revolutionary War was the laying of the foundation of a slave society. The first major shaking of that foundation came with the Revolutionary War. An examination of the census, which shows the numbers of slaves, reveals the impact of the Revolution. If the period of the Slavery Regime from 1680 is compared with 1770 and 1790, we can appreciate the growth of the peculiar institution and the challenge to it the Revolutionary War provided. From 1770 to 1790, Virginia, North Carolina, South Carolina and Georgia decreased significantly in the slave population. Although the Enlightenment had erupted in Europe and influenced the thinking of the leaders of the colonies, questioning the validity of torture, capital punishment, slavery and other accepted social institutions, it was the event of the Revolutionary War that made freedom possible for the slaves whose escape is reflected in the census. An examination of the initial cracks in the foundation of the Slave Regime provides an understanding of how the slaves capitalized on the situation of the two warring white societies as well as giving a foreshadowing of what it would take to eradicate the institution—another, more terrible war in 1861.

The Founding Fathers were members of the Colonial elite. John Adams, Benjamin Franklin, Thomas Paine were matched in the South by the planter class—George Washington, Thomas Jefferson, James Madison and Patrick Henry, who were also among the largest slave holders of the day. Already engaged in Enlightenment ideas, these men were sped upon the course of events by the outbreak of the war.

The British Colonial governor of Virginia, John Murry, the Earl of Dunmore, proclaimed freedom for all slaves who would fight against the rebellion. The Southern slave masters were alarmed by this challenge. During the war, British destruction in the Chesapeake region and in South Carolina and Georgia provided opportunity for slaves to flee. The fighting by the two white ruling classes enabled thousands of slaves to make their bid for freedom. In addition to the thousands who went north, ten thousand left when the British evacuated Savannah and Charleston, and thousands more left via New York City's harbor.

Perhaps as important as the physical freedom for the thousands who escaped during the war was the reality of the idea of freedom. The Founding Fathers and the patriots spoke out against the tyranny of Britain and the slavery they suffered at the hands of the British. Liberty became a prized quality, extolled throughout the land, regardless of color. Within thirty years of the war, slavery was gradually outlawed in the North.

Thomas Jefferson's original draft of the Declaration of Independence contained language strongly critical of slavery. He blamed King George III for forcing slavery on the colonies, describing the king as a ruler who "waged cruel war against human nature itself, violating the most sacred right of life and liberty in the persons of a distant people who never offended him, captivating and carrying them into slavery in another hemisphere, or to a miserable death in their transportation thither." This attitude proved too strong for Jefferson's colleagues who deleted the language condemning slavery from the final version of the Declaration of Independence.

In 1787, the Constitutional Convention was held in Philadelphia. Although the response of the white elite to Jefferson's strong views against slavery in the Declaration of Independence indicated the route slavery would probably take in the new political framework, it was still an open question at the convention.

The Constitutional Convention ratified the "three-fifths rule" regarding representing slaves in the electoral process. The notion that a slave constituted "three-fifths" for representation and taxation purposes was initially found in an amendment to the revenue act of the Congress of Confederation in 1783. The committee of the whole at the Constitutional Convention amended it to the Virginia plan, it was embodied in the New Jersey plan, and became a part to the Great Compromise. It was a minor part in the discussion on proportional representation. However, James Madison warned the convention that it was not the size of the states but "the danger to our general government is the great southern and northern interests of the continent, being opposed to each other."

The new Constitution prohibited Congress from outlawing the slave trade for twenty years, recognized the rights of masters to reclaim fugitive slaves, as well as establishing the "three-fifths rule." An immediate result was the dramatic increase of the importation of slaves from 1788 to 1808. In order to make it through the window of opportunity, slave traders imported more slaves in that period than at any other twenty year period of U.S. history. And this came on the heels of the increased slave trade during the Revolutionary War.

Vincent Harding describes what the new Constitution meant for black people:

> This basic set of national laws shielded the slave trade against any legislative prohibition for a minimum of twenty years; at the same time it made provision for the federal government to levy import fees on each new African who survived the middle passage. In the document the black population was included in the determination of Congressional representation, based on a formula which allowed enslaved people to be counted as three-fifths a person. The Constitution also guaranteed the right of slave owners to track down black fugitives across state lines and have them delivered back into captivity. It promised the use of federal armed forces in any struggle against insurrections. It fact, so firmly etched was the guarantee of black bondage that only a grim and bloody war would begin to expunge it from the laws. Thus the revolution for white liberty ended with black slavery carefully protected in the basic document of the new, "free" nation . . . The white American Revolution was not ours. (*There Is a River*)

Although moderating forces thought the ban on importing slaves after 1808, the increased manumission rates among several upper South states, and the gradual abolition of slavery in the North augured the end of the peculiar institution, such optimism proved misplaced. Rather, the Constitution placed the power of the federal government behind the institution of slavery. The moderate attitude also failed to reckon with the invention of the cotton gin by Eli Whitney in 1793. This one technological advance threw open the door to mass-produced cotton in the South, especially in the new states that joined through the Louisiana Purchase n 1803. Given the natural population growth among slaves, the upper South states began selling their slaves to provide labor for the lower South states, especially after the ban on importation took place in 1808. Slavery boomed and the once hopeful prospect of abolition receded among thousands of blacks toiling the cotton fields of Alabama, Mississippi, Louisiana, South Carolina and Georgia. Madison's premonition of the differing interests of North and South was proving prophetic. A free black, industrialized North and a slave, agrarian South grew further apart.

The Constitution established a government of white men, by white men and for white men. The white majority was truly a tyranny because there was no acknowledgment and protection of rights of the two racial minorities— African American and Native Americans. The governing document of the United States of America did not consider them fully human and thus, they were defined as undeserving of basic rights. As a matter of fact, though slaves were acknowledged as valuable in terms of property, no mention was made of Indians because they were considered to have no rights, either political or human. (It would take until 1923 for Indians to achieve an official status under the law.) In order to understand how such a situation developed, we look to the most well known and perhaps most enlightened of all the patriot leaders, Thomas Jefferson.

CHAPTER 4. THOMAS JEFFERSON (1743–1826)

Thomas Jefferson, the only white individual selected for a chapter in this work, was chosen for who he was and who he was not. The author of Declaration of Independence, he was an exponent of the quintessential position on religious freedom, opponent of slavery, third President of the United States of America, and in many ways was a beacon of Enlightenment thought. Yet the other dimension of the dialectic of Thomas Jefferson's thought is equally significant. He was a slave owner who, unlike George Washington, did not free his slaves upon his death. He felt deeply that black people were inferior to white people, emphasizing intellectual and moral limitations. Although an impassioned advocate of the abolition of slavery early in his career, in his old age he actually supported increasing the slave population through the western territories to insure the Southern balance of power in Congress.

We examine Jefferson as a person who illuminates many aspects of our national character. By discerning his attitudes, in many ways the most enlightened of the white majority in the United States, we are instructed as to how Americans could consider themselves the most freedom loving people on earth and at the same time have a government that was a Slave Regime subjecting nearly four million blacks to chattel slavery by 1860. On a personal level, he maintained a 38-year affair with Sally Hemmings, his slave, and did not acknowledge her as his equal or his mistress.

Finally, we consider Jefferson's attitude toward the Native Americans to see how America's other racial minority fared. For it was through his presidential administration (1801–1809) that the policy of Indian removal was articulated by a president.

In 1776, when Thomas Jefferson penned the Declaration of Independence, there were over two hundred thousand slaves in his native state of Virginia. Indeed, one third of the signers of the Declaration of Independence were slave owners. Yet, Jefferson stated he was opposed to the enslavement of human beings.

In 1774, Jefferson submitted his thoughts about the rights of colonial citizens vis-à-vis the English crown to the Virginia House of Burgesses. "Summary View of the Rights of British Americans" repudiated the rights of British Parliament in the colonies. Additionally, Jefferson declared that the abolition of slavery was the great desire of the colonists. Given the position of his fellow Virginians, who later rejected similar language before signing the Declaration of Independence, Jefferson was clearly speaking of his own deeply felt beliefs issuing from his study of Enlightenment ideas and not representing his colleagues' thinking.

Thomas Jefferson considered slavery a "hideous evil" and incompatible with the republican government he labored to create. He was a man of the eighteenth century, a slave owner who abhorred slavery, a man who had drunk deeply from the cup of Enlightenment thinking, but also a Virginian who never overcame the prejudices that permeated his time period regarding black people. It was as if his world of ideals warred with his physical environment at Monticello. The struggle between a Virginia planter and a humanist thinker reflected in his thought on slavery and blacks.

It is important to remember that at the time "Summary View" was written, as well as the Declaration of Independence, Jefferson's vilifying of King George and Parliament for the slave trade conveniently ignored certain facts. Approximately two thousand British and American ships were transporting forty to fifty thousand Africans annually to the Western hemisphere. Huge profits were made through this enterprise in America, by the ship builders and shippers in the North and the slave buyers in the South, and Britain also reaped enormous profits.

Despite rebuffs of his abolitionist slavery language in the Declaration of Independence, Jefferson focused on his plan for Virginia's government. His version of the Virginia constitution provided for the gradual abolition of slavery. In rejecting this plan, Jefferson thought his colleagues in the Virginia legislature were enacting a "legislative despotism" that left slavery intact.

Jefferson labored in Virginia for eight years, after returning from Philadelphia, in order to make the principles of the Declaration of Independence real in the establishment of the government of Virginia. In terms of slavery, his best successes came in 1778 when Virginia abolished the slave trade and in 1782 when the manumission laws were broadened.

In 1779, Jefferson was elected Governor of Virginia. During the Revolutionary War he opposed the using of slaves for soldiers, despite Lord Dunmore's enticing offer of freedom for slaves if they fought with the British. Jefferson feared arming slaves might lead to eventual insurrection and that Negroes, because of their degraded status in slavery, would not make fit soldiers. When the war ended, Jefferson accepted election to the Continental Congress, weary of the politics of his native Virginia.

The question of western territories came before the Congress. Jefferson led the effort to exclude slavery from any territory that entered the union. This motion failed by one vote. The entire Virginia delegation voted against him and only one other Southerner joined him. In 1787, the Northwest Ordinance banned slavery after 1800 from the region north of the Ohio. This action came two years after Jefferson had journeyed to France as the American minister replacing Benjamin Franklin. It reflected his feelings and efforts from the prior struggle to ban slavery from states joining the Union.

While in Paris, Jefferson's only book, *Notes on Virginia*, was published in 1785. In it Jefferson criticized the Virginia of 1776, totally condemned slavery, but expressed doubts about the intelligence of black people. It provides a revealing insight into Jefferson's conflicted attitude regarding slavery and black people.

Jefferson made it quite clear in *Notes on Virginia* that the ownership of human beings was uncivilized and, aside from war, the most degrading behavior imaginable was a result of this institution. "The whole commerce between master and slave is a perpetual exercise of the most boisterous passions, the most unremitting despotism of the (one) part, and degrading submission on the other." Slavery was an evil, destructive to master and slave alike. Indeed, it brought him to pen the words regarding slavery that echo today as a comment on the relationship of black to white in America: "I tremble for my country when I reflect that God is just."

But abolition of slavery did not translate into thinking that blacks were equal to whites. Jefferson summed up his feelings about the racial inferiority of blacks with one revealing line: "It is not their condition, then, but nature, which has produced the distinction." This conclusion came after a comparative study of whites and blacks in *Notes on Virginia*; a study conducted in the name of scientific inquiry, which produced the subjective and unscientific conclusion that it was the Negro's nature, which has produced their inferiority, not their conditions of confinement.

In order to subject his blacks to a condition of servitude, Jefferson had to believe they were not the equal of whites, regardless of slavery. He pointed out there were no black poets (dismissing Phyliss Wheatley). He maintained blacks could not do mathematics. He grasped at every "rational" straw he could find to justify his own lifestyle. By defining blacks as inferior to whites, he could rationalize his enslaving of them. So it was that the young Jefferson, who strongly called for the abolition of slavery, became the middle-aged man who would allow the issue to wait for the ripening of time. Finally, in his later years the capitulation was completed when he became a spokesman for actual expansion of slavery in order to keep the South's balance of power in Congress. His fear of Northern industrial and commercial interests dominating the nation and usurping his dream of the yeoman farmer blinded him to the power of the Southern aristocracy in the 1820s. A fierce opponent of the Virginia aristocracy as a young man and a vigorous proponent of the Rights of Man, Jefferson became a defender of the Slave Regime in his old age. It was an irony not lost on Lafayette, who visited Jefferson in the United States in 1825, one year before Jefferson's death. Lafayette concluded after his visit to Jefferson and America that the ideal for which he assumed the Revolutionary war was waged—"a great and noble principle—the freedom of mankind"—was really only that of freedom for the white man.

The first federal census in 1790 counted 697,897 slaves. By 1810, the number had increased to 1,191,354. Cotton, the new king of Southern agriculture, expanded from 6,000 bales in 1792 to 17,000 bales in 1796, 73,000 bales in 1800, 146,000 bales in 1805, and 178,000 bales in 1810. To meet the cotton demand, slavery was flourishing, not gradually diminishing as Jefferson had hoped. Indeed, by 1860, there were 3,953,760 slaves in the United States, virtually all in the South. The Slavery Regime, found only in the United States, Brazil, Cuba, and Puerto Rico in this hemisphere, was a booming business built on the backs and blood of black people. Its power and influence rested on chattel slavery, an institution Thomas Jefferson abhorred but would not challenge when he returned to the United States from France. Indeed, he felt it the obligation of the younger generation to finish the task. As the rapid increase in slaves reveals, the younger generation in the South neither sought such a job nor considered it their calling. The tide had shifted the other direction and Jefferson went with it.

Thomas Jefferson died in 1826. Two hundred and seven years earlier, the initial twenty Africans had arrived in Virginia at Jamestown. Jefferson went to his grave a strong but nominal opponent of slavery, despite the wobbling over the western territories issue, and with an equally strong belief in the inferiority of black people. The latter belief manifested itself in his concern that upon emancipation blacks be expatriated to another country, perhaps in the Caribbean. He failed to see what the earliest white settlers of Virginia realized—the racial difference was of no consequence for the indentured servants. Rather, it became an issue only when white planters created the laws mandating racial separation and slavery.

The reason this man of the Enlightenment could not glimpse what the early settlers of Virginia lived as a reality was that a racialist society had been created by Jefferson's time, which imbued him and other whites with a sense of superiority due to the color of their skin. This prejudice was planted and cultivated, as carefully as the tobacco, and really blossomed from 1662 onward. The emotive force of such racism grew so great, wrapped around the fears of sex and insurrection, it crippled Jefferson intellectually. He spoke of keeping the races apart—"beyond the reach of mixture"—even as he carried on an affair with Sally Hemmings and she bore him children. The man who viewed miscegenation a blight on the white race did not practice what he preached. Such ideas would not have been practiced in the 1630s because the concept of white superiority did not exist in Virginia. Rather, people were Christians, or savages or heathens.

The racialist society came about by the 1660s and it obliterated the historical beginning of the initial Africans working off their servitude, owning land, becoming Christians, marrying and bringing children to be baptized in the Christian church. The ideology of racism destroyed that beginning and poisoned the well of racial harmony for Jefferson, his successors, and all Americans since 1662.

Jefferson and the Other Minority: The Indians

If Jefferson represented the best and the worst of the best of white people in his appraisal and relationships with the black minority, his relationship with the other minority, the Indians, proves an interesting comparison.

Jefferson considered Indians to be the equals of whites, the Indian differences attributable to the environment rather than genetics. Marriage between Indians and whites was permissible as opposed to his thinking of marriage between blacks and whites as a pollution of the white race. For Jefferson, the Indian was the noble savage. An early document he signed indicating his attitudes toward Indians was one he initialed as Secretary of State, when George Washington was President. Given Washington's strong anti-Indian views, it certainly reflects Jefferson's influence:

Proclamation

By the President of the United States

Whereas I have received authentic information, that certain lawless and wicked persons of the western frontier, in the State of Georgia, did lately invade, burn, and destroy a town belonging to the Cherokee Nation, although in amity with the United States, and put to death several Indians of that Nation, and whereas such outrageous conduct, not only violates the rights of humanity, but also endangers the public peace, and it highly becomes the honour and good faith of the United States to pursue all legal means for the punishment of those atrocious offenders, I have therefore thought fit to issue this my proclamation, hereby exhorting all citizens of the United States, and requiring all the officers thereof, according to their respective stations, to use their utmost endeavors to apprehend and bring those offenders to justice. And, I do moreover offer a reward to Five Hundred Dollars, for each and every one of the above-named persons, who shall be so apprehended and brought to justice, and shall be provided to have assumed or exercised any command or authority among the perpetrators of the crime aforesaid, at the time of committing the same.

In testimony whereof, I have caused the seal of the United States to be affixed to these presents, and signed the same with my hand. Done at the city of Philadelphia, the twelfth of December, in the year of our Lord, one thousand seven hundred and ninety two, and of the Independence of the United States in the seventeenth.

By the president—George Washington

—Thomas Jefferson (Secretary of State)

Of course, no one claimed the five hundred dollar reward.

When Jefferson became President he saw himself as the Great Father to the Indians. He sought to do what was "just and liberal . . . within the bounds of reason." He told one Indian chief: "We, like you, are Americans, born in the same land, and having the same interests."

In terms of policy, Jefferson promoted the conversion of Indians into farmers rather than continuing as hunter/gatherers. If that failed, he thought they should be provided fair cash value for their land and transported to the western territories. The federal government played a protective role for the most part under Jefferson's presidency, not the role of annihilator. But his policy of making the Indians dependent on the goods of white people, thus obtaining their land when they could not pay, revealed he always saw the fate of the Indian as a consequence of white expansion. "The Indians could "incorporate with us" if they chose to accept 'civilization.' Those who preferred the hunter's life and the old ways of their ancestors would have to withdraw to the west, beyond the Mississippi, as game was depleted and hunting grounds were sold in the east. Eventually they too would have to adopt civilization or perish, as the Louisiana Territory itself and the lands beyond were settled."(*Jefferson and the Indian* by Anthony F.C. Wallace) Hence the Jefferson-created ". . . state was not an empire; it was egalitarian, democratic, and ethnically exclusive." (Wallace)

Ten years after Jefferson's death, the Frenchman Alexis de Tocqueville observed about the United States: "The Union treats the Indians with less cupidity and violence that the several states but the two governments are alike deficient in good faith." Seeking to understand the reasons for this situation, Tocqueville added: "The first of all distinctions in America is money." The quest for most Americans was to join the "moneyed aristocracy" (as Jefferson did). Seizing Indian land and initiating Indian wars was a sure way to attain such riches.

In 1818, President James Monroe, a fellow Virginian, described the Indian's status: "Experience has clearly demonstrated that independent savage communities can no long exist within the limits of a civilized population." Clearly, Jefferson's policy of Indian control and eventual submission to whites passed forward to President Monroe. Yet he too would be made to seem laggardly in his policy toward Indians with the aggressive actions of President Andrew Jackson in 1832.

In reviewing Thomas Jefferson's life, it is important to recall his beginnings. He was born in a simple wooden house in Virginia in the year 1743. Most important was the worldview of the Virginia into which he was born. Winthrop Jordan has helped explain that world view in *White Over Black*.

Jordan documents the Elizabethan English preference of the color white over black and the dislike of the color black. The preference helped establish the mindset for slavery, which was a reality in Virginia by the time of Jefferson's birth. This color bias, along with several other elements previously discussed, made white superiority possible.

> Englishmen did possess a concept of slavery, formed by the clustering of several rough but not illogical equations. The slave was treated like a beast. Slavery was inseparable from the evil in men; it was God's punishment upon Ham's (Noah's son) prurient disobedience. Enslavement was captivity, the loser's lot in a contest of power. Slaves were infidels and heathens. On every count, Negroes qualified.

The English Virginia planters stressed the heathen condition of the Negroes before legislating the slave laws of the 1660s. Jordan comments:

> It may be said, however, that the heathen condition of the Negroes seemed of considerable importance to the English settlers in America— more so than to English voyagers on the coasts of Africa—and that heathenism was associated in some settlers' minds with the condition of slavery.

After 1662, when "white" came to replace "Christian" as an identifier of the sellers, Jordan notes:

> [F]rom the first, then, vis-à-vis the Negro the concept embedded in the terms Christian seems to have conveyed much of the idea and feeling of we as against they, to be a Christian was to be civilized rather than barbarous. English rather than African, white rather than black . . . What may have been his two most striking characteristics,

his heathenism and his appearance, were probably prerequisite to this complete abasement.

The racial die was cast by the time of Jefferson's birth. The early mixing of races had given way to racial caste system in Virginia. Slavery as an institution rested upon a deep animus toward black people, which was created by whites. In this poisoned social atmosphere Thomas Jefferson lived and breathed. The Marquis de Chastellux, a French visitor at the end of the Revolutionary War, clearly saw the problem. In contrast to the ancient slave societies of Greece and Rome where, upon manumission, slaves could meld into society with their former masters, such was not possible in America: "But in the present case, it is not only the slave who is beneath his master, it is the Negro who is beneath the white man. No act of enfranchisement can effect this unfortunate distinction."

Simply because Thomas Jefferson was born and reared in a slave society in Virginia, he was blinded to the fully human qualities of black people. (Of course, with an intellect like Jefferson's, one would have hoped he would penetrate the Slave Regime but the *gestalt* of that Regime cloaked him.) It was why Jefferson, who cherished education as a value among the highest, could not bring himself to be concerned about educating blacks. It was also the reason he could make such comments as the following from *Notes on Virginia*:

> In general, their existence appears to participate more of sensation than reflection. To this must be ascribed their disposition to sleep when abstracted from their diversions, and unemployed in labour. An animal whose body is at rest, and who does not reflect, must be disposed to sleep of course . . .

> Comparing them by their faculties of memory, reason and imagination, it appears to me, that in memory they are equal to the whites; in reason inferior, as I think one could scarcely be found to capable of tracing and, comprehending the investigations of Euclid; and that in the imagination they are dull, tasteless, and anomalous . . . But never yet could I find that a black had uttered a thought above the level of plain narration; never see even an elementary trait of painting or sculpture.

We have singled Thomas Jefferson out for examination because of his fundamental influence on his contemporaries and Americans subsequent to his generation. Probably no other patriot was as widely read nor had as much influence as Jefferson. His views on race were key in the continuing development of the American understanding of white over black.

Jefferson's well-known slavery view was expressed in his metaphor of the wolf: "We have the wolf by the ears, and we can neither hold him, nor safely let him go. Justice is in one case, and self-preservation in the other."

It is noteworthy that this description was written in 1820, near the end of Jefferson's life. The early Jefferson's desire for abolition of slavery had given way to a political realism that rests on the political interests of the South. Yet, underneath it all is Jefferson's Enlightenment ideas of abolition tangled up with the deep soil of racism from which he sprung. He truly was the best of white American and, simultaneously, the worst of the best in his attitudes towards black people.

What the historical period we have considered thus far, from the arrival of Africans in 1619 to Thomas Jefferson's death in 1826, teaches us is how America became a country powered by the ideology of race. Indeed, the primacy of race—the inferiority of blacks and their enslavement and the extermination of the Native Americans—was such a given that, when Jefferson wrote the immortal words in the Declaration of Independence, "We hold these truths to be self-evident . . . etc.," he and his colleagues in the Continental Congress understood he was speaking of a government of white men, by white men, for white men. Others may have understood it broadly, but the intent of the Continental Congress was not universality of application in terms of people but universality of natural rights for particular people, that is, white men.

The Malevolence of Innocence

We have considered the defining of blacks as inferior in the calculus of slavery and will consider the permutations of destruction for the American Indian. However, there is another quality that emerges from the period that enabled this tyranny of the majority to triumph. It is a quality that sustains itself today, as does the problem of the color line. It is a contradiction that enabled the United States simultaneously to view itself as a "city upon a hill" in terms of liberty yet to enslave millions of human beings. It is the quality of innocence.

Innocence as defined here is not in the sense of naiveté. Rather, it is innocence in the purity of the ideal. It is this dimension of innocence, protesting to the British for treating colonists as slaves without linking tyranny to the colonists' slavery of blacks, which has a malevolent effect, even as it sustained the social ideas of a new government. It is a dimension we name the malevolence of innocence. The malevolence of innocence is a major feature of our national character and is rooted in the beginnings of white over black and red in the United States.

Tim O'Brien observed this phenomenon while reflecting on his role in a modern morality tale, the Vietnam Conflict. In a return trip to the area of Vietnam in which he fought twenty-five years earlier, which included the village of My Lai where Vietnamese civilians were massacred by American troops, O'Brien remarks:

> Evil has no place it seems, in our national mythology. We erase it. We use ellipses. We salute ourselves and take pride in America the White Knight, America the Lone Ranger, America's sleek laser-guided weaponry beating up on Saddam and his legion of devils . . . I know what occurred here, yes, but I also feel betrayed by a nation that so widely shrugs off barbarity, by a military judicial system that treats murderers and common soldiers as one and the same. Apparently we're all innocent—those who exercise moral restraint and those who do not, officers who control their troops and officers who do not. In a way, America has declared itself innocent. (*The New York Times Magazine*, October 2, 1994)

O'Brien has it almost correct. Only there is no "apparently" to it and it is not merely the military judicial system that renders everyone innocent. Rather, since near our inception as pre-Victorian era English Puritans in Massachusetts and Christians in Virginia, we have willed ourselves innocent. Initially relying upon centuries of Christian church history, which asserted the innocence of the Christian vis-à-vis the infidel while destroying the Jew and the Moor, we willed ourselves the purity of the religious ideal. We were the New Jerusalem, a city upon a hill in Massachusetts and the new people of God in Virginia. The religious impetus drove us strongly to will our innocence. With the Revolutionary War and the Continental Congress we witnessed an apotheosis. The religious innocence became secular as well. We became the champions of liberty, the upholder of inalienable rights, the number one advocate for the Rights of Man. If Søren Kierkegaard is correct in defining "purity of heart is to will one thing," then we are pure for we have truly willed our national innocence.

The phenomenon of willing innocence becomes malevolent because it enables us to utterly destroy those who oppose us without reflection upon conscience. From Indian destruction and African enslavement through the massacre of My Lai, this secular malevolence of innocence powers our national engine.

Of course, innocence itself cannot be malevolent. Rather, innocence just exists. Or one who is innocent is so by being, not by doing or action. But it is the innocence that springs from religious or secular volition, our willing to be innocent, that is so dangerous. In this created state we can perpetuate whatever horror we wish with a pure conscience. How? Because we are innocent by self-definition and will.

As odd as it seems, Thomas Jefferson and the whites of his period operated on this principle of innocence toward the racial minorities. The whites had a right to Indian land and a right to own property (i.e. slaves), and to keep blacks separate from whites. This was possible because the whites believed they were better, purer, chosen by God or Nature to lead the way. This belief was an innocence they willed with all their hearts and minds. It enabled them to write epochal words about individual rights and limitation of government with an innocence that simultaneously allowed them to practice slavery and genocide. This malevolence of innocence manifests itself repeatedly in our history, yet we blindly perpetuate it by remaining intentionally confined within it through our belief. We are innocent because we will to be innocent translates into the evils of slavery, Wounded Knee, Auschwitz, Hiroshima and My Lai.

It is difficult for us to perceive the quality of malevolent innocence because we have become so secular in our language and world view. The Puritans, however, would recognize this dimension of our national life. Their religious language would enable them to understand that our will to innocence is truly an act of idolatry. By locating within ourselves absolute righteousness we are able to act as we see fit, regardless of considerations of justice in the sense of what God might require of us. Our motives—profit, expedience, racial purity—become a means for a greater end in the making of the United States. Anything is possible when we become god.

For Thomas Jefferson, the malevolence of innocence revealed itself regarding African Americans. Jefferson truly believed, with all his heart and mind, that African Americans were inferior to whites. The depth and purity of this feeling was unshaken throughout his life. As a result, he could not free his slaves nor could the Enlightenment thinker overcome his prejudice. Thus, slavery, an institution he loathed, would remain unchallenged by him in his mature years. He relegated it to the succeeding generations to address. So it was that Thomas Jefferson, an advocate for the abolition of slavery, would die without freeing his slaves.

CHAPTER 5. THE SOUTH AND THE DEATH PENALTY: 1984

The next journey I took to the Florida State Prison, after John Spenkelink's electrocution on May 25, 1979, was in the summer of 1979. I was feeling somewhat recovered from the trauma of John's killing. The post traumatic stress disorder I experienced from the ordeal of the late May slaughter seemed to have dispersed. I was no longer driving through red stop lights and almost having accidents, as I did after my return from John's killing. The nightmares had subsided.

So, I made the journey to Starke again. This time it would be an opportunity for renewed friendships with other guys on the Row. We could grieve together, share the loss of a dear friend and try, as they say in the country, to read the chicken entrails to divine the future. We all knew the killing had just begun.

Of course, I had made the trip so many times it was virtually automatic for me. I flew into Jacksonville, rented a car and began driving southwest to the prison. Everything went as expected as I was driving the rental car across Florida.

Frankly, to this day I do not understand what happened. I was driving with no awareness of anything unusual until suddenly I spotted a sign saying that St. Augustine was less than 30 miles away. St. Augustine? I slowed down and pulled over. How could I be close to St. Augustine? It was in an entirely different direction from Starke. I noticed my hands were trembling. Then it dawned upon me what was transpiring. My unconscious mind would not allow me to go back to the scene of so much pain, suffering and heartbreak. It was silently screaming: NO! Don't go back! For your own good, don't go back.

I chuckled to myself and thought, "Joe, you're in great shape! Complete control, my man!" A few tears welled in my eyes and rolled down my cheeks. And I thought I had overcome the ordeal of John's execution.

Then I thought of the guys who were expecting my visits, which I had begun at the Florida State Prison in 1977. Their faces flitted through my consciousness: Black, brown, white, funny, sad, mentally ill and all poor as church mice. I had to see them. They were expecting me over the next three days beginning tomorrow. I was seeing them as much for myself as I was for them. I needed to be with them. It was the painful truth of death row ministry: More often than not I was the one who received the ministry.

2. James Adams on death watch at the Florida State Prison. Photo by Joe Ingle

Those of us fighting the death penalty in the South knew we were in a life and death struggle. We had few weapons and the power of the state seemed overwhelming at times. But we were, as the apostle Paul put it, "seeing through a glass darkly." We did not know what lay ahead. John Spenkelink had been our baptism in the blood of state killing. And our lack of foresight was a great blessing; for if we had known what awaited us on the road ahead, we would have all turned back.

We were in a desperate struggle with few resources fighting state governments across the South as they sought to execute prisoners. By hard work, state incompetence and the grace of God, only a few were killed by the state machinery of death until 1984. Indeed, in 1983 five had been executed and two were my friends, people I worked with closely: John Evans in Alabama and Jimmy Lee Gray in Mississippi. Then came 1984. It was a year of slaughter in the South. From Texas to Virginia, the state-sanctioned killing machine was well underway. Personally, by the beginning of 1984 I had already lost the following friends to the executioner: John Spenkelink in Florida, Frank Coppola in Virginia, John Evans in Alabama, Jimmy Lee Gray in Mississippi, Bob Sullivan in Florida and Robert Wayne Williams in Louisiana (all described by the author in *Last Rights: 13 Fatal Encounters with the States Justice*). I had also protested Charlie Brook's execution in Texas and Gary Gilmore in Utah.

None of this prepared me for what was about to befall us throughout the South in 1984. We were swirling about the heart of the beast, and the gyre sucked us toward oblivion.

My native state of North Carolina executed its first prisoner in twenty years—James Hutchins. I had grown fond of James in my visits to North Carolina's death row in Raleigh, where I attended high school. His wife Geneva was the proverbial salt of the earth and I truly treasured her companionship. She was heartbroken when James was killed in March. (See *Last Rights*.)

The first week of May I was ensconced in the Florida State Prison with a fellow Tennessean, James Adams. James was innocent of the crime he was charged with, a victim of poor defense representation and being a black man in Florida, but that was of no interest to the state of Florida. He received no binding relief from any court, state or federal. As with virtually all death row cases, James's case was circumscribed by a trial court record poorly made by his lawyer. The courts, especially the U.S. Supreme Court under Chief Justice William Rehnquist, made the presentation of exculpatory evidence post trial exceedingly difficult. Thus, I found myself at the side an innocent man who was set for execution at 7:00 a.m. on May 10, 1984.

On May 9th at 8:00 p.m., I was visiting with James. His stay of execution had been dissolved. He told me how badly it was going for his neighbor on death watch, Alvin Ford, who was in a holding cell near the electric chair. I listened to James concern for Alvin, who was mentally disintegrating, but I had to bracket Alvin from my mind. His execution was not until later in the month. James had only eight hours to live. "James, has there been any other time in your life when you thought you were going to die?," I inquired. His dark eyebrows came together as he concentrated, trying to recall.

"Yes, I remember now," he replied. "I was a youngster, maybe barely a teenager. I really felt I was going to die. I was real sick."

"Can you remember anything else about it?" I asked.

"It was like a dream, Joe. It was like a dream. I was walking away from my own body. I could look back and see Momma, Daddy, everyone around my bed. I could even see the cracks in the floorboard. But I was leaving them all. I knew I was all right, but I couldn't let them know. Then I felt a pulling on my ankles, on my feet, bringing me back. Then I was back."

James looked up and smiled. "You know, I haven't thought of that dream in years. I knew I was dying, but they dragged me back. Where I was heading I don't know, but there was a light. A bright light. That's what I was moving toward when I came back."

There was little I could add to the conversation. Whatever the dream meant to James, it became a buoy for him to hold onto in those last few hours. Maybe there was a bright light, a white light. I didn't know. What I did know with all my trembling soul was that James Adams was in the hands of the Lord. No matter what happened in that electric chair, God's spirit was felt through the life of James Adams. As I considered the good James had done for others, even in the hellhole of F.S.P., I knew "Tennessee" Adams would be home shortly.

James thanked me for our friendship. He said: "I don't mind the dying. It's the killing, the slaughter, which bothers me."

James was slaughtered in the Florida electric chair at 7:00 a.m. on May 10, 1984.

Perhaps I was stunned after James was killed. I don't know. I knew I had to head home to recover a bit before returning in late May for Alvin Ford, whose execution was set for May 31st.

It was strange returning to the killing ground of Florida in late May. I was reminded of my first trip back to the Florida State Prison after John Spenkelink was electrocuted in 1979. This time I consciously concentrated on driving to Starke from Jacksonville. There would be no detour toward St. Augustine.

I was experiencing the same powerful mental undertow I felt almost five years previously. It was exhausting, numbing and I really did not want to go on this final visit to Alvin. But Alvin Ford could not defend himself and those of us who cared about him had to be there to do what we could for him and his family.

Although I had witnessed Alvin's mental deterioration over the months, I was not prepared for the man I encountered now. Alvin was emaciated because he had not eaten since the death warrant was signed and he had been moved to Q-wing. I recalled the slightly depressed but cogent Alvin I had met in 1979. The starving countenance before me, mumbling incoherently, eyes closed and then fluttering involuntarily, did not seem to be the same man.

Alvin's vocabulary had not changed much since our last visit. "RS, pipe alley, destiny, Pope II," a cascading whisper of indecipherable code that enabled Alvin to navigate the trauma of death row. All I could do was express my support, let him know he was loved and listen to an unintelligible language from a man whose appearance suggested an African apparition more than a dear friend. It was thirty days since he had stopped eating, upon his removal to Q-wing when his death warrant was signed.

A community of people had gathered around Alvin as he descended into madness. Larry Wallen, a professor at Florida State University, Gail Rowland, a paralegal, Margaret Vandiver, his lawyers and me. His mother, Connie Ford, visited from south Florida whenever she could. Additionally, the guys on the Row were looking out for him, trying to help him as best they could. Two of them, Jacob Dugan and Elwood Barclay, were sitting on either side of him in the holding cage when Margaret, Gail and I came to visit. They were gently talking to him, telling him everything was going to be all right. "Here come Gail, Margaret and Joe to see you." Clearly, the news we received late the previous night of the U.S. Supreme Court granting a stay of execution had not penetrated Alvin's mind. He sat in the corner of the cage, eyes fluttering, gaunt, being ministered to by his death row brothers.

Our trio entered the Colonel's room and asked the guards to bring Alvin in to join us. Alvin came in, handcuffed, and sat down opposite us. Once again, we began the painful process of trying to communicate with an insane man we dearly loved.

As Alvin babbled, Margaret, Gail and I sat across from him trying to connect with him. After a roller coaster ride in the appellate courts, the U.S. Supreme Court had just given Alvin a stay of execution and decided to take his case to determine whether or not it was constitutional to execute the insane in the United States. *Ford v. Wainwright* would become landmark constitutional law. The stay had come hours before his scheduled electrocution.

As we sought to reach Alvin, to let him know the good news, the words of the psychiatric report done by the state's panel of mental health experts kept rising in my mind. Until this moment, I thought I understood the power of self-interest as a motivating force for an individual. But to think that a panel of three psychiatrists found the man mumbling before me to be competent to be executed was a withering indictment of the medical profession. The Hippocratic oath, admonishing physicians to do no harm, appeared to have not penetrated the Florida border.

Yet as I gazed at Alvin, I believed that somewhere, deep inside, beneath the rambling nonsense, behind the vacant stare and the fluttering eyelids, the Alvin I loved was there. I tried to focus on that person as I spoke.

> Alvin, they are not going to kill you. They aren't going to kill you. You have a stay. Do you hear me? Do you understand? They are not going to kill you.

Gail would try to communicate. Then Margaret had a go. We sat close to Alvin, held his manacled hands, peered into those shuttered, fluttering eyes. But nothing we said or did appeared to pierce the gibberish. Finally, as the morning wore on to completion, I stood up. I looked through the glass windows to the larger Colonel's room. The prisoner runners bringing the luncheon trays to the prisoners with visitors were busy unloading their cart. I stepped outside the interview room, stretched and looked at the trays.

Acting on intuition, I asked the runner to give Alvin a tray. He looked at me like I was crazy because he knew Alvin had been refusing to eat. I opened the door to the interview room and he placed the food tray at Alvin's feet. I told Alvin we were going to have a prayer. Gail held one hand, I another and Margaret linked Gail and me together. I uttered a short prayer of thanksgiving for Alvin's life. After completing the prayer, Alvin, without responding beyond his usual unintelligible rambling, leaned over and picked the tray up. He then began shoveling the food into his mouth, eating with the lust of the starving man he was. Gail, Margaret and I looked at each other. We knew that Alvin knew and we wept. The eating signified he understood he would live, and tears of joy, rage, and relief rolled down my cheeks. Alvin Ford would live beyond Florida's latest attempt to electrocute an insane man. Thank God.

Gail, Margaret and I joined other members of the defense team for Alvin for a celebratory dinner in a local eatery. We laughed and cried, reviewing the story of working with a man over the years who had been driven into insanity by the machinery of state killing.

On June 26, 1986, the U.S. Supreme Court ruled in *Ford v. Wainwright* that the constitution of the United States prohibited the execution of the insane. The 5–4 decision meant Alvin Ford would live indefinitely unless the state could make him competent for execution through treatment. Then he could be executed. Justice Lewis Powell cast the key vote.

Alvin never came back from his descent into madness. Removed from the death watch area of Q-wing back to the "bug" area of Q-wing where guys with mental problems were kept, Alvin lingered on death row, carrying on his monologue of madness. Of course, the state made desultory attempts to have him ruled competent so they could kill him, but Alvin was too far gone to be reached.

The Context

Alvin Ford survived the year which saw more executions than any since 1962. As 1984 rolled on, I was back at F.S.P. in July for David Washington's electrocution. The U.S. Supreme Court used his case, *Strickland v. Washington*, to lower the level of defense lawyers' competency at trial to the nadir. As one lawyer put it, if someone puts a mirror before your face and vapor appears on it, you are now competent to try a death penalty case. David was killed on July 13, 1984. In September it was Louisiana and I walked Tim Baldwin to the electric chair on September 10, 1984. David guilty, Tim innocent, both good friends of mine. Back to my native state of North Carolina for dear Velma Barfield's execution on November 2, 1984. (These stories are recounted in *Last Rights: 13 Fatal Encounters with the State's Justice*.) The year of 1984 witnessed 21 executions. The beat goes on.

***

Alvin Ford died in February of 1991 while on Florida's death row. I was enjoying a Merrill Fellowship at Harvard University which provided a welcome break from the Southern killing ground. I received a telephone call from Margaret Vandiver, who told me of the strange circumstances of Alvin's death.

3. Alvin Ford, Florida State Prison, May 1984. Photo: The Florida Alligator.

Since the medical staff at the Florida State Prison regarded Alvin as a malingerer, they were in no hurry to come to his aid when a runner serving breakfast discovered Alvin unconscious in his cell. It took a good ten minutes to get a medical orderly to the cell and another thirty minutes to get the stretcher to carry him to the medical clinic. Then there was a ninety-minute delay before an ambulance arrived.

The arriving paramedics were unencumbered with the medical laxity that the prison health professionals brought to their cursory treatment of Alvin. They quickly determined his blood pressure was dangerously high and transported him to Shands Hospital in Gainesville. Two days later, on February 28, 1991, Alvin Ford died. Connie Ford, Alvin's mother, who had cherished her son through the ordeal of imprisonment and madness, did not learn of her son's hospitalization until she was notified of his death.

A strange symmetry emerged from the process of Alvin's disintegration into insanity. The young, sane Alvin had worked in the criminal justice system as a guard at Union Correctional Institution just down the road from the Florida State Prison. In his early days incarcerated at F.S.P., he talked of how he had hoped to make a difference with his life. He wished to make a contribution to society.

Although the sane Alvin was unable to make that positive difference, the descent into madness resulted in a precedent-setting case, *Ford v. Wainwright*.

Alvin made his contribution because he lost his mind and ultimately his life. A modicum of justice emerged from a cruel, crazy system which had no room for justice, only finality. It took a mad man to move the U.S. Supreme Court a step away from the madness of state sanctioned killing.

Chapter 6. The Tyranny of the Majority

As we have seen in reconsidering the initiation and development of the governing process in what would become the United States of America, almost from the inception it was limited to a government for European settlers. From the initial English colonies through the ratification of the Constitution of the United States, the African and Native American people were either excluded or defined in a manner that denied their humanity and political rights. We term this exercise of disfranchisement by the white majority of the racial minorities the tyranny of the majority.

The perception of a racial majoritarian tyranny of whites over minorities in the country was initially articulated by a Frenchman, Alexis de Tocqueville. It is worth examining Tocqueville and his classic work on government and customs in the United States, *Democracy in America*, in order to comprehend the phenomenon of the tyranny of the majority.

On May 9, 1831, Alexis de Tocqueville and his traveling companion, Gustave de Beaumont, arrived in Providence, Rhode Island from Havre, France. The two young men were magistrates on an eighteen month leave from their posts with the French Ministry of Justice. Their assignment was to observe and report on the American prison system, which was experimenting with new concepts of punishment and reform. Each man also harbored an abiding interest in the experiment of democracy underway in the young United States of America.

Tocqueville, not quite twenty-six years old upon arrival in America after his thirty-eight day sail from France, was funded on his leave by his family. The Ministry of Justice authorized the leaves of the two magistrates and expected a report but provided no funding for the journey.

The two friends embarked upon a steamer from Providence to New York City. Arriving in New York on the morning of May 11, 1831, they viewed a bit of the city then went to bed at 4:00 p.m., exhausted from their journey. Their mission began in earnest on May 12, 1831.

Tocqueville and Beaumont visited every important prison in the country in preparation for a full report to the Minister of Justice. Their task was to determine how best to reform prisoners as well as examine new policies such as solitary confinement. The report became the most complete done on American prison policy and advocated reform in France.

As significant as the prison report became in France, it was truly a subtext for a larger quest by the two magistrates. They were intrigued by the American democratic form of government and frustrated by the forced marriage of monarchy and democracy in France. They hoped through their observations and writing about the people and government in the United States to illustrate what France and the other European nations might borrow to assist them on the path to democracy. In order to complete this goal the duo traveled to every state east of the Mississippi except Maine, New Hampshire, Vermont, Florida, Indiana, and Illinois.

Shortly after returning to France, Beaumont was dismissed from his post for refusing to argue a case without merit. Tocqueville resigned the same day, disgusted at the French judiciary. They completed their prison report and submitted it to the Minister of Justice. Then each turned to his own writing project born from the visit to America.

Beaumont, moved by the racial discrimination he witnessed in America, wrote a novel: *Marie*. It was a poignant examination of a young Frenchman who falls in love with an American woman who appears white but is from a racially mixed background. The two lovers seek permission to marry and then flee the city for the wilderness to escape the approbation of white society. Their story chronicles the racial antipathy Beaumont observed in America.

Tocqueville wrote a two volume work entitled *Democracy in America*. Volume I was published in Paris in 1835 and Volume II in 1840. The work soon came to be regarded as the standard work on the government and people of the United States.

Although from an aristocratic background, Tocqueville was imbued with the ideas of the Enlightenment. The eighteenth century French philosophers moved him beyond the provincial interests of class and the Catholic church. He became animated by the liberal views of French contemporaries. The political notions of the *ancien regime*, of which his family was once a member, gave way to the political appeal of democracy. His appraisal of Thomas Jefferson in *Democracy in America*: "I am glad to cite the opinion of Jefferson upon the subject rather than that of any other, because I consider him the most powerful advocate democracy has ever had" revealed not only a deep appreciation for democracy but the recognition of a kindred spirit.

Democracy in America is a praiseworthy evaluation of government in the United States. However, in Chapter XV of Volume 1, Tocqueville raises a fundamental concern. The chapter is entitled: "Unlimited Power of the Majority in the United States, and its Consequences." Within this chapter Tocqueville expresses his fear of the "possible tyranny of the majority." He also discusses why the majority is "omnipotent" in America. As one historian remarks "Throughout both parts of the *Democracy* this inquiry runs as a continuous thread in the design, a recurrent element in the whole pattern. It is not too much to say that is the real *raison d*'être for the writing of the *Democracy* (Phillips Bradley).

Tocqueville's keen insight enabled him to see that a democracy did not mean everyone's rights were respected but only those of the majority. "I have already observed that the advantage of democracy is not as has been sometimes asserted, that it protects the interests of all, but simply that it protects those of the majority." It was this perspective he brought to analyzing the racial composition of the United States and how it played out politically.

In Chapter XVIII, "The Present and Probable Future Condition of the Three Races that Inhabit the Territory of the United States," observing the geographic breadth of the United States, Tocqueville comments on its inhabitants:

> The human beings who are scattered over this space do not form, as in Europe, so many branches of the same stock. Three races, naturally distinct, and, I might almost say, hostile to each other, are discoverable among them at the first glance. Almost insurmountable barriers had been raised between them by education and law, as well as by their origin and outward characteristics, but fortune has brought them together on the same soil, where, although they are mixed, they do not amalgamate, and each race fulfills its destiny apart.

Tocqueville proceeds to analyze the races:

> Among these widely differing families of men, the first that attracts attention, the superior in intelligence, in power, and in enjoyment, is the white, or European, the MAN pre-eminently so called; below him appear the Negro and the Indian. These two unhappy races have nothing in common, neither birth, nor features, nor languages, nor habits. Their only resemblance lies in their misfortunes. Both of them occupy an equally inferior position in the country they inhabit; both suffer from tyranny; and if their wrongs are not the same, they originate from the same authors.

Tocqueville clearly declares that the minority races "both suffer from tyranny." The source of their tyranny is the European whites:

> We should almost say that the European is to the other races of mankind what man himself is to the lower animals: he makes them subservient to his use, and when he cannot subdue he destroys them. Oppression has, at one stroke, deprived the descendants of the Africans of almost all the privileges of humanity . . . Oppression has been no less fatal to the Indian than to the Negro race, but its effects are different. The Europeans, having dispersed the Indian tribes and driven them into the deserts, condemned them to a wandering life, full of inexpressible sufferings.

He concludes:

> European tyranny rendered them more disorderly and less civilized than they were before.

Tocqueville absorbed the fate of the Cherokee at the hands of the state of Georgia and the United States government during his travels through America. Indeed, he included a lengthy quote from the Cherokee petition to Congress in Chapter XVIII. He succinctly describes the treatment of the Indians by the state and federal governments: "Thus tyranny of the states obliges the savages to retire; the Union, by its promises and resources, facilitates them retreat; and these measures tend to precisely the same end." A more decorous description of the Indian Removal Act was never rendered.

In concluding his consideration of the Indians, Tocqueville compares the fate of the Indians in the hands of the Spanish with their demise under white Americans:

> The Spaniards were unable to exterminate the Indian race by those unparalleled atrocities which brand them with indelible shame, nor did they succeed even in wholly depriving it of its rights; but the Americans of the United States have accomplished this twofold purpose with singular felicity, tranquility, legally, philanthropically, without shedding blood; and without violating a single great principle of morality in the eyes of the world. It is impossible to destroy men with more respect for the laws of humanity.

The perspective of history has allowed us a more thorough consideration of how fairly white Americans treated Native Americans and our rendering of judgment is more critical than Tocqueville. However, the profundity of his insight from a visit of nine months over one hundred and eighty years ago is startling. Indeed, white Americans convinced themselves and the world what they did to the Indians was unavoidable and for the best interest of the Indians. As Tocqueville so eloquently expressed the spirit of the day: "It is impossible to destroy men with more respect for the laws of humanity."

And after treating the Indians, Tocqueville ponders the plight of the black population. It is a grim and prophetic vision he proclaims:

> The Indians will perish in the same isolated condition in which they have lived, but the destiny of the Negroes is in some measure interwoven with that of the Europeans. These two faces are fastened to each other without intermingling; and they are alike unable to separate entirely or to combine. The most formidable of all the ills that threaten the future of the Union arises from the presence of a black population upon its territory; and in contemplating the cause of the present embarrassments, or the future dangers on the United States, the observer is invariably led to this as a primary fact.

The lurking schism beneath the surface calm of the United States was perceived by Tocqueville. This racial tension, the evil polarity of slavery, the Jim Crow society in the North, were all taken in by the perspicacious Frenchman.

In reviewing slavery of the South, Tocqueville compared it with the slavery of classical times:

> The only means by which the ancients maintained slavery was fetters and death; the Americans of the South of the Union have discovered more intellectual securities for the duration of their power. They have employed their despotism and their violence against the human mind. In antiquity precautions were taken to prevent the slave from breaking his chains; at the present day measures are adopted to deprive him even of the desire for freedom. The ancients kept the bodies of their slaves in bondage, but placed no restraint upon the mind and no check upon education; and they acted consistently with their established principle, since a natural termination of slavery then existed, and one day or other the slave might be set free and become the equal of his master. But the Americans of the South, who do not admit that the Negroes can ever be commingled with themselves, have forbidden them, under severe penalties, to be taught to read or write, and as they will not raise them to their own level, they sink them nearly as possible to that of the brutes.

The Civil War to come was foreseen by Tocqueville. "Whatever may be the efforts of the Americans of the South to maintain slavery, they will not always succeed. Slavery, now confined to a single tract of the civilized earth, attacked by Christianity as unjust and by political economy as prejudicial, and now contrasted with democratic liberty and the intelligence of our age, cannot survive."

More profound than the glimpse of the future was Tocqueville's discerning what kind of future awaited Americans after the abolition of slavery:

> If I were called upon to predict the future, I should say that the abolition of slavery in the South will, in the common course of things, increase the repugnance of the white population for the blacks. I base this opinion upon the analogous observation I already made in the North. I have remarked that the white inhabitants of the North avoid the Negroes with increasing care in proportion as the legal barriers of separation are removed by the legislature; and why should not the same result take place in the South? In the North the whites are deterred from intermingling with the blacks by an imaginary danger; in the South, where the danger would be real, I cannot believe that the fear would be less.

Tocqueville quotes Thomas Jefferson to substantiate his fears of the fate of blacks after abolition: "Nothing is more clearly written in the book of destiny than the emancipation of the blacks; and it is equally certain, that the two races will never live in a state of equal freedom under the same government, so insurmountable are the barriers which nature, habit and opinion have established between them."

Democracy in America illuminates American life as no other work has done. As Robert Bellah has reminded us in *Habits of the Heart*, perhaps its greatest insight is into the manners, customs, or what Tocqueville refers to as "the habits of the heart." For it is in the plumbing of the morals, not merely the laws, Tocqueville discovers Americans' greatest strength and gravest folly. He clearly sees the habits of the heart of white Americans for blacks are rooted in a hostility that festers long past legal equality.

> I see that in a certain portion of the territory of the United States at the present day the legal barrier which separated the two races is falling away, but not that which exists in the manners of the country; slavery recedes, but the prejudice to which it has given birth is immovable. Whoever has inhabited the United States must have perceived that in those parts of the Union in which the Negroes are no longer slaves they have in no wise drawn nearer to the whites. On the contrary, the prejudice of race appears to be stronger in the states that have abolished slavery than in those where it still exists; and nowhere is it so intolerant as in those states where servitude has never been known.

Why is this the case? Again, Tocqueville returns to the slavery of antiquity for instruction:

> The greatest difficulty in antiquity was that of altering the law; among the moderns it is that of altering the customs, and as far as we are concerned, the real obstacles begin where those of the ancients left off. This arises from the circumstances that among the moderns the abstract and transient fact of slavery is fatally united with the physical and permanent fact of color. The tradition of slavery dishonors the race,

and the peculiarity of the race perpetuates the tradition of slavery. No African has ever voluntarily emigrated to the shores of the New World, whence it follows that all the blacks who are found there are either slaves or freedmen. Thus the Negro transmits the eternal mark of his ignominy to all his descendants; and although the law may abolish slavery, God alone can obliterate the traces of its existence . . . The moderns, then, after they have abolished slavery, have three prejudices to contend against, which are less easy to attack and far less easy to conquer than the mere fact of servitude; the prejudice of the master, the prejudice of the race, and the prejudice of color.

Although Tocqueville could not anticipate how insidious the attempt to maintain blacks in peonage and servitude would become after the abolition of slavery, he clearly recognized the power of prejudice of the whites toward the blacks. It is a force that has manifested itself to the present day. In many ways, we are grappling with the habit of racial prejudice today as were those dwelling in the late nineteenth century. The tyranny of the white majority, so strong in Tocqueville's day is still a tidal wave in social customs and political exercise today.

Tocqueville's ground-breaking work in *Democracy in America* chronicled, in Chapter XVIII, "The Three Races in the United States," the racial tension and conflict in America. He mentions "the tyranny" and "oppression" the Indians and Africans suffer at the hands of the white state and federal governments. In Chapter XV, "Unlimited Power of the Majority in the United States and its Consequences," Tocqueville examines the political mechanism that enables such tyranny to occur. After sketching the three branches of government-the executive, the legislative and the judicial—he comments on the majority propelling the political process:

"The majority in that country, therefore, exercise a prodigious actual authority, and a power of opinion which is nearly as great; no obstacles exist which can impede or even retard its progress, so as to make it heed the complaints of those whom it crushes upon its path. This state of things is harmful in itself and dangerous for the future."

Tocqueville feared "the Unlimited Power of the Majority" even as he knew social power must be vested somewhere. So even though he was an advocate of democracy, he proclaimed it with fear and trembling: "In my opinion, the main evil of the present democratic institutions of the United States does not arise, as is often asserted in Europe, from their weakness, but from their irresistible strength. I am not so much alarmed at the excessive liberty which reigns in that country as at the inadequate securities which one finds there against tyranny."

As Tocqueville aptly describes the dilemma:

When an individual or a party is wronged in the United States to whom can he apply for redress? If to public opinion, public opinion constitutes the majority, if to the legislature, it represents the majority and implicitly obeys it; if to the executive power, it is appointed by the majority and serves as a passive tool in its hands. The public force consists of the majority under arms; the jury is majority invested with the right of hearing judicial cases; and in certain states even the judges are elected by the majority. How ever iniquitous or absurd the measure of which you complain, you must submit to it as well as you can.

Coupled with Chapter XVIII, Chapter XV provides a searing indictment of how a majoritarian tyranny has and does function in the United States. Yet Tocqueville states in Chapter XV, "I do not say that there is a frequent use of tyranny in America at the present day, but I maintain that there is no sure barrier against it and that the causes which mitigate the government there are to be found in the circumstances and manners of the country more than its laws."

Tocqueville, the eloquent recorder of the oppression of the African and the Indian, finds, however an infrequent "use of tyranny in America at the present day." It is certainly not infrequent use of tyranny when viewed from the perspective of the racial minorities. For the democratic Frenchman, as with his model Jefferson, it was the white majorities right to own and, if necessary, tyrannize the Africans and the Indians. The presumption of manifest destiny by the white majority creates the very despotism Tocqueville and Jefferson feared. Yet neither Jefferson, who would not free his slaves, nor Tocqueville, a champion of democracy from aristocracy, would advocate the equality of humanity necessary to prevent a majoritarian tyranny.

In closing the section of the power of the tyranny of the majority, Tocqueville sounds a warning for the future of the young democracy. "Absolute monarchies had dishonored despotism; let us beware lest democratic republics should reinstate it and render it less odious and degrading in the eyes of the many by making it still more onerous to the few." It would be one hundred and eighty plus years before perspective was gained through the consideration of history and the experience of the majoritarian tyranny to consider how the odious democratic despotism Tocqueville warned about had come to pass in the United States.

CHAPTER 7. THE GENOCIDE REGIME (1830–1890)

At the time of the first meaningful European contact with the native people of North America in 1492, current estimates place their population at approximately 40 million. By 1890, when the massacre at Wounded Knee culminated the European conquest of the native inhabitants of the continent, the population was approximately 250,000. This staggering destruction of life, liberty and culture was accomplished with weapons, diseases and wholesale slaughter.

Although some would use the word "genocide" to describe this entire period, my own view limits the genocidal period between 1830 and 1890. The boundaries are the 1830 passage of the Indian Removal Act by Congress with President Andrew Jackson signing it into law and the 1890 massacre at Wounded Knee. There can be no doubt about the intent of the government of the United States from the passage of the Indian Removal Act to Wounded Knee. The Indian Removal Act fulfills the formal definition of genocide: "The systematic, planned annihilation of a racial, political or cultural group." Wounded Knee was its final act of slaughter.

The twentieth century experience with the Holocaust serves as our primary example of genocide. As one writer described it: "The Third Reich accomplished in twelve years what the Christian church had been trying to do for 1,200 years." (Raul Hilberg, *The Destruction of the European Jews*) A similar claim could be made against the United States government. From 1830 to 1890, the government systematically implemented what had been a sustained but episodic campaign against the Indians since 1607. As with the Jews of Europe and their extermination by the Nazi's, when it was all over the Indians were in camps (reservations) or dead. The Indian holocaust was complete.

The Cherokee

A few events preceding the Indian Removal Act chronicle the changing plight of the Indian of the South. On December 21, 1808, six Cherokee chiefs, who had journeyed to see President Thomas Jefferson in Washington, D.C. gave him the following report:

> Father—The underwritten, chiefs of the Cherokee Nation instructed by their national council to come to the city of Washington and there to take by the hand their father the President , and express to him in behalf of their nation their sincere sentiments of gratitude and to say to him—that, for nearly eight years they have experienced his protecting and fostering hand, under which they progressed in agriculture and domestic manufactures much beyond their own expectations or the expectations of their white Brethren of the United States and that by the schools many of their children have made great advancement in the useful facts of English education, such as reading, writing, and arithmetic—that by means of these acquisitions the desirable work of civilization advances and will in future be accelerated and knowledge diffused more easily and widely amongst their people provided the same measures shall be [pursued] by your successor in office, which they please themselves will be the case and that he will also hold them fast by the hand and that the magnanimity of the U. States will not suffer ten thousand human being [to] be lost between whom and the white people the great Spirit has made no difference, for they believe that the great Spirit loves his red children and as well as his white children and looks with equal eye on the works of his hands, and that their final destination is the same.

> Father—

> When you retire from the Administration of the great business which has been committed to your hand by our white Brethren, a consciousness of upright intentions will be your reward; a reward beyond the lash of contingencies—that the great Spirit will add yet many years to your useful life and that it may be happy is the affectionate wish of the red people whom we represent.

The War of 1812 would force the major southern tribes—the Cherokee, the Choctaw, the Chickasaw, and the Creek—to choose which white warring faction to join: British or American. The Creeks were already split into Upper Creek (anti-American) and Lower Creek. On August 30, 1813, the Upper Creeks destroyed Fort Mims in lower Alabama and killed more than 350 people. This event led the Lower Creeks, Choctaws, and Cherokees to join the American forces.

The American militia was headed by Andrew Jackson of Tennessee. He organized a force of 2,500 volunteers to attack the Upper Creeks. He welcomed the Indian tribes who volunteered to assist in the campaign. John Ridge, a Cherokee leader who had been one of the six chiefs who had journeyed to meet President Jefferson in Washington, brought two hundred warriors with him. The Cherokees met the Upper Creeks at Talladega and defeated them. However, the Red Sticks (as the Upper Creek were called for the red sticks they carried into battle) retreated to regroup. As the winter set in, the Cherokees had led the fighting and the Tennessee militia was unhappy with its own lack of action. The soldiers began to return home and, in January, Jackson was down to less than 200 men. The Cherokees also left to return to their homes but provided Jackson's men the corn they needed to survive the winter.

In March, the Cherokees rejoined General Jackson. By mid-March, his white forces had risen as well so that he had a command of five thousand soldiers to pursue the Creeks. Traveling deep into Creek country, Jackson's forces encountered the Red Sticks who were fortified behind breastworks on the Tallapoosa River. Earlier, Jackson had divided his force to search for the Red Sticks so now he faced an entrenched enemy of a thousand warriors and he no longer had the overwhelming numerical support he favored.

The Cherokees under John Ridge opened the battle by swimming across the river and stealing the Red Sticks' canoes. Once the canoes were brought to the Cherokee side, the Indians clambered aboard and paddled to the attack against their foes. The Creeks retreated behind the breastworks after trying to defend the canoes. General Jackson ordered a flanking attack on the breast works. The Red Sticks, caught in a pincers, fought long and valiantly. After five hours, with half the Creeks dead and the breastworks on fire, the remaining Red Sticks dashed to the river. The Cherokees met them and the battle ended in the Tallapoosa River. No Creeks surrendered. The final count of the corpses was 907 Red Stick warriors dead. An unspecified number of squaws were also dead. A hundred or so wounded warriors escaped. For the Cherokees there were eighteen dead and forty-six wounded, while the Tennessee militia lost thirty-two dead and ninety-nine wounded. The final total was a triumphant victory for Jackson who dubbed it the Battle of Horseshoe Bend. This victory along with the Battle of New Orleans in 1815 catapulted him into national prominence. It would not have been accomplished without the assistance of the Cherokee nation.

The Red Sticks who survived fled to Florida and allied themselves with the Seminoles. The Lower Creeks, who aided Jackson against their brethren, were forced to relinquish nearly eight million acres to the U.S. government. In 1818 General Jackson once again took the field against the Indians. Supported by the Lower Creeks, he campaigned against the Seminoles and Red Sticks in Florida. Although unable to defeat the Indians conclusively, he conquered enough of Florida to force Spain to yield Florida to the United States. By 1835 the Red Sticks and Seminoles had waged a seven year war against the U.S., which cost 1,500 American lives and approximately $60,000,000. Although 4,000 Indians were captured and sent west, the government abandoned the war. To this day descendants of Seminoles and Mikasukis dwell in the freedom of the Everglades, unconquered by government troops.

Andrew Jackson took office as President of the United States in 1829. In July of that year, whites learned of gold on Cherokee land in Georgia. By the fall of 1829 they were pouring into the Cherokee land seeking the gold nuggets in the streams of the north Georgia mountains. It was the richest gold strike since an earlier one in North Carolina, the previous gold capital of the United States. Instead of driving the miners out, the Cherokee awaited the assistance of their Great Father in Washington, D.C.

On December 8, 1929, President Andrew Jackson sent his first message to Congress and asked for removal of Indians from the eastern United States, "voluntary, for it would be cruel and unjust to compel them to abandon the graves of their fathers and seek a home in a distant world." In effect, he sided with Georgia's claim to the Cherokee land because he ordered no mobilization of troops to protect them.

The Georgia legislature, taking note of President's Jackson's leanings, convened in mid-December and began passing laws to ensure its right to the gold found on the Cherokee land. It forbade the Cherokee "in digging for gold in said land, and taking therefrom great amounts of value, thereby appropriating riches to themselves which of right equally belong to very other citizen of the state." John Ehle details the extent of the greed of the white Georgians:

> They passed a law that further denied Indians rights in a court, declaring that an Indian cannot testify at a trial involving white men; that no Indian testimony was valid without at least two white witnesses, that no Indian contract was valid without at least two witnesses. They voted through a bill making it unlawful 'for any person or body of persons . . . to prevent, or deter any Indian, head man, chief, or warrior of said Nation . . . from selling or ceding to the United States, for the use of Georgia, the whole or any part of said territory'. The penalty was a sentence in the Georgia penitentiary, at hard labor, for up to four years. They passed a bill making it illegal for any person or body of person to prevent, by threat of force or threat, Cherokees from agreeing to emigrate or from moving to the West. They passed in this same bill a provision outlawing all the meetings of the Cherokee council and all political assemblies of Indians in Georgia, except for purposes of ceding land. These measures were to take effect in June of 1830—only six months away. (*Trail of Tears*)

The new Georgia laws stood in direct conflict with the action of the Cherokee council in the fall of 1829. In response to the white onslaught on their lands, the Cherokee affirmed an age old law by putting it in writing:

> Whereas a Law has been in existence for many years, but not committed to writing, that if any citizen or citizens of this nation treat and dispose of any lands belonging to this nation without special permission from the national authorities, he or they shall suffer death; therefore, resolved, by the Committee and Council, in General Council convened, that any person or persons who shall, contrary to the will and consent of the legislative Council of this nation in General Council convened, enter into a treaty with any commissioner or commissioners of the United States, or any officers instructed for the purpose, and agree to sell or dispose of any part or portion of the national lands defined in the constitution of this nation, he or they so offending, upon conviction before any of the circuit judges of the Supreme Court [the Cherokee had constructed a Supreme Court, modeled after the U.S., out of wood in New Echota, Georgia], shall suffer death; and any of the circuit judges aforesaid are authorized to call a court for the trial of any such person or persons so transgressing. Be it further resolved, that any person or persons, who shall violate the provisions of this act, and shall refuse, by resistance, to appear at the place designated for trial, or abscond, are hereby declare to be outlaws; and any person or persons, citizens of this nation, may kill him or them so offending, in any manner most convenient, within the limits of this nation, and shall not be held accountable for the same.

Clearly, the state of Georgia and the Cherokee nation were on a collision course. Who would prevail would be decided by the U.S. Supreme Court and President Jackson.

On May 28, 1830, the Indian Removal bill was passed by Congress. It had been pushed hard by the Jackson administration. William Wirt accepted retainer by the Cherokees to challenge their treatment by Georgia and the United States. He filed an appeal to the U.S. Supreme Court in conjunction with a case where a Cherokee had been sentenced to die by Georgia. Chief Justice John Marshall ordered the state of Georgia to show cause why the Court should not issue a notice of error. Instead, the governor of Georgia asked the legislature for advice. The elected body of white men, what Jefferson once termed 'legislative despotism' in Virginia, told the governor to ignore the Supreme Court and proceed with haste to execute the prisoner. The prisoner was hanged.

The action of the Georgia legislature was consistent with the white policy of taking Indian land. Although Thomas Jefferson had sought to make sure there was a valid cash equivalent paid for the land, he acknowledged the white right to the land if the Indians refused to become farmers. Of course, Georgia was not concerned with giving anything for the land but simply taking it. The fact that the Cherokee were prosperous farmers was also beside the point. Gold had been discovered on Indian land and it was, therefore, the right of the whites to take it.

The Cherokee, an advanced tribe with their own alphabet created by Sequoyah, began publishing a newspaper in 1828 entitled the *Phoenix*. Its editor, Elias Boudinot, described the situation aptly: "Here is the secret. Full license to our oppressors, and every avenue of justice closed to us. Yes, this is the bitter cup prepared for us by a republican and religious government— we shall drink it to the very dregs." Although the Cherokees were standing firm on their land, the Choctaws gave in and moved west.

In March of 1831, the U.S. Supreme Court heard oral argument from William Wirt regarding the Cherokee conflict with Georgia. Mr. Wirt argued eloquently before the Court:

> We know that whatever can be properly done for this unfortunate people will be done by this honorable court. Their cause is one that must come home to every honest and feeling heart. They have been true and faithful to us and have a right to expect a corresponding fidelity on our part. Through a long course of years they have followed our counsel with the docility of children. Our wish has been their law. We asked them to become civilized, and they became so. They assumed our dress, copied our names, pursued our course of education, adopted our form of government, embraced our religion, and have been proud to imitate us in everything in their power. They have watched the progress of our prosperity with the strongest interest, and have marked the rising grandeur of our nation with as much pride as if the belonged to us. They have even adopted our resentments, and in our war with the Seminole tribes, they voluntarily joined our arms, and gave effectual aid in driving back those barbarians from the very state that now oppresses them. They threw upon the field, in that war, a body of men who descend from the noble race that were once the lords of these extensive forests—men worthy to associate with the 'lion', who, in their own language, 'walks upon the mountain tops.' They fought side by side with our present chief magistrate, and received his personal thanks for their gallantry and bravery.

Chief Justice John Marshall read the Supreme Court's decision on July 18, 1831. Despite stating his personal admiration of the Cherokee, he could not accept their claim to be an independent, indeed, foreign nation. Granted they were a separate state but they were "a domestic, dependent nation." At every turn—the Congress, the Supreme Court, the President—the Cherokee were denied. The Indian Removal Act would commence but the Georgians could not wait. They began incursions on Cherokee land with militia support. John Ridge described the Cherokee situation:

You asked us to throw off the hunter and warrior state. We did so—you asked us to form a republican government; We did so—adopting your own as a model. You asked us to cultivate the earth, and learn the mechanic arts: We did so. You asked us to learn to read: We did so. You asked us to cast away our idols, and worship your God. We did so.

In 1832 another case reached the Supreme Court: *Worcester and Butler v. Georgia*. The Supreme Court ruled it was unconstitutional for Georgia to imprison missionaries to the Cherokee and declared the Indian code passed by Georgia invalid:

The Cherokee Nation then is a distinct community, occupying its own territory, with boundaries accurately described, in which the laws of Georgia can have no force, and which the citizens of Georgia have no right to enter but with the assent of the Cherokees themselves or in conformity with treaties and acts of Congress.

President Jackson, who owed his career and even his life to the Cherokee, would have none of it. He was quoted as saying, "Chief Justice Marshall has made his ruling; now let him enforce it. I have soldiers, he doesn't."

The President had urged a Georgia senator to "build a fire under them. When it gets hot enough, they'll move." John Ridge, his old comrade in arms, made a personal appeal for assistance to the Cherokees by stopping the depredations of the Georgians; Jackson said no. He urged Ridge to return home and tell the Cherokee "that their only hope of relief was in abandoning their country and moving to the West." The state of Georgia staged a lottery to decide what Cherokee land would be acquired by Georgians.

For the next several years the Cherokees struggled amongst themselves in various councils. One group, led by John Ridge and Elias Boudinot, felt the inevitable point had been reached. A negotiated settlement with the government, on the best terms possible including cash for land, was the only option they realistically foresaw. John Ross headed another Cherokee group against accepting any settlement. Finally, a treaty was approved by the Ridge-Boudinot faction and forwarded to Congress, where it passed by one vote on May 17, 1836. President Jackson declared it law on May 23, 1836. The Ridge-Boudinot faction had struck a deal for the best they could get for the Cherokees. John Ross and his group declared their lives forfeit for such treachery and continued to work for their own deal.

Indian Removal

In September 1836, General Wool had arrived in Georgia with troops to enforce the treaty and the Indian Removal Act. Expecting the worst of the Cherokee, he was surprised to find a people so acculturated that war was no longer a possibility. He wrote to the Secretary of War, Lewis Cass:

The duty I have to perform is far from pleasant . . . Only made tolerable with the hope that I may stay cruelty and injustice, and assist the wretched and deluded beings called Cherokees, who are only the prey of the most profligate and most vicious of white men . . . The whole scene, since I have been in this country, has been nothing but a fear-rending one, and such a one as I would be glad to be rid of as soon as circumstances permit . . . If I could, and I could not do them a greater kindness, I would remove every Indian tomorrow, beyond the reach of the white men, who like vultures, are watching, ready to pounce upon their prey, and strip them of everything they have or expect to have from the government . . . Nineteen-twentieths, if not 99 of every hundred, will go pennyless to the west.

An Englishman, George W. Featherstonehaugh, traveled among the Cherokee in 1837. His subsequent book describes what he witnessed:

August 5th— . . . A whole Indian nation abandons the pagan practices of their ancestors, adopts the Christian religion, uses books printed in their own language, submits to the government of their elders, builds houses and temples of worship, relies upon agriculture for their support, and produces men of great ability to rule over them, and to whom they give willing obedience. Are not these the great principles of civilization? They are driven from their religious and social state then, not because they cannot be civilized, but because a pseudo set of civilized beings, who are too strong for them, want their possessions! What a bitter reflection it will be to the religiously disposed portion of the people, who shall hereafter live here, that the country they will be so proud of and so blest in was torn from the Aboriginals in this wrongful manner.

May 23, 1838, the deadline for the Indian removal came. By this time, 4,000 to 5,000 Cherokee (including Sequoyah, Ridge and Boudinot with their families) had already departed. The latest three groups, comprising another thousand, had also left. (A total of thirteen groups would depart.)

General Nathaniel Smith was in command of the final removal. The Georgians, however, were not pleased with the lack of alacrity General Smith displayed so they lobbied for another appointment. General Winfield Scott, the veteran of the Mexican War, assumed command to ensure the Cherokee would be dispatched west expeditiously.

By mid-summer of 1838, General Scott had reached a deal with John Ross and his Cherokee council. They would cooperate in removing the remaining 11,000 Cherokees. What was to be known as "The Trail Where We Cried" or "The Trail of Tears" commenced. Beginning on August 28th, more than 700 Cherokee began marching west. The following days brought twelve more groups from north Georgia assembled for departure. They marched, inadequately provisioned, through drought, cold, and without shelter. Fifty days into the journey found them less than half way to their destination. One hundred twenty days found them making a mere five miles a day, many collapsing from exhaustion, malnutrition and exposure. On March 14, 1839, group number ten arrived in Cherokee territory after 189 days on the trail.

How many died on the trail? Some estimate 2,000 and others 4,000. Who really knows? The forced march decimated the Cherokee. The suffering and loss of that nine to ten month trek was an ordeal resulting from official U.S. policy enforced by all three branches of government. It was genocide. President Martin van Buren described it thusly in a message to Congress:

> It affords me sincere pleasure to be able to apprise you of the entire removal of the Cherokee Nation of Indians to their new homes west of the Mississippi. The measures authorized by Congress with a view to the long-standing controversy with them have had the happiest effect, and they have emigrated without any apparent resistance.

And so it goes.

In 1837–38, the Chickasaws became the last of the southern tribes to move west. The Indian Removal Act was utilized against northern tribes as well. Among others the following were forced west of the Mississippi River: Ottawas, Miamis, Shawnee, Sauk and Fox, and Delaware tribes. A total of over 90,000 eastern Indians were forcibly relocated to what would become the Oklahoma territory.

Indian Disfranchisement of Life and Liberty Continues

The Civil War forced the tribes to choose which side to fight with as the whites divided North and South. As usual in a war between whites, Indians always lost. After the Civil War, tribal councils were outlawed. Indian lands shrunk and Indian territory opened for white settlement. Finally, the land the eastern tribes had been promised by President Jackson, "an ample district west of the Mississippi to be guaranteed to the Indian tribes, as long as they shall occupy it," was up for grabs. Congress, on June 30, 1834, in an act to Regulate Trade and Intercourse with the Indian Tribes and to Preserve Peace on the Frontiers, described the Indian land and made its future intent clear:

> All that part of the United States west of the Mississippi and not within the states of Missouri and Louisiana or the Territory of Arkansas would be Indian country. No white persons would be permitted to trade in Indian country without a license. No white traders of bad character would be permitted to reside in the Indian country. The military force of the United States would be employed in the apprehension of any white person who was found in violation of provisions of the act.

This land, designated for the Indian by presidential decree and congressional action became the state of Oklahoma in 1907.

We have examined the Cherokee in depth, more so than any other tribe in this look at the Genocide Regime, because they are the example par excellence of doing exactly what the whites asked them to do. They became so acculturated that from agriculture (including some slaves), to religion, to a court system with a Supreme Court, to fighting with whites against other Indians, it is difficult to imagine a more cooperative tribe. And what was the result of their effort? The Trail of Tears.

Supreme Court decisions. Acts of Congress. Presidential utterances. The three branches of government acted and the tyranny of the white majority was manifest. Treaties were treated as a legal fiction to pacify and expedite possession of Indian land by whites. The "lawful offenses" begun in the Seventeenth century carried through to the last third of the Nineteenth century. There was only one remaining question: Would this pattern and policy continue as the whites pushed farther west? As the Cherokee revealed the white policy so clearly in the East, the Sioux would do so in the West.

The Plains Indians

On March 1, 1867, Nebraska became the thirty-seventh state in the Union. From 1860 to 1900, more than 400 million acres would be added to the farming area of the United States. On May, 10, 1869, the last spike in the transcontinental railroad was driven. Yet, one date more than any other spoke volumes of what was to come. In an effort to extend citizenship to African Americans in the wake of the Civil War, Congress overcame President Andrew Johnson's veto and passed the Civil Rights Act on April 9, 1866. The legislation, which became the Fourteenth Amendment to the Constitution, extended rights of citizenship to all people born in the United States and bestowed certain rights and privileges. The legislation specifically exempted American Indians.

The Plains Indians were comprised of southern and northern groups. These Indians were a horse culture dependent upon buffalo for hunting. Among the most prominent of the southern Plains Indians were the Cheyenne, Arapaho, Kiowa, Comanche, Crow, Manda, Assinibones, Hidastsas, Shoshoni, Pawnee, Blackfeet and Arikaras. They became a horse culture through trading and raiding with the Pueblo and other southwestern tribes who had driven the Spanish out in 1680 and seized the Spanish horses.

In 1858 and 1859 gold was discovered by whites at the foot of the Colorado Rockies. Denver became a boom town and the hunting grounds of the Cheyenne, Kiowa, Arapaho, Sioux and Comanche were invaded. The Indians were divided about how to respond.

Black Kettle and White Antelope, Cheyenne chiefs, wanted peace. They had been to Washington, D.C. and met President Abraham Lincoln, who had given them a large American flag as a gift. But, by 1864, warriors were trying to drive the whites out of the buffalo hunting grounds. Black Kettle and other leaders went to Denver to meet with Governor John Evans and the military commander of Colorado, Colonel John Chivington. Upon the chiefs' return and informing the tribesmen of their discussions, the Cheyenne Dog Soldiers left to travel north and join the Sioux. They did not believe the assurances given the chiefs by Governor Evans and Colonel Chivington.

Black Kettle led his remaining followers to camp near Ft. Lyon, at Sand Creek. Governor Evans and Colonel Chivington had designated this place as one where the Indians could dwell in peace. Black Kettle flew the large American flag, the gift of President Lincoln, outside his lodge. It was unmistakable to the Colorado volunteers, commanded by Colonel Chivington, who stormed into the sleeping village at dawn on November 29th. Colonel Chivington, who had already spoken publicly of the need to destroy Indians, including children, and to do so by scalping them, summed up his position: "Nits make lice!"

Despite the Indians' raising of a white flag as soon as they awakened to the surprise attack, the massacre continued. Most of the warriors were gone on a hunting expedition so the camp consisted of the elderly, women and the young. They had felt so secure they had posted no sentinels. By nightfall, the slaughter was completed, with 105 women and children along with 28 men killed, including White Antelope. Black Kettle and his wife, who was shot seven times, miraculously escaped. Robert Bent, riding with Colonel Chivington, observed:

> I saw the American flag waving and heard Black Kettle tell the Indians to stand around the flag, and there they were huddled— men, women and children. This was when we were within fifty yards of the Indians. I also saw a white flag raised. These flags were in so conspicuous a position that they must have been seen. When the troops fired, the Indians ran, some of the men into their lodges, probably to get their arms . . . I think there were six hundred Indians in all. I think there were thirty-five braves and some old men, about sixty in all . . . the rest of the men were away from camp, hunting . . . After the firing the warriors put the squaws and children together, and surrounded them to protect them. I saw five squaws under a bank for shelter. When the troops came up to them they ran out and showed their persons to let the soldiers know they were squaws and begged for mercy, but the soldiers shot them all. I saw one squaw lying on the bank whose leg had been broken by a shell; a soldier came up to her with a drawn saber; she raised her arm to protect herself, when he struck, breaking her arm; she rolled over and raised her other

arm, when he struck, breaking it, and then left her without killing her. There seemed to be indiscriminate slaughter of men, women and children. There were some thirty or forty squaws collected in a hole for protection; they sent out a little girl about six years old with a white flag on a stick; she had not proceeded but a few steps when she was shot and killed. All the squaws in that hole were afterwards killed, and four or five bucks outside. The squaws offered no resistance. Every one I saw dead was scalped. I saw one squaw cut open with an unborn child, as I thought, lying by her side. Captain Soule afterwards told me that such was the fact. I saw the body of White Antelope with the privates cut out.

I saw a little girl about five years of age who had been hid in the sand, two soldiers discovered her, drew their pistols and shot her, and then pulled her out of the sand by the arm. I saw quite a number of infants in arms killed with their mothers.

Lieutenant James Conner recounted what he witnessed:

In going over the battleground the next day I did not see a body of man, woman, or child but was scalped, and in many instances their bodies were mutilated in the most horrible manner—men, women and children's privates were cut out, etc; I heard one man say that he had cut out a woman's private parts and had them for exhibition of a stick; I heard another man say that he had cut the fingers off an Indian to get the rings on the hand; according to the best of my knowledge and belief these atrocities that were committed were with the knowledge of J.M. Chivington, and I do not know of his taking any measures to prevent them; I heard of one instance of a child a few months old being thrown in the feedbox of a wagon, and after being carried some distance left on the ground to perish; I also head of numerous instances in which men had cut out the private parts of females and stretched them over the saddle-bows and wore them over their hats while riding in the ranks.

Indeed, the private parts of Indian females killed at Sand Creek were displayed on hats worn at the Denver Opera House.

Black Kettle and his wife survived. White Antelope was killed standing by the white flag. The Cheyenne chiefs who had urged peace were discredited or dead. The repercussions of Sand Creek rumbled through the Plains. How could the whites be trusted when they guarantee your safety and then slaughter your village?

After the Civil War the government set aside two large reservations for tribes of the southern Plains. Although many Indians, Cheyenne Dog Soldiers among them, refused the offer to go to the reservation, Black Kettle led his people onto the reservation by the Washita River. Many of the young men left to join the Dog Soldiers but Black Kettle and the remaining Cheyenne camped by the Washita.

On November 27, 1868, Colonel George Armstrong Custer led the 7th Cavalry in a dawn attack on Black Kettle's peaceful southern Cheyenne. Custer had pursued a raiding party and mistakenly assumed the Indians came from Black Kettle. An eyewitness account described what happened:

> Black Kettle mounted a horse and helped his wife up behind him and started to cross the Washita River, but both the chief and his wife fell at the river riddled with bullets . . . The soldiers rode right over Black Kettle and his wife and their horses as they lay dead on the ground, and their bodies were all splashed with mud by the charging soldiers.

Along with Black Kettle and his wife, 101 other southern Cheyenne were killed. Within four years Black Kettle, who only desired peace with the whites, suffered two massacres of his people without provocation. The peace of death was the only peace the whites provided Black Kettle and the southern Cheyenne.

As a result of new tanning technique in the East, buffalo hides became very valuable. From 1872-1874, four million buffalo were slaughtered. The Plains Indians' bond with the shaggy beast was shattered, as the herds rapidly diminished under the white buffalo hunters onslaught. Of course, the whites saw this as a positive development. General Phil Sheridan, leader of the western campaign against the Indians, spoke to the Texas legislature: "(They) have done . . . more to settle the vexed Indians questions than the entire regular army. They are destroying the Indian's community. For the sake of lasting peace, let them kill, skin and sell until the buffaloes are exterminated."

General Sheridan saw the granting of his wish. By 1886, there were fewer than a thousand buffalo remaining on the Plains from the thirty million population that thrived prior to the arrival of the whites. On another occasion General Sheridan had stated: "The only good Indians I ever saw were dead." He and his colleagues transformed the statement of belief into one of actual fact with the destruction of the southern Plains Indians. By 1874, the Indian resistance was broken, and posterity preserved General Sheridan's remarks as: "The only good Indian is a dead Indian."

The northern Plains were dominated by the Sioux. The three branches of the Sioux were the Santee, the Yankton and the Yanktoni, and the Teton or Lakota. The Santee dwelt in the woodlands and farm country of Minnesota. The whites slowly took more and more of their land and they rebelled, killing 350 whites. Soldiers were dispatched from the Civil War in 1862 to destroy the Santee. The troopers crushed them and hanged thirty eight Indians publicly in Mankato. Each hanging was personally approved by President Abraham Lincoln. The Santees fled west to their Sioux relatives and also to Canada.

In the summers of 1863 and 1864, Army troops pursued the Santee into western Sioux territory. The soldiers slaughtered unsuspecting villages of the Lakota in a vain attempt to punish the Santee. Along with the Sand Creek massacre of the Arapaho and Cheyenne in Colorado, the white depredations were too much for the Sioux, Cheyenne Dog Soldiers and Arapaho. With swift effectiveness they struck along the Platte River, downing telegraph lines, stopping stages, mail and supply trains, and wreaking havoc. They cut off Denver, Salt Lake City, and San Francisco from the East. The Indians broke off the conflict in the spring and moved to their summer hunting grounds in the Powder River country. The government fielded a force to try to punish the Sioux but it failed due to Indian guerilla tactics.

On June 5, 1866, the peace commissioner met with Oglala leaders Red Cloud and Man Afraid of His Horse, along with Sicangu chiefs Sinte Gleshka and Swift Bear. The Indians had come to Fort Laramie to see what the whites had to offer. Unbeknownst to them, a decision to establish a series of forts in the Powder River country to protect the Bozeman Trail, a primary route for whites flocking west after the Civil War, had been implemented simultaneously with the peace parley. Although the Oglala war leader Crazy Horse, Chief Sitting Bull of the Hunkpapas, and the Miniconjous refused to come to Fort Laramie, Red Cloud and the other chiefs in attendance represented leadership among their tribes and had successfully driven the whites away thus far. They heard the commissioner's appeal to use a designated road through the Powder River country "as may be deemed necessary for the public service and for the emigrant to mining districts in the West." The payments for such access were significant enough to ponder, so the meeting was adjourned until June 13th.

After reconvening on June 13th the meeting was interrupted by Colonel Covington's arrival with 700 troopers en route to establish the forts. When informed of Covington's mission to proceed into Powder River country and build forts without permission, the Indians felt betrayed. Their anger was clear in Red Cloud's words: "Great Father sends us presents and wants new road. But white chief goes with soldiers to steal road before the Indian says yes or no!" Red Cloud told his fellow Indians:

> The white men have crowded the Indians back year by year until we are forced to live in a small country north of the Platte, and now our last hunting ground, the home of the People, is to be taken from us. Our women and children will starve, but for my part I prefer to die fighting rather than by starvation.

Red Cloud led the Indians out of the negotiations in order to defend their land.

Colonel Covington constructed three forts in Powder River country. Building them was one matter, making them viable proved an altogether different problem.

The Sioux had harassed the fort builders but, once winter came, their campaign began in earnest. Fort Phil Kearney was surrounded, and a foolish effort by Captain Fetterman to rescue a group of wood cutters resulted in his death along with the eighty men under his command. General Sherman's response was firm: "We must act with vindictive earnestness against the Sioux even to their extermination, man, woman and children."

Reality proved more difficult than talk. In the spring and summer of 1867, the Indian attacks continued and with the troops penned into the forts there was no protection for the settlers who wanted to travel the Bozeman Trail. In 1868, the government gave up and withdrew from the forts. The Army left Powder River country. Red Cloud had won. He came and signed a treaty at Fort Laramie, which he thought guaranteed the Indians the Powder River country as well as trade and hunting south to the Platte. The whites would stay away.

The U.S. government, however, had other ideas about the treaty. A reservation was to be established in what is today all of South Dakota and the Sioux forced to report to Fort Randall at the southwestern tip, far from the buffalo country. It became clear to the Sioux that the whites were not to be trusted. Red Cloud's leadership was faulted as the whites began to encroach once again. The Army and Navy Journal best expressed the reality of governmental policy to the Indians: "We go to (the Indians) Janus faced. One of our hands holds the rifle and the other the peace-pipe."

In 1874, responding to the demands of miners who found gold in the Black Hills, General Sheridan ordered George Armstrong Custer on an expeditionary force into the Black Hills, or Paha Sapa, as the Sioux called them. The Indians had driven the miners out of Paha Sapa because it was their sacred ground, the center of their universe. Custer cut a trail into the Black Hills for his supply wagons and it became known as "the Thieves Road." Custer reported finding gold and the rush resumed into Paha Sapa for gold.

The treaty of Fort Laramie in 1868 stated: "No white person or persons shall be permitted to settle upon or occupy any portion of the territory, or without consent of the Indians to pass through the same." The words of Crazy Horse of the Oglalas and Sitting Bull of the Hunkpapas were clear. Crazy Horse: "One does not sell the earth upon which the people walk." Sitting Bull: "We want no white men here. The Black Hills belong to me. If the whites try to take them, I will fight."

Yet in the spring of 1875, miners were swarming the Black Hills. The Indians resisted and as the United States prepared to celebrate its centennial anniversary in 1876, General Sheridan set a battle plan to attack the Sioux and force them into reservation life.

On June 16, 1876, Crazy Horse fought General George Crook's forces on the Rosebud River. The first of the three-prong attack, designed by General Sheridan, was stalled. Crazy Horse joined Sitting Bull and 6,000 others in an enormous encampment along the Little Bighorn River. The Indians, feeling safe, had posted no lookouts so when the 7th Cavalry, commanded by George Custer, galloped toward camp, the Indians were taken by surprise. The soldiers attacked the Hunkpapas encampment initially and the war chief Gall rallied the Indians who repelled the soldiers. Then the remainder of the Sioux, Cheyenne, and other tribes joined the battle.

The bravery of Gall and the Hunkpapas stopped a column of soldiers led by Major Reno and drove them into the woods. Those troops opening volley had killed Gall's family and he was enraged as he was brave. As a result of forcing Reno to retreat, which soon became a rout, Gall was able to send hundreds of his warriors to charge Custer's force. As Gall's warriors rode headlong toward Custer, Crazy Horse and Two Moon led attacks on the flank and rear.

Within thirty minutes, the Battle of the Little Big Horn was over. George Armstrong Custer, leader of the massacre at Washita and carver of the Thieves' Road into Paha Sapa, was dead with his entire command. Only Major Reno, whom Custer ordered to attack separately, survived with some soldiers behind the bluffs. After attacking Reno several times, scouts brought word to Sitting Bull that the third prong of Sheridan's attack, General Terry, was approaching. The Indians struck camp.

Today it is difficult to fathom why Custer divided his command and sought to attack a superior force. One can only suspect his hubris and low opinion of the Indians accounting for such a foolhardy maneuver. Washita may have been one thing Custer "achieved" but the Little Big Horn was an entirely different deal. But on July 4, 1876, when word reached the East of the Battle of the Little Big Horn, it was deemed a "massacre." The hundredth anniversary of the white majority government in the United States was an inconvenient time to learn of the Native Americans successfully defending their land. The white reaction was one of rage and it was directed at the Indians, not the foolish Custer. Revenge was swift.

On July 22, 1876, General Sherman took authority over all reservations in Sioux country and was granted the power to treat the Sioux as prisoners of war. On August 15 the Sioux were forced to give up the Powder River country and the Black Hills. Throughout the territory soldiers were exacting revenge, attacking Indian camps. (Not unlike the white reaction to Nat

Turner's slave rebellion in Southampton County, Virginia in 1831.) Iron Teeth of the Cheyenne shared her experience:

> When the snow had fallen deep, a great band of soldiers came. They rode right into our camp and shot women and children, as well as men. Crows, Pawnees, Shoshonis, some Arapahoes and other Indians were with them. We who could do so ran away . . . As our family were going out of camp, my husband and our older son kept behind and fought off the soldiers . . . I saw [my husband fall] . . . I wanted to go back to him, but my two sons made me go on . . . From the hilltops we Cheyennes looked back and saw all of our lodges and everything in them being burned into nothing but smoke and ashes. When spring came, all of the Cheyennes surrendered to soldiers.

The fall and winter of 1876-77 was a terrible one for the Indians. Time and again soldiers attacked villages, without regard to whether or not the Indians were reservation Indians or had ever been at the Little Big Horn. Finally, in May 1877, Crazy Horse led 900 proud Oglala into the Red Cloud agency. Starving and exhausted from fighting, Crazy Horse led them in so they could survive. On September 5, 1877, Crazy Horse was bayoneted by soldiers as they tried to arrest him. His parents buried him at Wounded Knee creek.

Sitting Bull had led the Hunkpapas into Canada in May, 1877. He described his situation eloquently:

> When I was a boy the [Lakota] owned the world; the sun rose and set on their land . . . Where are the warriors today? Who slew them? Where are our lands? Who owns them? What law have I broken? Is it wrong for me to love my own? Is it wicked for me because my skin is red? Because I am a [Lakota]; because I was born where my father lived; because I would die for my people and my country?

The Dawes Act, passed in 1887, allowed the President of the United States "whenever he pleases" to require the Indians to give up their reservations, which they had been herded into so assiduously, for individual allotments of private property.

By 1888, The Plains Indians were broken, confined on reservations, coerced into signing treaties, in reality a colonized people. Sitting Bull had brought the Hunkpapas back from Canada and was on the Standing Rock reservation. Alvin Josephy describes the situation:

> So began a period of deliberate deculturation. In 1887, an unseemly alliance of eastern reformers and western land grabbers pushed through Congress the Dawes General Allotment Act, which broke up communal tribal reservation lands into small plots that were then assigned to individual Indians. The reformers' motive was to destroy the group-oriented institution of tribes and chiefs by turning the

Indians into independent landowning farmers. Whatever land was left over after all the allotments had been made could be sold to whites—which was the western land grabbers' motive. Their foresight was correct. In 1887, the Indian nations in the United States still owned 138 million acres. By 1934, when the Allotment Act ended, 90 million had become white owned and a large part of the remainder leased to whites.

In 1889, Congress was not content with the destruction of the tribes and the Dawes Act, so it authored a new plan to steal land from the Indians. This was the infamous Jerome Commission, a three-man panel appointed the task of meeting the tribes west of the 96th meridian, with the goal to gain "the cession to the United States of all of their title." Due to intense negotiation by the Commanche leader Quanah Parker, the best terms possible were obtained but bleak they were: The Indians would get 160 acres of land for each individual and whatever land was left over the government would buy for $2,000,000.

Also in 1889, Thomas Jefferson Morgan, Commissioner of Indian Affairs, declared what his solution to the Indian problem would be:

> The logic of events demands the absorption of the Indians into our national life, not as Indians, but as American citizens . . . The Indian must conform to "the white man's ways," peaceably if they will, forcibly if they must. They must . . . conform their mode of living substantially to our civilization. This civilization may not be the best possible, but it is the best the Indians can get. They cannot escape it, and must either conform to it or be crushed by it.
>
> The initial tribal relations should be broken up, socialism destroyed, and the family and the autonomy of the individual substituted.

Perhaps no more poignant description of the Americanizing of the Indian can be given than Commissioner Morgan's declaration of how Indian children should be separated from their parents and placed in far-off boarding schools:

> I would . . . use the Indian police if necessary. I would withhold from [the Indian adults] rations and supplies . . . and when every other means was exhausted, I would send a troop of United States soldiers, not to seize them, but simply to be present as an expression of power of the government. Then I would say to these people, "Put your children in school"; and they would do it.

Given the annihilation of their way of life, it was no surprise that the Plains Indians seized upon the message of a Paiute named Wovoka, proclaiming the coming of a messiah who would restore the old Indian way of life. Wovoka and his followers led dances, songs, and prayers lasting all night and sometimes several days. A young Lakota told of what he saw:

They danced without rest, on and on . . . Occasionally someone thoroughly exhausted and dizzy fell unconscious into the center of and lay there "dead" . . . After a while, many lay about in that condition. They were not "dead" and seeing their dear ones . . . The visions . . . ended the same way, like a chorus describing a great encampment of all the Lakotas who had ever died, where . . . there was no sorrow but only joy, where relatives thronged out with happy laughter.

The people went on and on and could not stop, day or night, hoping . . . to get a vision of their own dead . . . And so I suppose the authorities did think they were crazy—but they weren't. They were only terribly unhappy.

4. Horses Grazing at Wounded Knee. Photo by: Marty Stuart.

The whites dubbed this ritual the Ghost Dance and feared it augured Indians on the warpath again. Overacting, the whites sent Sioux Indian police to arrest Sitting Bull on December 15, 1890. Awakened from his sleep, he came outside and was murdered by those sent to arrest him.

The Hunkpapas fled Standing Rock reservation after Sitting Bull's death. About a hundred reached Big Foot's Miniconjous camp near Cherry Creek. Once Big Foot heard of Sitting Bull's death, he started his people on a winter march in the bitter cold to Pine Ridge, in hopes of Red Cloud protecting them. Big Foot became ill with pneumonia and was carried in an open wagon with a white flag flying on it. The Indians were intercepted by the 7th Cavalry a day's ride from Pine Ridge. Big Foot agreed to surrender to the former command of Custer. The next day, the soldiers disarmed the Sioux. In attempting to take the rifle of Black Coyote, a deaf Indian, it accidentally discharged. The Indians, totally surrounded and with six Hotchkiss guns mounted on the hills pointed down at them, came under a withering fire.

Rough Feather described the soldier's fire as "like the sound of tearing canvas, that was the crash [sound]." A few Indians tried to fight the soldiers but most fled. As they ran, the Hotchkiss guns opened up, destroying the entire Indian camp. Louise Weasel Bear recalled: "We tried to run but they shot us like we were buffalo . . . the soldiers must be mean to shoot children and women."

In the ensuing confusion and melee, soldiers shot their own men. When the firing ceased, the grim body count totaled: Of the 350 people in Big Foot's band, 153 bodies were found and countless others died in the snow after crawling away. Approximately 300 of the 350 people perished. The 7th Cavalry lost twenty-five dead and thirty-one wounded, nearly all shot by fellow soldiers.

The wounded Sioux were carried in wagons to Pine Ridge. The survivors, four men and forty seven women and children, were taken to an Episcopal mission, which was opened for them. Benches were removed and hay spread upon the floor so the wounded Indians could have a measure of comfort. As the injured and dying lay in the hay, four days after Christmas, they could see a banner proclaiming:

"PEACE ON EARTH, GOOD WILL TO MEN."

Black Elk, then a young boy who witnessed the massacre at Wounded Knee, later put into words the final dying of an age:

> I did not know then how much was ended. When I look back now from this high hill of my old age, I can still see the butchered women and children lying heaped and scattered all along the crooked gulch as plain as when I saw them with eyes still young. And I can see that something else died there in the bloody mud, and was buried in the blizzard. A people's dream died there. It was a beautiful dream . . . the nation's hoop is broken and scattered. There is no center any longer, and the sacred tree is dead.

The massacre at Wounded Knee marked the end of the Indian holocaust in the sense of slaughter. But the years that followed were a Dark Age for the Indian culture. The white majority reduced them to a caricature, continued to confiscate their lands, removed and educated their children in white schools, and designated them as detritus of Western civilization in America. The Native American population was reduced to 250,000 by 1892, from the thirty to forty million natives who inhabited North American in 1492.

Crazy Horse, before going into battle, would rally his warriors with the affirmation: "Today is a good day to die." The expression is an apt description of each day from 1830 to 1890 regarding the Native American contact with whites. Truly, under the Genocide Regime, each day was a good day to die.

Chapter 8. Reconstruction (1866–1876)

In the course of American history, there have been two periods of time when the white majority's grip was loosened by the racial minority in alliance with whites willing to change. In each instance, the United States government moved closer to fulfilling its democratic promise as it responded to the pressure from its African-American minority. We term these segments of American history the First Reconstruction (1866–76) and the Second Reconstruction (1954–1976). (Due to the genocidal campaign against American Indians, we have yet to see a similar period of American history where the Native American was responded to by the government.)

Although each era of Reconstruction was followed by a significant white majoritarian backlash against the gains made through Reconstruction, the First and Second Reconstructions proved the finest hours of fulfillment of the dream of democracy in America. It is no accident that the locale for the struggle for democracy was the South and the agents of change African-Americans. Let us turn to the initial chapter where the white majority frees the slaves and enfranchises the African-American minority in response to its bid for political recognition and humanity.

In April of 1865, two events occurred within one week that altered the course of American history. On April 9th, 1865, General Robert E. Lee, commander of the Army of Northern Virginia, surrendered to General Ulysses S. Grant, commander of the Armies of the United States. The two met at the MacLean house in Appomattox Court House, Virginia, and ended the bloodiest military campaign, in terms of casualties, in the history of the United States. In order to comprehend the magnitude of the conflict, the number of Americans killed in the Civil War totals more than all the combined casualties in all wars fought by the United

States excepting the last 10,000 losses during the Vietnam Conflict. The exchange of surrender papers at 3:45 p.m. on Palm Sunday halted a terrible slaughter.

On April 15, 1865, President Abraham Lincoln was shot, on Good Friday, while attending a play at the Ford Theater in Washington, D.C. Lincoln's death meant Andrew Johnson of Tennessee, the Vice-President, would fulfill the remainder of Lincoln's presidential term. President Lincoln died on Saturday and the country was grief stricken.

When Andrew Johnson assumed the mantle of the presidency, his native land of the South had been destroyed by four years of war. Before the Civil War, much of the South was a frontier. After the War, it was a desolate frontier. The economic engine ignited by war production in the North was ready to expand South and West. There were also four million slaves who were now free. The question became: What was to be done?

Fortunately for the United States, Andrew Johnson alone would not decide the fate of Reconstruction. Indeed, as his actions in the spring and summer of 1865 revealed, he had abandoned his earlier declared good intentions for poor people to obtain abandoned and confiscated plantation land in the South. Rather, President Johnson succumbed to the flattery and guile of the former slave masters, people he had bitterly opposed for much of his political career as governor and senator from Tennessee. The planters flocked to visit Johnson in Washington and tapped into Johnson's animus against black people.

Because Congress was in recess, President Johnson held immense power. He gave his blessing as ex-Confederates assembled in all-white conventions throughout the South to reclaim the reins of power. Johnson's about face occurred when he realized that if poor people did indeed obtain plantation land, the poor would include many of the four million slaves who had worked the land. Andrew Johnson, like so many aspiring white southerners of poor background, fell victim to the ugly grip of racism. He would not permit black land ownership even if it meant denying it to poor whites as well.

Andrew Johnson was not alone in his concept of the inabilities of slaves to be productive citizens. The Chief Justice of the U.S. Supreme Court, Roger Taney, articulated the governing philosophy in the United States in 1857 in delivering the majority opinion in *Dred Scott v. Sanford*. Blacks were regarded "as having no rights which a white man was bound to respect." Despite President Lincoln's Emancipation Proclamation on January 1, 1863, the passage of the 13th Amendment to the constitution which abolished slavery, Chief Justice Taney's opinion prevailed in much of the United States.

The North utilized Taney's legal dictum to sanction a Jim Crow society while the South pointed to the Supreme Court as justification for the continuance of chattel slavery for four million people. After the Civil War, *Dred Scott* was used as justification to establish Reconstruction on the state level without federal involvement, an effort aptly termed "Confederate Style Reconstruction," by historian John Hope Franklin. Two of the three branches of government, the executive and the judicial, were prepared for an all white reconstruction effort. Only the Congress remained as a vehicle for enfranchising the former slaves.

Report from the Conquered South

The progress of African-Americans from slaves, to freedmen, to soldiers in the U.S. Army, forced the government into a policy of rewarding and supporting the black contribution to winning the Civil War. Although President Johnson became determined to limit the role of blacks in Reconstruction and allow the white oligarchy to return to power, other forces were at work. Those interests relied on information President Johnson chose to ignore, such as the report of General Carl Schurz, whom the President commissioned to survey the South and report back on its status after the war. Johnson ignored the report once Schurz presented it but it became a useful appraisal of the South in the aftermath of the Civil War. Schurz observed four classes existing in the South:

"1. Those who, although having yielded submission to the national government only when obliged to do so, have a clear perception of the irreversible changes produced by the war, and honestly endeavor to accommodate themselves to the new order of things.

2. Those whose principal object is to have the states without delay restored to their position and influence in the Union and the people of the states to the absolute control of their home concerns. They are ready in order to attain that object to make any ostensible concession that will not prevent them from arranging things to suit their taste as soon as the object is attained.

3. The incorrigibles, who still indulge in the swagger which was so customary before and during the war, and still hope for a time when the Southern confederacy will achieve its independence.

4. The multitude of people who have no definite ideas about the circumstances under which they live and about the course they have to follow, whose intellects are weak, but whose prejudices and impulses are strong, and who are apt to be carried along by those who know how to appeal to the latter."

But as soon as the struggle was finally decided, and our forces were scattered about in detachments to occupy the country, the so far unmoved masses began to stir. The report went among them that their liberation was no longer a mere contingency, but a fixed fact. Large numbers of colored people left the plantations, many flocked to our military posts and camps to obtain the certainty of their freedom, and others walked away merely for the purpose of leaving the places on which they had been held in slavery, and because they could not go with impunity. Still others, and their number was by no means inconsiderable, remained with their former masters and continued their work in the field, but under new and as yet unsettled conditions, and under the agitating influence of a feeling of restlessness.

In some localities, however, where our troops had not yet penetrated and where no military post was within reach, planters endeavored and partially succeeded in maintaining between themselves and the Negroes the relation of master and slave partly by concealing from them the great changes that had taken place, and partly by terrorizing them into submission to their behests. But aside from these exceptions, the country found itself thrown into that confusion which is naturally inseparable from a change so great and so sudden. The white people were afraid of the Negroes, and the Negroes did not trust the white people; the military power of the national government stood there, and was looked up to, as the protector of both.

One might have thought that after the violence and suffering of a brutal and bitter war, the peace following it might be truly calm. However, power was up for grabs and that meant peace was to give way to terror and violence as whites sought to regain control in the South. The Black Codes were instituted by the white Reconstruction legislatures in every Southern state. Laboring blacks were termed "servants" and the contractor "master." The written contract required white judicial approval and white supervision. Vagrancy laws were passed to punish blacks not under contract. These and other laws placed the freed slave into a state of peonage.

General Carl Schurz described the environment of the South in his tour:

[It] looked for many miles like a broad black streak of ruin and desolation—the fences all gone; lonesome smoke stacks, surrounded by dark heaps of ashes and cinders, marking the spots where human habitations had stood; the fields along the roads wildly overgrown by weeds, with here and there a sickly patch of cotton and corn cultivated by Negro squatters . . . [Cities were] a wilderness of crumbling walls, naked chimneys and trees killed by flames.

General Otis Howard, the commissioner of the Freedman's Bureau, termed the war a "shattering (of) the prevailing existing social system," "old industries" destroyed, and a threat of "a reign of anarchy." In this wasteland the freedman was trying to discern what to do and where to go. The master was grabbing for the reins of power through the Black Codes.

Although Abraham Lincoln never fully unveiled his vision of Reconstruction, he was clear about slavery. In December 1864, he stated:

> While I remain in my present position I shall not attempt to retract or modify the Emancipation Proclamation. Nor shall I return to slavery any person who is free by the terms of that Proclamation, or by any of the Acts of Congress. If the people should, by whatever mode or means, make it an Executive duty to re-enslave such persons, another, and not I, must be the instrument to perform it.

The Black Codes would have been anathema to Lincoln because they were a thinly veiled attempt (except in Mississippi, which merely changed the word slave to servant in its slave code in obvious disregard of Congress so it was not even a thinly veiled effort but a naked one) to maintain slavery without using the name. Johnson, unlike Lincoln, had no problem with the Black Codes as long as the states approved the Thirteenth Amendment abolishing slavery.

President Johnson's friendliness with the white ruling class of the South and chilly attitude toward blacks was too much for the leaders of Congress. They watched in horror as the Southern constitutional conventions, lily white and emboldened by President Johnson's command to the Freedman's Bureau to return confiscated plantation land given to freedman back to the planters, enact the Black Codes, and return to power politically unscathed. It truly was a Confederate style Reconstruction. Southerners, despite their defeat, reverted to their old ways of doing business. Ex-Confederate colonels and other officers were elected to the constitutional conventions. Indeed, when Congress returned from recess in December 1865, it was greeted by Southern Congressmen and Senators chosen in all-white elections, which elected many who had served as officers in the Confederate army, its cabinet, and even the Vice President of the Confederacy, to go to Congress. The effrontery of this effort seemed not to have crossed the Southerners' minds and their blatant attempt to reinstitute black servitude in the Black Codes was worn as a badge of honor. The events of the last few months since President Lincoln's death stirred what W.E.B. Du Bois called the "abolition/democracy" wing of the Republican Party.

Wendell Phillips, a leading abolitionist with William Lloyd Garrison, parted company with Garrison when the latter proved content with simple abolition. Phillips urged much more on President Lincoln, of whom he said: "He may wish the end—peace and freedom—but is wholly unwilling to use the means which can secure that end." For Wendell Phillips the goal was clear: "the safety beyond peril; and the equality without a doubt of the colored race of this country." Such an effort demanded "not charity, not patronage, but justice." And justice meant the vote, education and land:

"Confiscation [of the land] is mere naked justice to the former slave. Who brought the land into cultivation? Whose sweat and toil are mixed with it forever? Who cleared those forests? Whose wages are invested in those warehouses and towns? Of course, the Negro's. Why should he not have a share of his inheritance?"

Frederick Douglass spoke of the need for the South to be a scene of "National Regeneration. Nothing less than radical revolution in all the modes of thought which have flourished under the slave system."

Frederick Douglass and Wendell Phillips were leaders with a view that encompassed more than the abolition of slavery. But they were outside the realm of direct power. Inside the political arena, two other men of vision sought the political means to implement the dream of black equality with white: Charles Sumner of Massachusetts in the Senate and Thaddeus Stevens of Pennsylvania in the House of Representatives.

Check and Checkmate

Charles Sumner pushed not only for abolition but for land and the vote for the freedman. Thaddeus Stevens also championed this course from his position as chairman of the House Ways and Means Committee. It was these two men who rallied Congress, while in recess, to oppose President Johnson's Confederate Reconstruction. The Thirty Ninth Congress would decide which road the country would take in Reconstruction: The executive or legislative.

When Congress returned to Washington, D.C. in early December 1865, Thaddeus Stevens summoned key senators and representatives to his hotel room. Stevens and Sumner were the leaders of the abolition/democracy wing of the Republican Party. The group was influential but a minority in Congress. However, with President Johnson's determination to persevere in a Confederate Reconstruction manifest to all, Stevens had a plan to seize the hour and take control of Reconstruction.

Stevens' political ingenuity called for a super-committee, composed of nine members of the House and six members of the Senate. It would have the power to examine all of Reconstruction and then recommend legislation. No debate would be allowed on any Reconstruction matter unless it came through the Committee of Fifteen. The mechanism was approved on December 2nd by the Republican caucus, which controlled Congress. On December 4, Thaddeus Stevens laid out the Joint Congressional Committee of Fifteen before the House and barred the Johnson Confederate Reconstruction representatives from Congress. Two weeks later he plainly declared: "The future condition of the conquered power depends on the will of the conqueror." The seceded states would not be allowed admission again until they had served an apprenticeship as territorial governments:

> [They] ought never to be recognized as capable of acting in the Union, or of being counted as valid states, until the Constitution shall have been so amended as to make it what its framers intended; and so to secure perpetual ascendancy to the party of the Union; and so render our republican Government firm and stable for ever.

Stevens knew his colleagues in the House were not motivated primarily out of concern for rectifying the evil done the slaves. Rather, the freeing of the slaves translated into four million new votes and future representation in the House would be determined by those voters. If the South was allowed to return to the Union under Johnson's plan, the region would actually come back stronger politically than when it seceded. Stevens put the dilemma to his Republican colleagues: "With the basis unchanged, the 83 Southern members with the Democrats that will in the best times be elected from the North, will always give them a majority in Congress and in the Electoral College. I need not depict the ruin that would follow."

At this point, Thaddeus Stevens summoned his radical, democratic social vision and shared it with his stunned colleagues: "Governor Perry of South Carolina and other provisional governors and orators proclaim that 'this is the white man's government . . . 'Demagogues of all parties, even some in high authority, gravely shout, 'This is the white man's government.' . . . [One] race of men are to have the exclusive rights forever to rule this nation, and to exercise all acts of sovereignty, while all other races . . . are to be their subjects, and have no voice in making the laws and choosing [their]rulers . . . "

No, Stevens spoke out, "our fathers repudiated the whole doctrine of the legal superiority of families or races and proclaimed the equality of men before the law. Upon that they created a revolution and built a Republic. They were prevented by slavery from perfecting the superstructures whose foundation they had thus broadly laid."

And now, he continued, "It is our duty to complete their work if this Republic is not now made to stand on their great principles . . . the Father of all men will shake it to its center."

To call ours a "white man's government is," Stevens argued, "political blasphemy, for it violates the fundamental principles of our gospel of liberty."

As 1866 began, Congress faced following Johnson's Reconstruction plan, with whites carrying out Reconstruction after abolishing slavery with no requirement of civil rights or enfranchisement for freedman. The alternatives were: 1. A territorial plan, which Stevens hinted in his speech, in which governments would continue in the South until an interracial society had been created; 2. Dividing the South into five military districts with the army enforcing black rights. The North was not truly interested in the first option so the Congressional Reconstruction settled on the latter possibility, which included black suffrage and federally guaranteed civil rights.

In 1866, the struggle between President Johnson and Congress crystallized the issues. Congress passed legislation establishing the Freedmen's Bureau and a Civil Rights bill. Johnson vetoed both legislative initiatives and did so with language that further antagonized the moderates in Congress. President Johnson said the acts discriminated against whites because they put in place "for the security of the colored race safeguards which go infinitely beyond any that the General Government have ever provided for the white race." One wonders, who did Johnson think had been under the heel of oppression for two hundred years via chattel slavery, and how would the freedman be protected without specific provisions for their welfare? In a later speech, Johnson revealed his true animosity to black people. He considered it "worse than madness" to provide black people the means to rule the white race, make and administer state laws, elect presidents and members of Congress, and shape a greater or lesser extent the future of the country:

> It is the glory of the white man to know that they have had those qualities in sufficient measure to build upon this continent a great political fabric and to preserve its stability for more than ninety years, while in every part of the world all similar experiments have failed. But if anything can be proved by known facts, if all reasoning upon evidence is not abandoned, it must be acknowledged that in the progress of nations Negroes have shown less capability for government than any other race of people. No independent government of any form has ever been successful in their hands. On the contrary, wherever they have been left to their own devices they have shown a constant tendency to relapse into barbarism.

Congress passes the Civil Rights Act over Johnson's veto

As the congressional campaign election of 1866 loomed, President Johnson took to the campaign trail and made speeches that would have been well received in his native Tennessee. White power was a tried and true formula in the South. However, in the light of the Black Codes passed by Johnson's Confederate style Reconstruction, the South sending former Confederate army officers and cabinet members, as well as the former Confederate Vice President to take seats in Congress in an audacious, naked grasping of power when in reality the South had no power-no army, no capital, no industry-resulted in a Republican campaign sweep. The violence of Confederate style Reconstruction was seen with whites terrorizing blacks: In Norfolk, Virginia, three were killed and others severely injured on

April 16; in Memphis, Tennessee, where forty- six were killed and thirty-five wounded; and in New Orleans, Louisiana, where a mob of mostly policemen killed forty people and injured a hundred and fifty to prevent freedman and progressive whites from holding a constitutional convention. General Philip Sheridan, commander of Louisiana, described the slaughter: "It was not a riot; it was an absolute massacre . . . a murder which the mayor and the police of the city perpetrated without the shadow of necessity."

So the South, emboldened by a Southern president, ignored political reality and through its behavior once again precipitated the demise of whatever chance it had in the political process. The Republicans took two-thirds of the majority in the House and the Senate. The battle for the course of Reconstruction was joined with a vengeance in the second session of the Thirty Ninth Congress.

Meanwhile in the South, terror was becoming a way of life. From the end of the Civil War in April of 1865 through the congressional elections of 1866, President Andrew Johnson and the Confederate style Reconstruction reigned in the South. General Howard, head of the Freedman's Bureau, aptly portrayed the situation in the region:

> The planters in the main are determined to try to coerce both black labor and white, without outside interference of any sort. They proposed to enact and enforce the black codes. They were going to replace legal slavery by customary serfdom and caste. And they were going to do all this because they could not conceive of civilization in the South with free Negro workers, or soldiers or voters.

Ex-Slaves Speak

Southern whites had not regarded slaves as human beings. An entire psychological world view must be changed along with the political and social relations. But the Southern white would not change despite defeat in the Civil War. The freedman experienced the harsh reality of Confederate style Reconstruction, as recounted by former slave Henry Adams of Louisiana:

"The white men read a paper to all of us colored people telling us that we were free and could go where we pleased and work for who we pleased. The man I belonged to told me it was best to stay with him. He said, 'The bad white men was mad with the Negroes because they were free and they would kill you all for fun.' He said, stay where we are living and we could get protection from our old masters.

> I told him I thought that every man, when he was free, could have his rights and protect themselves. He said, 'The colored people could never protect themselves among the white people. So you had all better stay with the white people who raised you and make contracts

with them to work by the year for one-fifth of all you make. And next year you get one-third, and the next you maybe work for one-half you make. We have contracts for you all to sign, to work for one-twentieth you make from now until the crop is ended, and then next year you all can make another crop and get more of it.'

I told him I would not sign anything. I said, 'I might sign to be killed. I believe the white people is trying to fool us.' But he said again, 'Sign this contract so I can take it to the Yankees and have it recorded.' All our colored people signed it but myself and a boy named Samuel Jefferson. All who lived on the place was about sixty, young and old.

On the day after all had signed the contracts, we went to cutting oats. I asked the boss, 'Could we get any of the oats?' He said, 'No; the oats were made before you were free.' After that he told us to get timber to build a sugar mill to make molasses. We did so. On the 13th day of July 1865 we started to pull fodder. I asked the boss would he make a bargain to give us half of all the fodder we would pull. He said we may pull two or three stacks and could have the other. I told him we wanted half, so if we only pulled two or three stacks we would get half of that. He said, "All right." We got that and part of the corn we made. We made five bales of cotton but we did not get a pound of that. We made two or three hundred gallons of molasses and only got what we could eat. We made about eight hundred bushel of potatoes; we got a few to eat. We split rails three or four weeks and got not a cent for that.

In September I asked the boss to let me go to Shreveport. He said, "All right, when will you come back?" I told him "next week." He said, "you had better carry a pass." I said, "I will see whether I am free by going without a pass."

I met four white men about six miles south of Keachie, De Soto Parish. One of them asked me who I belonged to. I told him no one. So him and two others struck me with a stick and told me they were going to kill me and every other Negro who told them that they did not belong to anyone. One of them who knew me told the others, "Let Henry alone for he is a hard-working nigger and a good nigger." They left me and I then went to Shreveport. I seen over twelve colored men and women beat, shot and hung between there and Shreveport.

Sunday I went back home. The boss was not at home. I asked the madame where was the boss? She says, "Now, the boss; now, the boss! You should say 'master' and 'mistress'—and shall or leave. We will not have no nigger here on our place who cannot say 'mistress' and 'master.' You all are not free yet and will not be until Congress sits, and you shall call every white lady 'missus' and every white man 'master.'"

During that same week the madame taken a stick and beat one of the young colored girls, who was about fifteen years of age and who is my sister, and split her back. The boss came next day and take this same girl (my sister) and whipped her nearly to death, but in the contracts he was to hit no one any more. After the whipping a large number of young colored people taken a notion to leave. On the 18th of September I and eleven men and boys left that place and started for Shreveport. I had my horse along. My brother was riding him, and all of our things was packed on him. Out come about forty armed men (white) and shot at us and taken my horse. Said they were going to kill every nigger they found leaving their masters; and taking all of our clothes and bed-clothing and money. I had to work away to get a white man to get my horse.

Then I got a wagon and went to peddling, and had to get a pass, according to the laws of the parishes, to do so. In October I was searched for pistols and robbed of $250 by a large crowd of white men and the law would do nothing about it. The same crowd of white men broke up five churches (colored). When any of us would leave the white people, they would take everything we had, all the money that we made on their places. They killed many hundreds of my race when they were running away to get freedom.

After they told us we were free—even then they would not let us live as man and wife together. And when we would run away to be free, the white people would not let us come to their places to see our mothers, wives, sisters, or fathers. We was made to leave or go back and live as slaves. To my own knowledge there was over two thousand colored people killed trying to get away after the white people told us we were free in 1865. This was between Shreveport and Logansport. (Henry Adams, Senate report 693, 46th Congress, 2nd Session)

From Savannah, Georgia comes another accounting, on January 4, 1865:

I have been here for some days. The colored people did not seem to realize that they were free, as their status was not announced by any proclamation. The scarcity of provisions, the unsettled state of things, no employment—all these had the effect of causing our people to stand on the threshold of freedom like the rescued passengers of a ship on a barren sea-shore, wet and shivering with the cold blast of the tempest. They wanted encouragement, advice, and strength to go forward and assume the responsibilities of free men. (James Lynch, *The National Freedman*, February 1, 1865)

An ex-slave looking back on his first experience of freedom, wrote the following:

At the close of the war they were set free without a dollar, without a foot of land and without the wherewithal to get the next meal even.

The labor of these people had for two hundred years cleared away the forests and produced crops that brought millions of dollars annually. It does seem to me that a Christian nation would, at least, have given them one year's support, forty acres of land and a mule each.

Did they get that or any portion of it? Not a cent. Four million people turned loose without a dollar and told to 'Root, hog or die!' Now, whose duty was it to feed them? Was it the former masters' or that of the government, which had conquered the masters, and freed the slaves? My opinion is that the government should have done it. (H.C. Bruce, *The New Man*, York, Pennsylvania, 1895).

General William T. Sherman's March to the Sea resulted in tens of thousands of slaves following his army across Georgia. Secretary of War Stanton and Sherman met with twenty of Savannah's black leaders to see what they most needed. The interview is preserved:

Q—State in what manner you think you can take care of yourselves.

A—The way we can best take care of ourselves is to have land, and turn it and till it by our labor. We can soon maintain ourselves and have something to spare. We want to be placed on land until we are able to buy it or make our own.

Q—State in what manner you would rather live; whether scattered among the whites or in colonies by yourselves.

A—I would prefer to live by ourselves. There is a prejudice against us in the South that will take years to get over, but I do not know that I can answer for my brethren. (Mr. Lynch says he thinks they should not be separated, but live together. All the other persons present, being questioned one by one, answer that they agree with Bro. Frazier.)

Q—Do you think that there is intelligence enough among the slaves to maintain themselves under the Government and maintain good and peaceable relations among yourselves and your neighbors?

A—I think there is sufficient intelligence among us to do so. (*The National Freedman*, April 1, 1865)

Sherman issued Special Field Order No. 10. It provided for forty acres of land for each freedman and his family as well as a self-governing black community. The Sea Islands, off the Georgia coast, were turned over to the freedmen, many of the same slaves who worked the land in bondage in the previous years. Congress followed up by establishing the Bureau of Refugees, Freedmen and Abandoned Lands. Congress instructed the Freedmen's Bureau to set aside the abandoned plantation land for freedmen and local white refugees.

The challenge of providing land to freedmen was more than most Republicans could swallow. Thus, when President Johnson ordered the land given back to the plantation owners, the Republicans supported the President. Land, the most critical element of Reconstruction, was deleted from the equation within months. In the spring of 1866, black troops evicted freedmen from the Sea Islands. Reconstruction, the most inclusive experiment in democracy in the United States, was mortally wounded from its beginnings by the failure to provide land as restitution for slavery. By the end of 1866, only 1,565 of the forty thousand freedmen who received land still maintained it.

A letter dated December 30, 1865, described the common treatment of freedmen by white contractors:

Laura Perry (col'd)—abbreviation for "colored" in the Congressional Record—represents as follows:

> Her husband Robert Perry and herself were formerly owned by William Turno who lives in the town of Pendleton. They had planted a crop for Turno and worked it till it was ready to 'lay by' when, Laura states, Turno proposed to them with others to sign a contract for their lifetime. They with two others, Novel and Richard, refused to sign such contract and Turno drove them away without food or any compensation for their labor.

> They proceeded toward Columbia and had reached a place called Rocky Mill when they were overtaken by two white men who had been sent by Turno. They shot Robert, killing him instantly. They did the same to Novel. Richard ran to a creek, plunged in, was shot at but succeeded in making his escape. They then took Laura, stripped her bare, gave her fifty lashes upon the bare back and compelled her to walk back to Pendleton, some 25 miles. They then put her at the plow by day and confined her in the 'dark house' by night for one week, giving her nothing to eat. An officer from Anderson happened at the place. When Laura revealed to him her terrible situation said officer took her and her two children in a cart to where her husband and Novel had been shot, found remnants of their bodies and buried them and then placed Laura and her children on board the cars for Charleston. Soon after reaching this city Laura gave birth to a dead infant. [National Archives].

As a result of the physical abuse, political outrages, and the whites' insistence on treating blacks as 'niggers', the freedmen assembled in North and South Carolina, Maryland, Virginia, Tennessee, Florida, Louisiana, and Georgia, forwarding petitions of protest to Congress and the President. These conventions served as counterpoints to the white Confederate style Reconstruction conventions.

The Freedmen's Bureau was the first social welfare effort of the United States government. The Bureau helped organize schools, churches, and medical clinics and served as a dispenser of justice as well as much needed provisions. General Howard performed yeoman's work in organizing the Bureau with an inadequate budget and, along with the federal troops, served as a counter to the Confederate style Reconstruction governments from 1866 through 1876. Despite the Freedmen's Bureau and troops, terror stalked the black community.

Jane Sneed, wife of a black soldier, comments:

> On Wednesday, they came into my house and searched for arms and not finding any, went away. Before they came to my house they went to Adam Lock's, right alongside mine. With Rachel, my daughter, I went out to help get the things out of his house. The house had been set on fire and was burning. There was a man in the house asleep and some of the people asked me to go and wake him. When I went back, I walked upon the body of Rachel. She was dead and the blood running out of her mouth. Her clothes were all burned off from her.
>
> Q—How old was your daughter?
>
> A—About fourteen years old. [Eyewitness testimony, House Report No. 101, 39th Congress, 1st Session]

Government Intervention

The authorization for the Freedman's Bureau came despite Andrew Johnson's veto. And the Fourteenth Amendment likewise passed over Johnson's veto. Charles Sumner described the political situation in a letter to a friend:

> The suffering in the South is great, through the misconduct of the President. His course has kept the rebel spirit alive, and depressed the loyal, white and black. It makes me very sad to say this. Considering the difficulties of their position, the blacks have done wonderfully well. They should have had a Moses as a President, but they had found a Pharaoh.

It was the same Charles Sumner who left the Senate chambers to weep when colleagues refused to allow freedman land as restitution for slavery.

The winter of 1866-67 found the South, not unexpectedly, rejecting the Fourteenth Amendment in state after state. Johnson's white conventions could not abide enfranchising the black man. Only Tennessee accepted it.

In February of 1867, the South was divided into five military districts, with a general and troops assigned to each district. After much maneuvering in the Senate by Sumner, the Reconstruction bill passed and was forwarded to President Johnson. The President held it until two days before Congress adjourned and then vetoed it. Congress overrode the veto and the

Reconstruction bill was law. Johnson's Confederate style Reconstruction was ended.

But Andrew Johnson was not through. He had the power to appoint the generals in the military districts and he wanted to appoint those sympathetic to the white South. Congress, meeting in extraordinary session, convened one day after the end of the 39th Congress, and passed a supplemental Reconstruction bill to thwart Johnson's appointment powers. The bill provided for all male citizens twenty-one and over to be registered to vote, take the loyalty oath, and for the commanding generals to order elections and choose delegates for a constitutional convention. Of course, Johnson vetoed immediately, and was again overridden.

The showdown with President Johnson and Congress culminated with the impeachment effort of 1868. Johnson had exercised his veto twenty-three times in three years, more than double of Andrew Jackson's eleven vetoes in eight years. The impeachment trial began on March 30, 1868 and lasted until May 6. Over two-thirds of the House of Representatives and thirty-nine of fifty-four senators voted for impeachment. The effort failed by the lack of one vote in the Senate.

W.E.B. Du Bois describes the forces at work during Reconstruction:

Reconstruction was an economic revolution on a mighty scale . . . not simply a fight between white and black races . . . It was much more subtle, it involved more than this. There have been repeated and continued attempts to paint this era as an interlude of petty politics or nightmare of race hate instead of viewing it slowly and broadly as tremendous series of efforts to earn a living in new and untried ways, to achieve economic security and to restore fatal losses of capital and investment. It was a vast labor movement of ignorant, earnest, and bewildered black men . . . ground in the mud by three awful centuries of degradation . . . who now staggered forward blindly in blood and tears amid . . . hate and hurt . . . . Reconstruction was a vast labor movement of ignorant, muddled and bewildered white men . . . disinherited of land and labor . . . hanging on the edge of poverty . . .chasing slaves and now lurching up to manhood.

Reconstruction was the turn of white Northern migration southward to new and sudden economic opportunity which followed the disaster and dislocation of war . . .

Finally Reconstruction was a desperate effort of a dislodged, maimed, impoverished and ruined oligarchy and monopoly to restore an anachronism in economic organization by force, fraud and slander, in defiance of law and order, and . . . in bitter strife with a new capitalism and a new political framework.

From the "Swing Around the Circle" of President Johnson until the economic panic and depression of 1873, Du Bois saw "seven mystic years (when) the majority of thinking Americans of the North believed in the equal manhood of the Negroes." Seven dramatic years in which a revolution played itself out within the framework of American politics. It was a magic time of professed equality between black and white. One of its highlights was the development of public education in America.

A dramatic development in the South was the freedman's thirst for knowledge. Schools sprang up wherever people could gather (Du Bois taught in one outside of Nashville); many volunteers-white and black-came down from the North to assist in educating the freedmen who had been forbidden by the slave codes from reading or writing. This growing wave of people providing learning joined with the political education campaign in the spring and summer of 1867 that registered people to vote. The Freedman's Bureau helped register the newly enfranchised citizens. As a result, state and local Republican parties were formed.

James Sims, an ex-slave speaking in Savannah to a gathering of seven thousand, was blunt:

> Colored men are not fools. They knew enough to fight right and they will vote right. I wish the white people to understand distinctly that we will not elect a Rebel Mayor or have any more brutal policemen.
>
> Offices should be filled by both white and colored men who are capable of serving with honor. I would have white and colored aldermen and white and colored policemen and the sooner people know it the better. Some people might be surprised to see white and colored men working shoulder to shoulder in the political field—I am not. I have children at school in Massachusetts and expect to see them in Congress some day. (*The New Orleans Tribune*, April 13, 1867)

As a result of such organizing throughout the South, by the fall of 1867, seven hundred thousand blacks and six hundred sixty thousand whites had registered to vote. This led to the elections of the state constitutional conventions. The press, dominated by the old white oligarchy, was vicious in describing these conventions: Delegates were "baboons" and "monkeys" while the conventions were "The Menagerie," the "Black and Tans," or the "Ring-Streaked and Striped Negro Convention."

The voter turnout in the South for the conventions in 1867 to reconstruct the states was an astonishing 1,363,640 people. In 1860, there had been only 721,191 whites voting. The 1867 elections saw 703,459 blacks voting and 660,181 whites doing so.

As the national presidential race geared up in May 1868, it became clear Reconstruction was on the table to be controlled by the victor. The Democrats chose Seymour and the Republicans picked Grant. President Johnson was a pitiful figure with little support for reelection.

The newly enfranchised blacks, with the strong support of northern efforts, elected Ulysses Grant as President of the United States. He received two hundred fourteen electoral votes to eighty such votes for Seymour. Grant won by a majority of three hundred and nine thousand votes. Almost five hundred thousand blacks voted for him and he polled a minority of the white vote. The Republican sweep of 1868 was made possible by the black vote.

The North, with its booming war economy, looked South and West for development. At this point, the leaders of the economic engine were not about to side with the Democrats who represented the white, agrarian, oligarchy of the South. Thus, the 40th Congress in its third session, fortified with overwhelming Republican mandates, initiated and passed the Fifteenth Amendment to the Constitution of the United States. The Republicans did not want a repeat of Grants narrow election and in 1870 passed the Fifteenth Amendment.

The Fifteenth Amendment

Section 1.1. The right of citizens of the United States to vote shall not be denied or abridged by the United States or by any State on account of race, color, or previous condition of servitude.

Section 2. The Congress shall have power to enforce this article by appropriate legislation.

It is instructive to examine one Southern state under Reconstruction to realize the dramatic social changes brought about by the federal legislation. We choose South Carolina because it provided the most promise and indeed went further than any other Reconstruction state to realize democracy for all people. In large measure this was due to its majority black representation at the state convention- 61%, followed by Louisiana with 50% black. All other Southern states averaged about one fourth, or less, of the state convention delegates being black.

In 1860, South Carolina had 412,329 black and 291,300 white inhabitants. About ten thousand blacks were free and thus became citizens. As a result of the 1867 election, the South Carolina Constitutional Convention was constituted with 48 white delegates and 76 black delegates. The convention was made up of mostly poor people, black and white, rather than the wealthy white planters. As W.E.B. Du Bois remarked:

Since the great majority of white people of the state had been kept in ignorance and poverty, and practically all the Negroes were slaves, whose education was a penal offense, one could hardly expect universal suffrage to put rich men in the legislature. It was singularly to the credit of these voters that poverty was so well represented.

Beverly Nash, a hotel waiter as a slave, told his colleagues in the South Carolina convention:

I believe, my friends and fellow citizens, we are not prepared for this suffrage. But we can learn. Give a man tools and let him commence to use them, and in time he will learn a trade. So it is with voting. We may not understand it at the start, but in time we shall learn to do our duty.

Beverly Nash and his colleagues soon established the truth of his statement.

In South Carolina, as throughout the South, there was no public education before the Civil War. Francis L. Cardozo, chairman of the Committee on Education, brought forth a bill establishing a statewide system of free public schools (with free textbooks), an insane asylum, an institution for the blind, deaf, and dumb, and the maintenance of a state university. Accompanying the bill was this proviso: "All the public schools, cottages and universities supported by public funds shall be free and open to all the children of the state without regard to race or color."

The South Carolina convention confronted the question of land. They knew that without economic enfranchisement, political enfranchisement was doomed to failure. Francis Cardozo spoke to the convention:

The poor freedmen were induced, by many Congressmen even, to expect confiscation. They held out the hope of confiscation. General Sherman did confiscate; gave the lands to the freedmen; and if it were not for President Johnson, they would have them now. The hopes of the freedmen have not been realized, and I do not think that asking for a loan of one million, to be paid by a mortgage upon the land, will be half as bad as has been supposed. I have been told by the Assistant Commissioner that he has been doing on a private scale what this petition proposes. I say every opportunity of helping the colored people should be seized upon. I think the adoption of this measure should be seized upon. We should certainly vote for some measure of relief for the colored men, as we have to the white man who mortgaged their property to perpetuate slavery, and whom they have liberated from their bonds.

After much debate, a petition was drawn asking Congress to buy land for the freedman. Such an action was deemed unlikely, so a state land commission for buying and selling land to the freedmen was established.

In working on their Bill of Rights, the convention abolished all distinctions based on race or color. Also, a divorce law was enacted for the first time and married women could not have their property sold to cover their husbands' debts. The convention also engaged in judicial reform. The entire new constitution was adopted by the convention on in April of 1868 and ratified by the voters.

As a result of the South Carolina constitutional convention, the state, along with Alabama, Florida, Georgia, Louisiana, North Carolina, and Arkansas, was admitted to the Union. Only Mississippi succumbed to the intimidation and terrorism of the White Leagues. Tennessee had previously been admitted and Texas was still writing its constitution.

The Reconstruction legislatures met to implement the constitutions ratified by the people. "The bottom rail was on top" and the planters, despite controlling the press and the Democratic Party, were not in power. The Republicans, the Freedmen's Bureau, and the Army ushered in a new day in Southern, indeed, American history.

Taxation in South Carolina was based on a uniform rate of assessment of all property in its full value. Prior to the Civil War, taxes were high on merchants, professions, and banking and low on land and slaves. The new tax base was equitable and provided the money to run the public institutions recently established.

The denunciation of the new tax system was vociferous, and significant amounts were not collected due to obfuscation and manipulation by the planters. Nonetheless, the tax changes indicated a revolution in the role of the state. W.E.B. Du Bois comments:

> It is said that the ante-bellum state was ruled by 180 great landlords. They had made the functions of the state just as few as possible, and did by private law and on private plantations most of the things which in other states were carried on by the local and state governments. The economic revolution, therefore, which universal suffrage envisaged for this state, was perhaps greater than any other Southern state. It was for this reason that the right of the masses to vote was so bitterly assailed, and expenditures for the new functions of the state denounced as waste and extravagance.

One of the realities of life in South Carolina and the nation was the rise of railroads. Investors flocked South and West to build what was regarded as a public highway, through which state appropriations enriched individuals extraordinarily. Into this web of speculation, malfeasance, and outright robbery, the Reconstruction government of South Carolina became entangled.

The economic troubles of South Carolina in Reconstruction were complex. Lerone Bennett summarizes it:

Yes, there was corruption in South Carolina between 1867 and 1877, as there was corruption in the same period in any lily-white governments of New York and Washington and as there is today . . . What I am concerned to emphasize here is that corruption is a constant variable in American politics—a constant that varies with socioeconomic conditions and the nature of political structures, rather than with the color of men's skins. Some black leaders were peripherally involved in corruption in South Carolina as receivers of bribes and improper pay certificates; but the major operators, by all accounts, were white Republicans and Democrats, some of the highly placed Confederates with impeccable connections in the Charleston Board of Trade and the Columbia Chamber of Commerce.

In 1871, the black legislators initiated a series of reforms to improve the economic chaos of the state. Despite the furor in the press and the white resentment of increased taxation, institutions for the insane and the deaf, blind and dumb were created. The public school system was under way from first grade through the University of South Carolina, with black and white welcomed at all levels.

Congressman Ransier summarized the economic and political situation on March 9, 1871:

I am no apologist for thieves; for if I were, I do not think I would have occupied for so long a time a place in your confidence. On the contrary, I am in favor of a most thorough investigation of the official conduct of any and every public officer in connection with the discharge of whose duties there is anything like well-grounded suspicion; and to this effect have I spoken time and again. Nor am I lukewarm on the subject of better government in South Carolina than that which seems to be bearing heavily on all classes and conditions of society today. Still, recognizing that which I believe to be true, that such is the determined opposition to the Republican Party and its doctrines by our opponents that no administration of our affairs, however honest, just and economical, would satisfy any considerable portion of the Democratic masses in the State of South Carolina.

Ransier was on target. The corruption in the Republican administration served as an excuse for the fusillade from the white Democrats who wanted to destroy the Republicans and regain power. The changes the Republicans had made in the state were weakening the white's bid for control because things were improving; from the economy to politics. The land commission was resettling freedmen on plantations—by 1880, thirty three thousand plantations of 1860 were divided among ninety three thousand small farmers. By 1873, the Freedmen's Bureau Bank had fifty-five hundred depositors, totaling $350,000; public schools, a penitentiary, the institutions for the physically disabled and mentally impaired were all established. South

Carolina, for the first time, actually had a functioning state government and it was in the aftermath of a halcyon of destruction through the Civil War.

Sir George Campbell, a Member of Parliament, described his visit South: "Before I went South, I certainly expected to find that the Southern states had been for a time a sort of Pandemonium in which a white man could barely live, yet it was certainly not so. 'Well, then,' I had gone on to ask, 'did the black legislatures make bad laws?' My informants could not say they did." What Sir Campbell discerned was that the corruption charges were hurled at Reconstruction governments by displaced whites. The same people, he also noted, organized the Ku Klux Klan and were trying to tear the government down through terror.

Nathan Bedford Forrest, a founder of the KKK, estimated it had half a million members in 1868. Through the KKK and other terrorist organizations the white South fought Reconstruction. The violence in Memphis, New Orleans and Norfolk underscored that, even with federal troops in a city, blacks were not safe. The countryside, where troops were sparse, was a scene of violent harassment. It's a scene Frederick Douglass portrayed:

> You emancipated us. You have; and I thank you for it. But what is emancipation?
>
> When the Israelites were emancipated they were told to go and borrow of their neighbors—borrow their coin, borrow their jewels, load themselves down with the means of subsistence; after, they should go free in the land which the Lord God gave them. When the Russian serfs had their chains broken and were given their liberty, the government of Russia—aye, the despotic government of Russia—gave to those poor emancipated serfs a few acres of land on which they could live and earn their bread.
>
> But when you turned us loose, you gave us no acres. You turned us loose to the sky, to the storm, to the whirlwind, and worst of all, you turned us loose to the wrath of our infuriated masters.

The ugly truth was that wealthy whites organized the KKK, stirred up the masses of poor whites to join them, and in the name of the Lost Cause carried on a reign of terror throughout the South.

White Flight in the North

By 1875, four states remained Republican-Mississippi, South Carolina, Florida and Louisiana. The Mississippi Plan was being executed even as the Civil Rights Act of 1875 passed through Congress. Charles Sumner's dying request that his colleagues "take care of the civil rights bill . . . don't let it fail" was honored by passage on March 1, 1875. It was too late for Mississippi and the rest of the South.

The Mississippi White League militarized every Democratic organization in the State. By massacring blacks and seizing control on the local level, the White League awaited the November elections with a pat hand. Despite a thirty thousand black majority in the state, the blacks of Mississippi were not well armed. They depended on the militia, which needed the Governor to mobilize it, and Governor Ames was not inclined to do so.

Governor Ames turned to President Grant who replied that the "whole public is tired of these annual autumnal outbreaks." As the election approached, Ames finally asked Charles Cardwell to provide outlying districts with arms for survival against the White League. Cardwell, by leading the militia, was condemned by his white foes.

White Leaguers, with cannon booming, marched and demanded that Ames disband the militia. He did so. On October 13, an agreement was signed that disbanded the militia and gained the White Leaguers' promise to disarm and allow free elections. It was a promise promptly broken; the election was characterized by armed men and artillery, along with cavalry from Alabama and Louisiana, intimidating and killing blacks who sought to vote.

Although President Grant later described the election: "Mississippi is governed today by officials chosen through fraud and violence, such as would scarcely be accredited to savages, much less to a civilized and Christian people," his words were gratuitous because when troops were requested of him earlier to prevent this violence, he responded with his infamous "annual autumnal outbreak" reply. The Senate, which took no action to challenge the results of the election, called it "one of the darkest chapters in American history."

Southern Retrenchment

Meanwhile, in Mississippi, Charles Cardwell was murdered. Governor Ames resigned after threatened impeachment by the Democratic legislature; the black Lieutenant Governor, Alexander K. Davis, was impeached, and Mississippi was no longer part of Reconstruction.

The Mississippi Plan was soon exported to South Carolina, Louisiana, and Florida. By 1876, the Democrats controlled the Louisiana House of Representatives and the Florida Senate, but South Carolina remained under black Republican control. In December 1875, the Charleston News and Observer gave a taste of what the New Year would bring to the Palmetto state with the following headline: "ORGANIZE! ORGANIZE! ORGANIZE!" The article stated: "Next year is the centennial year. (The) special task of South Carolina white men is to redeem, regenerate, and disenthrall their people and give them a new natal day, from which shall date, a second time, the freedom and independence of South Carolina." Lerone Bennett commented on the "redemption" of South Carolina:

> South Carolina was free—it would never be so free again. The state contained, at that juncture, 415,000 black people and 289,000 white people. There were seventy-seven black men in the state legislature, four of the eight state cabinet members were black, and one of the two most powerful men in the state was the young (thirty-four) Robert Brown Elliott, Speaker of the House of Representatives.

Heartened by the success of the Mississippi Plan, the South Carolina insurrectionary forces headed by General Gray consulted with Mississippi. Gray hatched a plan that the South Carolina "Red Shirts" pledged to carry out. It called for the following:

> Every Democrat must feel honor bound to control the vote of at least one Negro, by intimidation, purchase, keeping him away or as each individual may determine, how he may best accomplish it. Never threaten a man individually. If he deserves to be threatened, the necessities of the time require that he should die. A dead Radical is very harmless—a threatened Radical or one driven off by threats from the scene of his operations is often very troublesome, sometimes dangerous, always vindictive.

Rifle clubs were organized by whites throughout the state. Parades of thousands of red-shirted white men were featured. A letter to the New York Tribune conveys the scene in South Carolina:

> The air is filled with reports of outrages and murders which never appear in print. No prominent Republican of either color can safely leave a town. Let a hint that he intends to ride out into the country get wind and he is sure to be ambuscaded. But more than this. The whites regard a Republican of their color with tenfold the vindictiveness with which they look upon the Negro. Scores of white Republicans are hurrying in alarm to the newspaper offices to insert cards in which they renounce their party and profess conversion to Democracy. If these men hang back and refuse to neglect to join the precinct club or the nearest military company, their conduct is reported to the township meeting. A committee is appointed to request an explanation. They call on the suspected man at their earliest convenience. If he is sensible, he will submit profuse apologies and regrets, and hurriedly take up his rifle and follow them to the drill room.

As in Mississippi, blacks were killed and their meetings broken up. Black voters were lynched and massacres in Hamburg (five blacks killed) and Ellerton (thirty-nine blacks killed) highlighted the white exercise of terror.

In South Carolina, unlike Mississippi, the blacks composed a strong militia and it was activated. The militia fought back against the Red Shirts. President Grant ordered the rifle clubs disbanded on October 17 but they simply reorganized with new names. Grant sent troops to South Carolina in late October but the troops sided with the white Southerners who were very hospitable to them

The election "was one of the greatest farces ever seen," one native commented. White voters from Georgia and North Carolina crossed state lines to vote. But the blacks persisted.

South Carolina, Florida and Louisiana were deciding electors in the presidential race between the Republican Rutherford Hayes and the Democrat Samuel Tilden. The election boards certified Hayes the winner over Tilden. Whites refused to accept the result and appealed to Congress. For a few months, South Carolina and Louisiana had two governors and two legislatures. The Democrats in the federal House of Representatives filibustered and refused the proper accounting of the electoral votes.

In order to break the deadlock, someone had to yield. Hayes struck a deal with Southern Democrats. In exchange for their support, he would withdraw federal troops from the South and give them two Southerners on the Supreme Court. The white Southern Democrats deserted their party and Hayes was inaugurated on March 3, 1867. On April 10, he removed troops from Columbia, South Carolina and the government fell. On April 24, he did the same in Louisiana and its Republican government collapsed.

Thomas Miller, a black Republican in the South Carolina House of Representatives, summarized Reconstruction in South Carolina:

> We were eight years in power. We had built schoolhouses, established charitable institutions, built and maintained the penitentiary system, provided for the education of the deaf and dumb, rebuilt the jails and courthouses, rebuilt the bridges and reestablished the ferries. In short, we had reconstructed the State and placed it upon the road to prosperity and, at the same time, by our acts of financial reform, transmitted to the Hampton Government an indebtedness not greater by more than $2,500,000 than was the bonded debt of the state in 1868, before the Republican Negroes and their white allies came into power.

As W.E.B. Du Bois makes clear, the end of Reconstruction could not have come without the industrial wealth of the North aligning itself with the white southern Democrats. Frederick Douglass said it best: "The Republican party has gone from a party of morals to a party of money."

The best experiment in democracy in United States history came to a crashing halt because white wealth would no longer support black enfranchisement and equality. Hence, the end of the First Reconstruction and a return to peonage for blacks in the South. In the North, a Jim Crow society continued to exist. The tyranny of the racial majority had once again exerted itself and the Regime of Segregation had begun.

It is interesting to note that it was not because the experiment in democracy failed that it was discarded. The experiment had been an astounding success by all counts. The economy rebounded dramatically. Cotton in 1860 was at an all time high of 5,187,052 bales. By 1880, a mere fifteen years after total destruction during the Civil War, it surpassed the previous record with 5,575,659 bales. Farms had gone from an average of 335 acres in 1860 to 153 acres in 1880, signifying that more people were operating successful farms. The free public schools were in operation and the custodial institutions had been created.

What Du Bois said about South Carolina was true of the South and the nation:

> It seemed fairly clear that what South Carolina wanted was not reform even in its narrower sense . . . what it was attacking was not even stealing and corruption. If there was one thing that South Carolina feared more than bad Negro government it was good Negro government.

As we have seen throughout this work, the white majority dictated the lives of minorities in the name of democracy. As a result of civil war, the white abolition/democratic movement was able to launch the first real democratic government in the country in the conquered South. Indeed, those Southern states sent two black senators and fourteen congressmen to Washington, a black governor of Louisiana for a brief period of time, and proved to the world that blacks could participate in government. For this effort they were pilloried, defamed, terrorized, and murdered. Ultimately, they were sold out to what Du Bois termed "the new American industrial empire (whose concern) was not national well-being, but individual gain."

It is difficult for us to understand the betrayal of democracy, which the demise of the Reconstruction represented. Perhaps because it reveals our country in such a harsh light, we cannot abide it. But Du Bois shines that light for us clearly when he comments:

> What liberalism did not understand was that such a revolution was economic and involved force. Those who against the public weal have power cannot be expected to yield save to superior power. The North used its power in the Civil War to break the political power of the slave barons. During and after the war, it united its force with planters. It hoped with the high humanitarianism of Charles Sumner eventually to induce the planter to surrender his economic power peacefully, in return for complete political amnesty, and hoped that the North would use its federal police power to maintain the black man's civil rights in return for peaceful industry and increasing intelligence . . . Abolitionists failed to see that after the momentary exaltation of war, the nation did not want Negroes to have civil rights

and that national industry could get its way easier by alliance with Southern landholders than by sustaining Southern workers. They did not know that when they let the dictatorship of labor be overthrown in the South they surrendered the hope of democracy in America for all men.

A personal note is in order before closing the chapter on Reconstruction. As a white Southerner, I undertook the task of writing this chapter with a keen sense of humility. The historical record reflects a literary infatuation with the myth of Dixie after its demise. The image of the noble Lost Cause plagued historians well into the 20th century. W.E.B. Du Bois' epic *Black Reconstruction in America: 1860-1876*, published in 1935, did more to correct the historical narrative than any other work; but the myth persists still today.

I was born in Greenville, North Carolina, in 1946. A tobacco market town in eastern North Carolina, it was a segregated world. After my father's sudden death in 1954 while we were living in Jonesville, my mother moved our family back to Greenville to live with my maternal grandparents while my mother worked on her master's degree at East Carolina University.

The year following my father's heart attack was most difficult for me. My beloved Ma-Ma, Mayme Miller Gaston, frequently comforted me as I sobbed while lying on my bed. She would come to me and gently stroke my back with her hands and fingers, easing my pain amid the Southern evenings of sadness. Under Ma-Ma's tender care, I would slowly calm down. She told me stories of her maternal grandmother, and of her mother, to soothe me through the grief of my father's dying.

I first learned from Ma-Ma of carpetbaggers (Northerners—Yankees-who came South to make money after the War Between the States), scalawags (Southerners who cooperated with the Yankees), and the destruction and ruin of the South. Her view was colored by the fact that General Sherman's soldiers had marched through Cokesbury, South Carolina, and plundered the family plantation in the name of freeing the slaves. (One bit of family lore was that the slaves told the Yankee troops where the silver was hidden, in the well, with which they absconded).This action forced her grandmother, whose husband had died in Richmond and whose sister's husband died at Gettysburg, to move to Columbia. (The sisters had married brothers, a not uncommon practice in the frontier South.) In Columbia she rented rooms out, establishing a boarding house above a bank, as she and the town of Columbia struggled to survive Sherman's destructive force.

It was hard times for the Blackwell family, as it was for most Southerners, black or white. The family kept a barrel of Confederate money in the attic hoping for a better price for its redemption, but it was worthless. Many of the men, like her grandfather and grand-uncle, were dead. Others were maimed or missing in action in America's bloodiest war. The women, like Ma-Ma's mother and grandmother, endured.

Ma-Ma was a strong loving woman, proud of her family and a survivor herself. She birthed eight children and saw two die and one disappear. In the year 1954–55, while *Brown v. Board of Education* shook the segregated external world of the South, Ma-Ma reconstructed the internal world of the soul of a lost child, her grandson. It was a patient, loving task, which would take the better part of a year of back rubs and consoling songs and stories. Slowly, the sobs subsided.

As the boy, now a man, reads the record of Reconstruction, he finds an element of truth in the myth of his grandmother's view of the War Between the States. It was a difficult time for all and our family suffered grievous loss. Because of that traumatic experience, we absorbed the best and the worst of the South. A pride of family and a stubborn endurance in the face of overwhelming devastation; but also the ugly grip of racism, which wanted to blame "the niggers" for all the problems of the South. Whether it be the South of 1854 or the South of 1954, the blacks were easily blamed.

Sometime in the welter of experiences in Greenville, I used the word "nigger" (a word I had not heard Ma-Ma or Mother use) in the presence of my aunts, uncles, and grandparents. None of them appeared to notice because the term was loosely used by most of them. My mother, however, immediately pulled me from the kitchen, where the family was gathered telling stories, into my grandparent's bedroom. Sitting me down on their ancient cherry wood bed, she looked me in the eye and spoke directly to me. "Joe, we don't use that word in our family." Immediately, I responded: "Aunt Grace and Uncle Blue use it all the time." My mother's serious face was unmoved by my logic: "I don't care what they say. They're adults. You're my child, and we will not use that word. Do you understand?" I nodded my head affirmatively.

So it is with a mixed collection of feelings I have sought to address Reconstruction. Above all, I have sought to be fair to the record and let it point the way for all of us in this country so we may achieve a new appreciation for what happened then, who we became, and why the dream of democracy was betrayed to lie dormant for almost another one hundred years.

From 1883 until 1954, the judiciary turned its back on black people when the civil rights cases were struck down as unconstitutional by the Supreme Court. From 1875, when Charles Sumner's dying request for the Civil Rights Bill to be passed was granted by his colleagues, until 1957, no further civil rights action passed Congress. From President Rutherford B. Hayes's sell out of the Republican governments in the South in 1876 until Franklin Roosevelt's administration desegregated the federal government with one hundred administrative appointments beginning in 1933, no executive action was taken on behalf of blacks. The tyranny of the white majority was complete in all branches of government and remained virtually intact until the Second Reconstruction began in 1954. The Regime of Segregation was underway.

Chapter 9. The Regime of Segregation (1883–1953)

The executive and legislative branches of government pushed Reconstruction into the final act of the morality play centered on how the white majority would treat the black minority. The U.S. Supreme Court provided the denouement by ruling in the *Civil Rights Cases of 1883*.

Section I. The Supreme Court Revanchement on Civil Rights

The *Civil Rights Cases* were a consolidation of lower court decisions from Kansas, California, Missouri, New York and Tennessee. The question addressed by the Supreme Court was what did Congress mean when it passed the 1875 Civil Rights Act? Following the Thirteenth and Fourteenth Amendments to the Constitution, the Fifteenth Amendment ran into obstruction throughout the country, especially in the South. For many white Americans it was one thing to free slaves and provide them the vote but quite another matter to permit equal access to public conveyance and inns, which is what the Civil Rights Bill authorized. Many of the white majority felt that was surely going too far. The Supreme Court would decide if the country had endured the Civil War and constitutional changes to leave the freedman a second class citizen.

The majority ruling in the *Civil Rights Cases* concluded that Congress had not intended individuals and corporations to be prohibited from discrimination. Rather, the Civil Rights Act was interpreted to apply only to governments. Justice Harlan vehemently dissented:

> The [majority's] opinion ... [is] too narrow and artificial ... I cannot resist the conclusion that the substance and spirit of the recent amendments to

the Constitution have been sacrificed by a subtle and ingenious verbal criticism . . .

It proceeds as if "the purpose of the nation [in enacting the Thirteenth Amendment was] simply to destroy the institution [of slavery], and then remit the race . . . held in bondage to the several states for such protection . . . as those states in their discretion might choose to provide."

Justice Harlan continued:

> I hold since slavery . . . was the moving . . . cause of the adoption of [the Thirteenth] amendment and since [slavery] rested wholly upon the inferiority, as a race, those held in bondage, their freedom necessarily involved immunity from, and protection against, all discrimination against them, because of their race . . . [not only by the state but] also upon such individuals and corporations as exercise public functions and wield authority under the state.

If the Supreme Court majority was intent upon interpreting the Civil Rights Act honorably, the remembrance of the Senator who championed the act, Charles Sumner, would have been helpful. Senator Sumner's dying request to his colleagues was "to take care of my Civil Rights Act." This pillar of the rights of black people in the U.S. Senate once stated he regarded "any human right a constitutional right." The narrow restricting and perverse interpretation of the Supreme Court majority was an affront to all Sumner stood for in pushing for implementation of the Civil Rights Act.

Justice Harlan was from the border state of Kentucky. Although not a member of the Confederacy, Kentucky had slavery, and Harlan experienced the reality of slavery and segregation. He knew the *Civil Rights Cases* decision was a signal to the white majority to proceed back in the direction of the *Dred Scott* case, when blacks were legally deemed inferior to whites. Chief Justice Roger Taney was the author of *Dred Scott* and the *Civil Rights Cases* decisions.

Time would prove Justice Harlan a prophet in his dissent in both cases. It would be seventy one years from the *Civil Rights Cases* decision until blacks were granted equality under the law. As Harlan noted, black citizens were "left, in respect of their civil rights in question, practically at the mercy of corporations and individuals wielding power under the State."

Frederick Douglass Responds to the Civil Rights Cases Decision

Frederick Douglass knew all too well what the Supreme Court decision augured. He was a former slave and champion of the rights of black people. On October 22, 1883, he spoke to a mass meeting about the decision:

The cause which has brought us here tonight is neither common nor trivial. Few events in our national history have surpassed it in magnitude ... It has swept over the land like a moral cyclone, ...

I look upon [this decision in the Civil Rights cases] as one more shocking development of that moral weakness in high places which has attended the conflict between the spirit of liberty and the spirit of slavery from the beginning ...

Far down the ages, when men shall wish to inform themselves as to the real state of liberty, law, religion and civilization in the United States at this juncture of our history, they will ... read the decision declaring the Civil Rights [Act] unconstitutional and void.

The Supreme Court of the United States ... decided that the law intended to secure to colored people the civil rights guaranteed to them [null and void] ... and It presents the United States before the world as a Nation utterly destitute of power to protect the rights of its own citizens upon its own soil ... In the name of commonsense, I ask, what right have we to call ourselves a Nation, in view of this decision, and this utter destitution of power?

***

In the dark days of slavery, the Court, on all occasions, gave the greatest importance of intention as a guide to interpretation. The object and intention of the law, it was said, must prevail. Everything in favor of slavery and against the Negro was settled by this object and intention. The Constitution was construed according to its intention. We were over and over again referred to what the framers meant, and plain language was sacrificed that the so affirmed intention of these framers might be positively asserted ...

Fellow citizens! While slavery was the base line of American society, while it ruled the church and the state, while it was the interpreter of our law and the exponent of our religion, it admitted no quibbling, no narrow rules of legal or scriptural of Bible or Constitution. It sternly demanded its pound of flesh, no matter how much blood was shed in the taking of it. It was enough for it to be able to show the intention to get all it asked in the Courts or out of the Courts. But now slavery is abolished. Its reign was long, dark and bloody. Liberty now, is the base line of the Republic. Liberty has supplanted slavery, but I fear it has not supplanted the spirit or power of slavery. Where slavery was strong, liberty is now weak ...

***

... O for a Supreme Court which shall be as true, as vigilant, as active, and exacting in maintaining laws enacted for the protection of human rights as in other days was that Court for the destruction of human rights!

Ida Wells Fights Back

Although the three branches of government commenced the Regime of Segregation with the *Civil Rights* decision by the Supreme Court, it was not a fait accompli. Reconstruction had changed state and federal constitutions, altered social customs, and revived the Southern economy. But the *Civil Rights Cases* ruling added impetus to the movement toward a segregated society. One black citizen described her experience in Tennessee on May 4, 1884. The ripple of the *Civil Rights Cases* was no mere judicial history as Ida Wells sought to sit in the same railroad car as white people:

> When the train started and the conductor came along to collect tickets, he took my ticket, then handed it back to me and told me that he couldn't take my ticket there. I thought that if he didn't want the ticket I wouldn't bother about it so I went on reading. In a little while when he finished taking tickets, he came back and told me I would have to go in the other car. I refused, saying that the forward car was a smoker, and as I was in the ladies' car I proposed to stay. He tried to drag me out of the seat, but the moment he caught hold of my arm I fastened my teeth in the back of his hand.

> I had braced my feet against the seat in front and was holding to the back, and as he had already been badly bitten he didn't try again by himself. He went forward and got the baggageman and another man to help him and of course they succeeded in dragging me out. They were encouraged to do this by the attitude of the white ladies and gentlemen in the car; some of them even stood on the seats so that they could get a good view and continued applauding the conductor for his brave deed.

> By this time the train had stopped at the first station. When I saw that they were determined to drag me into the smoker, which was already filled with colored people and those who were smoking, I said I would get off the train rather than go in—which I did.

Until the *Civil Rights Cases* decision, Ida Wells could sit where she chose on the train. Indeed, it was a trip the school teacher had made many times previously to school. So, Ida Wells sued the railroad to get her rights back. The circuit judge in Memphis, Tennessee, a former federal officer from Minnesota, awarded her $500 damages. The *Memphis Daily Appeal* headline read: "A Darky Damsel Obtains a Verdict for Damages against the Chesapeake and Ohio Railroad—What It Costs to Put a Colored School Teacher in a Smoking Car—Verdict for $500."

Of course, the railroad appealed. The Tennessee Supreme Court ruled, not on the facts but on Ida Wells' supposed intent: "We think it is evident that the purpose of the defendant in error was to harass with a view to this suit, and that her persistence was not in good faith to obtain a comfortable seat for the short ride." Frederick Douglass's thoughts about intentions and how courts interpret such a word come readily to mind when reading the ruling by the Tennessee Supreme Court.

Despite the tumblers of the governmental lock falling into place in order to keep equality stowed away from black people, there were still areas of freedom remaining. By 1900, there were only four Southern states with segregated waiting rooms. The last black Congressman, George H. White, from North Carolina, left Congress in 1901. But the *Civil Rights Cases* painted the path for the white majority to pursue for a segregated society. In order for the Segregation Regime to become fully established another judicial decision was needed. In 1896, the Supreme Court rendered such a decision. In *Plessy v. Ferguson*, if any doubt remained, it became clear how onerous the future would be for the black minority at the hands of the white majority.

Plessy v. Ferguson

The majority decision in *Plessy v. Ferguson* began: "This case turns upon the constitutionality of an act of the General Assembly of the State of Louisiana, passed in 1890, providing for separate railway carriages for the white and colored persons." The factual description summarized the efforts of Plessy, an octoroon, to be seated in the white section of the passenger train. For his efforts he was forcibly removed and jailed. Plessy filed suit and it eventually reached the Supreme Court. The majority decision found a curious distinction: "The object of the (Fourteenth) amendment was undoubtedly to enforce absolute equality of the two races before the law, but in the nature of things it could not have been intended to abolish distinctions based upon color, or to enforce social, as distinguished from political, equality, or a commingling of the two races upon terms unsatisfactory to the other."

Once again we find the intentions argument noted by Frederick Douglass, only this time asserted with yet another subjective evaluation, "the nature of things." No matter the plain reading of the Fourteenth Amendment and subsequent efforts to enforce it such as the Enforcement Acts and the Civil Rights Act, the white majority perceived "the nature of things" and the intentions of the legislature in order to evade the meaning of the words themselves. This mischief would provide a beacon for all state legislatures and future Supreme Courts to follow for decades to avoid granting equality to black people. (Indeed, it is manifest in *McCleskey v. Kemp* on April 22, 1987.)

Plessy was a manifesto for segregation and it was acted upon accordingly by the Southern states.

Justice Harlan, the strong dissenter in the Civil Rights Cases decision, articulated an insightful and eloquent dissent in Plessy:

> The result of the whole matter is, that while this court has frequently adjudged and at the present term recognized the doctrine, that a State cannot, consistently with the Constitution of the United States, prevent white and black citizens, having the required qualifications for jury service, from sitting in the same jury box, it is now solemnly held that a State may prohibit white and black citizens from sitting in the same passenger coach.

This logical contradiction induced Justice Harlan to envision a scenario of farcical proportion which he painted for all to ponder. He then turned to the heart of the matter:

> I am of the opinion that the statute of Louisiana is inconsistent with the personal liberty of citizens, white and black, in that State, and hostile to both the spirit and letter of the Constitution of the United States . . . The white race deems itself to be the dominant race.'

After *Plessy v. Ferguson*, the Southern states continued unchecked in totally segregating blacks and whites. By the turn of the century, the Regime of Segregation was rendering Reconstruction a dim memory. Reconstruction had become, as Southerners' referred occasionally to the Civil War, "the late, great unpleasantness."

As blacks sank into a feudal state, terror became a way of life through lynching. Between 1889 and 1909 over seventeen hundred blacks were lynched. Race riots occurred in Washington, D.C. in 1886 and Atlanta, Georgia in 1906. One lynching provides a glimpse into the reality behind the statistics:

> 1918 in Valdosta, Georgia: Mary Turner hanged to a tree pregnant, doused with gasoline and motor oil and burned. As she dangled from the rope, a man stepped forward with a pocketknife and ripped open her abdomen in a crude Caesarean operation. Out tumbled the prematurely born child. Two feeble cries it gave—and received for an answer the heel of a stalwart man, as life was ground out of the tiny form. [Walter White, NAACP]

The pervasiveness of lynching (see *Thirty Years of Lynching in the United States, 1869-1918*, NAACP) as an enforcing mechanism for the white tyranny over black minority forced blacks to either "go along to get along" or to flee. Either was a means of survival. The decades reveal the black migration North: 1910-1920—300,000; 1920-1930—1.3 million; 1930-1940—1.5 million; 1940-1950—2.5 million.

With the death of Frederick Douglass in 1895, W.E.B. Du Bois emerged as the statesman of black rights. He remarked: "A belief in humanity required a belief in colored people." Although a truism, during the Segregation Regime Southerners were not willing to expand their definition of humanity to include black people. And if the truth be told, the federal government did little better. In 1913, under the Presidency of the Virginian Woodrow Wilson, the government was resegregated. Beginning with Republican President William McKinley in 1901, followed by Republican presidents Theodore Roosevelt and Howard Taft, the Republican Party abandoned the future of blacks to Southern Democrats. When a Democrat, Wilson, finally ascended the presidency, he merely formalized a de facto discrimination countenanced by the party of Lincoln.

In 1919 there were twenty-six race riots in the United States. It was called the Red Summer for the blood spilled. The KKK was strong in the South and Midwest, especially in the 1920s, (The largest KKK rally in the U.S. *history* was on July 4, 1923 in Kokomo, Indiana. Over a hundred thousand people assembled to see the installation of the Grand Dragon of the KKK.) Ironically, during this reign of terror the Negro Renaissance was underway in the 1920s. Harlem became a center of social critics, and black literary artists and musicians. From 1910 to 1923, Harlem tripled in population, increasing to over 180,000 blacks by 1923, mostly from the South. Into this schizophrenic world of artistic flowering and brutal oppression, Mahatma Gandhi delivered a timely message in July of 1929:

> Let not the 12,000,000 Negroes be ashamed of the fact that they are the grandchildren of slaves. There is no dishonor in being slaves. There is dishonor in being slave-owners. But let us not think of honour or dishonor in connection with the past. Let us realize that the future is with those who would be truthful, peaceful and loving. For, as the old wise men have said, truth ever is, untruth never was. Love alone binds and truth and love accrue only to the truly humble.

The Social Reality

The twentieth century in the United States of America gave every indication it would be the century of the whites. The Segregation Regime systematically oppressed blacks, North and South. A segregated society was fully in place in the South and Jim Crow society characterized the North. The political oppression rested on an economic structure that entrenched the white Southern oligarchy. At the turn of the century, the percentage of the national economy in terms of manufacturing capital and manufacturing establishments was the same in the South as in 1860. Per capita income in 1900 was 51 percent of the national average, the same as in 1860. C. Vann

Woodward provided an apt description: "Like republics below the Rio Grande, the South was limited largely to the role of the producer of raw materials, a tributary of industrial powers, an economy dominated by absentee landowners."

As in the antebellum South, cotton was still king. The average size farm decreased and tenancy increased in the 1890s. The world demand for cotton increased 3.5 percent a year for fifteen consecutive years. Textiles emerged as a burgeoning Southern industry. By 1915, the South had over 40 percent of the textile spindles in the United States. The northeastern textile owners moved their mills South to exploit the cheap labor available, which was provided by a feudal society.

When one examines fifteenth century Spain, there is an economic disparity virtually unfathomable to the modern mind. The nobility owned ninety-nine percent of the land, the merchant class and remaining workers were engaged in "root, hog or die." Although 1492 may seem a long time ago, it was more akin to the South of the early twentieth century than the South was to itself the latter third of the twentieth century. An examination of the Regime of Segregation will reveal it's parallel to medieval Spain.

John Egerton opens his epic history of the pre-Civil Rights South (*Speak Now Against the Day*) by providing a glimpse of the South in 1932:

> When America caught cold, the South got pneumonia, and when the nation was really sick, as it was in the Great Depression, its colonial states below the Mason-Dixon line were on their deathbed. (I call them colonial not because they harked back to the era before the American Revolution, though some of them did, but because they were still wards of the national government 150 years after the revolution had ended British domination) . . . the old deal had bankrupted tens of thousands of businesses, tripled the suicide rate, and driven millions of there-to-fore functional citizens to a nomadic search for their very survival. Historian William Manchester called 1932 "the Cruelest year," and he was right. It was the year the United States of America almost went belly-up.

The Depression was a difficult time for the country and a near impossible one for Southerners. The post-Reconstruction, white elite was known as Bourbons or Redeemers. Their world of segregation was complete. The blacks were at the bottom of the social order with poor whites right above them, according to the planters. Above all was the white oligarchy, which returned to power in 1877 with the withdrawal of federal troops from the South. Egerton describes the Southern economics of 1932:

> More than three-fourths of all Southerners had a standard of living . . . that would qualify them as paupers, as we would define the term today. Two-thirds of them lived on farms or small villages, and close

to two thirds of the farmers were share-croppers or tenants. The average gross income of farm families didn't reach $1,000 a year in nine Southern states, casting them to the bottom of the agriculture heap—but lest you think those were the poorest of the poor, keep in mind that they at least were employed and had a bare minimum of food and clothing and shelter to sustain them; millions of others were vagabonds with no resources at all.

In order to survive, millions of whites and blacks left the South from 1900 through 1950. The total was about five million immigrants of whom three million were black and two million white.

The pervasiveness of terror was documented by the Tuskegee Institute in Alabama. Founded by Booker T. Washington to teach blacks the mechanics of survival in a white world, Tuskegee also documented lynchings. Between 1890 and 1930, the Institute accounted for 2,771 lynchings in the United States. These figures are extremely conservative because they limited lynching by definition as mob violence against a person in custody or one being pursued for a supposed crime. Not counted were folks killed by deputized posses and others who "escaped from custody." It would not be untoward to double or triple the Tuskegee totals for a truer reading of the terror utilized to enforce the Segregation Regime. Almost all victims were black and over 75 percent black men.

As an example of an uncounted lynching statistic, Emile Joffrion recalled an incident from his youth in Laurel, Mississippi. (Emile was my father-in-law who grew up in Laurel in the 1920s and 30s.) Emile heard a commotion behind his house one evening that involved men and dogs chasing someone through the woods. The next day when he went to downtown Laurel, such as it was, there was a body part of the black man on display who had been caught and lynched the previous night. As Emile heard the story, he realized it was the man who had fled through the woods behind his house.

The Segregation Regime adopted the Jim Crow society of the North as a working model, seeking to keep everything separate. From the mid-1880s through 1901, one Southern state after another tore down Reconstruction and created an apartheid society. All of which was implemented by the executive, legislative and judicial branches of the state and federal government.

Egerton describes the reality of the renewed Confederate style Reconstruction:

> Segregation spread rapidly through the entire fabric of the society. The franchise was taken away, and elective office went with it . . . Poll taxes, white primaries, literacy tests, and other rules designed to remove blacks from voting had precisely that effect . . .
>
> In courtrooms, where black lawyers were exceedingly rare and black judges nonexistent, new restrictions were placed on the status

of blacks as plaintiffs, witnesses and jurors. Hospitals, where black doctors and nurses could not practice, denied admission to black patients. (Even blood was segregated.) Churches, which had split along racial lines before the Civil War, reaffirmed their separateness, as did schools and colleges. All types of public accommodations, from parks and theaters to restaurants and libraries, adopted segregation policies, and the same applied to toilets and water fountains. There were white and black newspapers. There were jobs and unions and even entire industries that catered to one race or the other, but not both. Cemeteries were either black or white. Interracial dating and marriage, of course, were strictly forbidden. In public discourse and in public print, blacks were commonly denied the courtesy of personal or professional titles (Dr., Mr., Mrs., Miss). In polite company, they were called colored people or Negroes (black was then considered a derogatory term and so was African-American. The most common and hated word was nigger; only slightly less cutting was negro, not capitalized and pronounced neg-ra), for it was a visible and explicit denial of any stature as a person.

It is difficult to convey the totality of exclusion and oppression of the black minority by the white majority after *Plessy v. Ferguson*. Neil McMillan summarizes the situation: "Once effectively stripped of their Fifteenth Amendment rights, blacks were driven from public office, refused equality under the law; excluded from place of accommodation and amusement and denied the public services for which they were taxed."

Five Southern states enacted a poll tax, registration, secret ballot, and other restrictions from 1889 to 1893. Mississippi amended its constitution in 1890 to disfranchise blacks and other Southern states soon followed. In 1910, Oklahoma became the last state to legally subject blacks. All Southern states approved oppressive measures to disfranchise blacks. The Solid South, a white oligarchy practicing the tyranny of the racial majority, became omnipresent.

Two Significant Political Events

Two events with national overtones impacted the South in the 1890s. The Populist Movement swept much of the South in the early 1890s. Georgia, Alabama, North Carolina, Arkansas, Tennessee and Texas were hotbeds of farmers demanding their rights over against Northern industry. The Populist revolt began as an exercise in racial equality, but as the years wore on, the movement broke up like a wave on the shoals of entrenched power. The Populists became subject to race baiting. Tom Watson of Georgia, a truly charismatic leader of much promise, abandoned his Populist roots to lead the Georgia Democratic Party and become an ardent racist. With the fall of

Populism, the political realignment of the 1890s found the Republicans in control nationally and the Democratic oligarchy running the South.

The second signal event was the Spanish–American War of 1898. The South demonstrated its patriotism by championing American interests in Cuba. Southerners extolled martial vigor, as they had in the Civil War, and saw their commitment to battle as a confirmation of their American, no longer Southern, duty. The Southern military heritage extended from the Civil War to the Spanish-American War and the region would continue to provide soldiers out of proportion to its population into twentieth century conflicts.

Spokesmen for the Negro

On February 20, 1895, Frederick Douglass died at home in Cedar Hill, near Washington, D.C. The runaway slave from Maryland had become one of the outstanding leaders in America, white or black. He had witnessed a civil war, Reconstruction, and the ascendancy of the white tyranny of the majority again. He observed shortly before his death: "The Supreme Court has surrendered. It has destroyed the Civil Rights Bill, and converted the Republican party into a party of money rather than a party of morals."

Two distinctly different black leaders emerged after Douglass's death. One, Booker T. Washington, gave a speech at the Atlanta Exposition in 1895. The speech, the Atlanta Compromise, advocated blacks in the South staying put, accepting segregation and the stripping of their rights. The phrase Washington used-"Cast down your bucket where you are"-meant blacks should rely on whites for their political future. Perhaps it was good that Frederick Douglass did not live to hear the speech. W.E.B. Du Bois was the second leader to stride forward after Douglass death. Although Booker T. Washington had founded Tuskegee Institute in 1881, Du Bois brought an intellect educated at Fisk, Harvard, and the University of Berlin. His writings were a force of nature. In 1903 with *The Souls of Black Folk* he gave classic expression to what it meant to be African and American. Du Bois named it "two-ness," the double nature of being a black person in the United States. In *The Souls of Black Folk*:

> It is a peculiar sensation, the double consciousness, this sense of always looking at one's self through the eyes of others, of measuring one's soul by the tape of a world that looks on in amused contempt and pity. One ever feels his two-ness—an American, a Negro; two souls, two thoughts, two unreconciled strivings; two warring ideals in one dark body, whose dogged strength alone keeps it from being torn asunder.

In addition to his writing, Du Bois helped found the NAACP in 1909 and worked for twenty-four years editing *Crisis* and being an outspoken champion of black rights.

Of course, the white majority did not want to hear Du Bois. Rather, the voice of accommodation of Booker T. Washington and the pro-business voice of white Atlantan Henry Grady, editor of the *Atlanta Constitution*, were the sirens in the air. Grady called for a "New South" built out of partnership with business forces in the North. Atlanta, the city torched by General Sherman, was emerging like a Phoenix from the ashes to concretize Grady's vision of a New South.

What Du Bois knew and articulated, was the white majority had once again sold out the black minority. New South or Old South, it was still a white man's South. And the South set the tone on how to handle blacks for the rest of the country.

Herbert Hoover continued the Republican domination of the White House, which had been interrupted by Woodrow Wilson. Hoover carried the country despite the South providing a solid Democratic vote. It would take the Depression and the election of Franklin Roosevelt to bring the Democrats back to the White House.

The United States in 1930 saw a concentration of wealth in the hands of a few, similar to the concentration of capital in the 21st century. Just as did the nobility of Spain in the 15th century, the wealthy elite had an ethnic problem. For Spain it was the Jews, for Americans it was black people. Each society created an apartheid society characterized by terror. The Jew was singled out, the victim of laws of segregation, exile and torture in Spain. The black was segregated, lynched, imprisoned and executed in the United States. Each minority was regarded as alien, foreign to the white, Christian rulers.

March of 1931 provided a vivid glimpse to the country of what undergirded the Southern Democratic oligarchy. Two white teenage girls reported to the police that while hitching a ride on a train in Alabama they were raped by young black men. In a matter of fifteen days, nine black males ages 13 to 20 were arrested, indicted, tried, convicted, and sentenced to death by electrocution in the Alabama electric chair. (Only the youngest escaped the death sentence due to his age.) The trial and conviction of the Scottsboro Boys resonated throughout the country as a clear example of the terror that lay beneath the tyranny of the white majority. Although all of the youngsters were innocent and the zealous defense of the NAACP, the Communist Party and other groups eventually freed them; the last case was not cleared until 1950.

The Scottsboro case tapped into the power of the myth of black men raping white women. This myth led to the defeat of all anti-lynching legislation by the Southern filibuster in Congress. Yet the reality of the repeated lynchings in the South told a different story. Fewer than one third of all lynchings claimed rape, and the number in which blacks were actually clearly identified was a mere fraction of the total. It led one to wonder, what is going on here?

Since the days of slavery, white masters had forcibly violated their black women slaves. The 1860 census identified 500,000 mulattoes and virtually all were a product of master/slave sexual activity. The factual evidence indicated what had really transpired, and it was white violating black, not vice versa.

The psychological illusion, however, was what the white elite fostered and disseminated. By portraying the sexual taboo of miscegenation as a reality because of black male aggression, any response could be punished in order to respond to the attack on white Southern womanhood. So the black/white rape story achieved mythic proportions in stark reversal of reality itself because it facilitated the ruthless oppression of a segregated people without recourse to law. An equation neatly describes the reality supporting the Segregation Regime: Black man allegedly rapes white woman=White terror on black community. The Scottsboro Boys were but one example of how factual innocence could quickly give way to the power of racial hatred in the rush for judgment.

From the New Deal to Truman

Franklin Delano Roosevelt became the second Democratic president of the century when he was inaugurated in March of 1933. His New Deal would restore American confidence and rescue the country from Depression. But it proved a slow-acting elixir for the South, a region that was still a rural frontier in 1933. It would take the massive industrialization of World War II to jump start the economy of the South into the twentieth century.

Roosevelt's New Deal, which offered so much possibility, also brought change. Change was not something the white leaders of the South had any interest in pursuing if it threatened their oligarchic rule. By virtue of seniority, they controlled the leadership in Congress, the House and the Senate, as well as the state legislatures. They took a guarded approach to their fellow Democrat who was now President. Although a Democrat, Roosevelt was also a Yankee from the state of New York.

For six years, from 1933 until 1939, Roosevelt worked his New Deal magic, even with the Southern leadership in Congress. The programs and agencies came into being to rescue the economy from Depression with the support of Southern whites, who occupied two thirds of the most important congressional committees in 1933. John Egerton describes how they came to occupy such a position of power:

They had succeeded in building an inner unity around an ideology of Southern nationalism—the Lost Cause lament, the code of honor, hatred of Yankees, and so forth. They maintained a monolithic society, the four corners of which were politics (Democratic), religion (Protestant), race (Caucasian), and livelihood (cotton), and through physical and intellectual isolation they shielded it from outside influence. They kept taxes low and public services at a minimum, and deflected criticism by pitting working-class whites and blacks against each other, thus leaving the middle and upper classes in positions of relative but perpetual advantage. And, finally, they controlled the political process so completely through malapportionment, poll taxes, and other limitations on voting that blacks, women, urban dwellers, and the generality of low-income people were either depreciated or left out of the process altogether. Incumbents thus could return themselves to office with the blessing of as little as ten percent of the age-eligible voting population.

Facing this entrenched block of power, Roosevelt moved the country economically but political movement was a more delicate operation. Harold Ickes, Secretary of the Interior, responded to pressure from progressive Southerners-white and black-and began appointing black people to key administrative posts. By desegregating the Department of Interior and the WPA, other cabinet officers followed his lead. For the first time in this century, a few blacks were appointed to positions of authority in the federal government. (One, William H. Hastie, became the first black federal judge in 1949, a Truman appointee.) However, it was Harry Hopkins, with the urging of Eleanor Roosevelt, who appointed Mary Cloud Bethune to the National Youth Administration in 1935. The sixty-year-old educator became the leading African-American in the Roosevelt administration. But aside from these key appointments involving no more than one hundred people, Roosevelt adopted a go-along-get-along approach with the Southern Democratic leadership of Congress in his first term. He steadfastly refused to exert any pressure for black civil or political rights.

In 1936 there was only one black representative in Congress—Arthur W. Mitchell, a Chicago Democrat. There would be no more until after World War II. The judiciary was still all white and the few appointments of blacks in the executive branch provided the only ripple of color in what was an all-white tyranny of the majority, albeit a progressive one nationally.

Economically, the South received about $2 billion through the New Deal. The programs increased the standard of living and created tens of thousands of new jobs. But for the Southern elite, this was a threat to their low-wage economy and they feared Roosevelt's "creeping socialism." Despite the people's love for the President, demonstrated through overwhelming support in his reelection, the rulers of the oligarchy felt threatened. John Egerton summarizes the political reality Roosevelt faced with the Southern oligarchy:

> In the final analysis, though, it was not court decisions or right-wing pressure groups or even rabble-rousing governors like Gene Talmadge (of Georgia) that dealt such crippling blows to Roosevelt and the New Deal; rather, it was the veteran Southerners in Congress, men as outwardly proper and respectable as Senator Russell and as unapologetically bigoted as his colleagues Cotton Ed Smith and Theodore Bilbo. Together—and with the acquiescence of their Northern lodge brothers in the House and Senate—they kept democracy at bay in the South for another generation. The people of this region have never spoken more clearly than they did at the polls in 1936—they gave FDR over seventy-five percent of their votes—but their voices have never been so effectively nullified as they were in the years that followed.

Unfortunately for the farmers, the early New Deal farm policy worsened their situation. Responding to the incentive to cut production, many large farmers simply let their tenants go so they wouldn't have to share the federal benefits with the tenants. Sharecroppers and tenants were thrown off the land. The transition from mules to tractors accelerated the eviction of tenants. During the decade of the 1930s, despite a depression throughout the country, more than 689,000 whites and 458,000 blacks left the South than migrated into the region.

The spirit of reform blossomed through the country in the 1930s. The labor movement became a force to be reckoned with by business. In the South, the poorest region, strikes in Gastonia, North Carolina, Elizabethtown, Tennessee, and other textile mills in 1929 reflected the growing strife between the ruling oligarchy in alliance with Northern industry and the Southern people. Despite the Labor Relations Act of 1935 and the Fair Labor Standards Act of 1938, the Southern labor pool remained poorly organized throughout the South. By 1940, the South had 74 percent of all cotton textile spindles in the United States and a union-free labor force.

But the New Deal had worsened the lot of the poor farmer. The work relief programs made survival possible for many farm families. The Fair Labor Standards Act raised wages through the minimum-wage provisions. Southern workers were so poorly paid that the Act resulted in hundreds of thousands of workers achieving improved earnings.

Native Southerners, black and white, pushed the region to reform in the 1930s. The Southern Tenant Farmers Union in Arkansas reached a membership of twenty-five thousand black and white farmers. The Highlander Folk School was founded in Tennessee to work with people in organizing around labor and civil rights issues. The Fellowship of Southern

Churchmen worked for equal opportunities of blacks. The names behind these organizations—H.L. Mitchell, Myles Horton, Claude Williams, Don West, Buck Kester, and other like minded spirits such as Lillian Smith, Benjamin Mays and James Dombrowski—advocated radical change in segregated South. Although it would be another generation before their dream began to be fulfilled, they worked against the Regime of Segregation at great cost.

President Roosevelt, at the urging of his wife Eleanor and Southern activists, wrote a preface to the National Emergency Council's Report on the Economic Condition of the South, which was published in 1938. The President declared: "The South presents right now the nation's No. 1 economic problem-the Nation's problem, not merely the South's. For we have an economic imbalance in the Nation as a whole, due to the very condition of the South." Relying heavily on the work of University of North Carolina sociologist, Howard Odum, President Roosevelt was willing to be so publicly open about the South because the Southern political leadership had made the New Deal increasingly difficult to achieve. The Southern oligarchy thwarted the changes Roosevelt indicated needed to occur. Roosevelt even dipped into state elections trying to affect the outcome to get a more supportive Congress from the South.

Despite all the dreams, the hard work, the calls for change, 1940 found the New South very much like the Old South in many ways. Black people were completely disfranchised and there appeared little hope for change. The New Deal ran aground on the reef of Southern Democratic reaction in 1938 and the feudal South seemed destined to remain so for a long time in the future.

Section II. The Black Response to the Segregation Regime

If the country and the South was determined the twentieth century would be an all-white experience, African-Americans were not so inclined. W.E.B. Du Bois, Walter White, and James Weldon Johnson had founded and run the N.A.A.C.P. since 1909. Du Bois edited *Crisis*, the magazine for N.A.A.C.P., and published numerous books advocating the rights of black people. James Weldon Johnson led the organization until he left for Fisk University in 1930 and Walter White succeeded him as executive director. Du Bois arrived at a point where he wanted black people to unite in a voluntary segregation from white society, building a strong economic base for equality. White attacked segregation directly, seeking to break down discrimination. The rift between the two grew so great that Du Bois left New York in 1934 to return to Atlanta University.

There had been no voice in America like W.E.B. Du Bois since the death of Frederick Douglass. Through his writings-*The Souls of Black Folk, Black Reconstruction in America, Black Folk, Then and Now, Dark of Dawn,* not to mention countless articles and editing *Crisis* and then *Phylon*—Du Bois' intellect unceasingly demanded the rights of black people. Unlike Douglass, Du Bois was not a great orator. His considerable influence was felt through his writings.

The man who came to the fore for the N.A.A.C.P. legally was the dean of the Howard University School of Law, Charles Hamilton Houston. In 1934 he established an aggressive legal program for the organization. He persuaded a recently graduated student, Thurgood Marshall, and the solicitor of the New Deal, William H. Hastie, to join him in the struggle for integration. The strategy Houston developed was simple and brilliant. If the country, particularly the South, insisted on separate but equal facilities for blacks, they would have to pay for them. The attack began on graduate schools and professional schools with the eventual goal "the abolition of all forms of segregation in public education." In 1934, Thurgood Marshall, with Charles Hamilton Houston as co-counsel, represented Donald Murray. Murray, a black applicant to the University of Maryland law school, had been denied admission because of his skin color. Marshall and Hamilton prevailed in court and Donald Murray entered law school in 1936 at the University of Maryland.

Donald Murray was the opening salvo of a systematic effort to dismantle segregation by making it prohibitively expensive. For the next eighteen years Thurgood Marshall (Houston returned to academe in 1938) and his colleagues pursued the course for integration from court to court. The Segregation Regime was successfully attacked through the legal system.

World politics soon dominated the attention of the country as Germany began swallowing Europe and Japan attacked Asia. With the bombing of Pearl Harbor on December 7, 1941, the United States entered World War II.

The Segregation Regime was intact and tyranny of the white majority nearly total on the eve of World War II. The reaction of Americans, not just Southerners, to the Japanese attack was clearly informed by racial bias. The Japanese became Japs, slant eyes, and were demonized through the press. Despite the horror stories of Nazi aggression in Europe, no German-Americans were interned in camps as were the 110,000 Japanese-American citizens in 1942. The internment of the Japanese-Americans was advocated by journalists including Walter Lippmann, the Attorney General of California Earl Warren; it was ordered by President Roosevelt and upheld by the Supreme Court. Despite this action, Japanese-Americans comprised one of the most decorated units in the European theater of the war. Officially, the United States government stated, "the Japanese race is the enemy race."

Southern whites and American blacks led the way in enlisting to fight in World War II. Despite the discrimination blacks faced daily during the Segregation Regime, they came forward to fight and work. A. Philip Randolph provided a glimpse of the future by organizing an effort to desegregate the armed forces and defense industry.

Initially Randolph, head of the Brotherhood of Sleeping Car Porters, Walter White, leader of the N.A.A.C.P., and T. Arnold Hill of the National Urban League, met with President Roosevelt in 1940 to discuss the two issues. The President reassured them but committed himself to nothing. After waiting five months for an indication from President Roosevelt that he might do something, Randolph took matters in hand.

In March 1941, Randolph publicly promised to put a hundred thousand blacks on the streets of Washington, D.C. to march for desegregation in the defense industry and the armed forces. Endorsed by black newspapers throughout the country, the pressure on Roosevelt mounted. The march was scheduled for July 1, 1941.

On June 18, Philip Randolph and Franklin Roosevelt met at the White House. Roosevelt indicated that with war imminent he would not desegregate the armed forces. The President offered to jawbone the defense industry into admitting blacks. Roosevelt looked at Randolph and asked, "What do you think?" Randolph replied, "[We] ask you say to the white workers and to management that we are American citizens and should be treated as equals. We ask no special privileges; all we ask for is that we be given equal opportunity with all other Americans for employment in those industries that are doing work for the government. We ask that you make it a requirement of any holder of a government contract that he hire workers without regard to race, creed or color." Roosevelt agreed and on June 25, 1941, he issued Executive Order 8802 prohibiting discrimination in government contracts. Randolph called off the March on Washington set for July 1.

Although the country was at war in six months, the Executive Order was implemented and it was an indication change was coming. The Segregation Regime was going to have to come to terms with its black constituency, either in the courts through the N.A.A.C.P. challenge or in the streets from civil rights advocates. War might delay consideration of the plight of black people but it would not make the issue disappear.

John Egerton described the Southern political scene on the eve of World War II in these terms:

> In war as in peace, the South was ravaged by the political equivalent of a plague of locusts. Informally bonded by philosophy and temperament—and by the acquired habits of power and privilege—

this undemocratic oligarchy of reactionary lawmakers held sway from the city halls and county seats to the state capitols and the halls of Congress. The pattern, established after Reconstruction, had continued virtually unaltered for more than sixty years: A relative handful of economically powerful white people controlled the region by excluding from the political process all except others similar to themselves.

An inventive variety of devices served to limit the franchise ... Every southern state had instituted a poll tax in the 1890s or early 1900s as a transparent means of taking the vote away from blacks and poor whites. The tax of one or two dollars a year was billed as a revenue raiser, but its only effective purpose was to restrict suffrage ... Some of the southern states abolished the poll tax in the 1940s or 50s, but others held on to it until it was banned by the 24th Amendment in 1964.

Next to the poll tax, exclusive party membership proved to be the favorite restrictive tool of the political process. There were so few Republicans and splinter-party members ... that the Democrats could control elections simply by excluding certain groups (blacks in particular) from the party ...

Election returns provided a dramatic picture of the consequences of all of these antidemocratic manipulations. In the 1940 general election, populous states such as New York, Illinois, and California counted about half as many votes as they had people ... In stark contrast were the Southern states, where an average of only fourteen percent of the population voted ...

(Before the Civil War, no blacks in the region were allowed to vote, but they became a majority of the electorate in five states during Reconstruction, when more than 670,000 blacks from Virginia to Texas were enfranchised; by 1920 their voting strength in the Deep South was almost back to zero.)

It was World War II that mobilized the resources of the country to truly escape the Depression. This was especially true in the South where $50 billion went for defense-related industry during the war. Although the armed forces were segregated, black units fought with distinction. Roosevelt's reelection to a fourth term in 1944 set the stage for a decisive consideration of an issue simmering below the surface of a united country in war. How would black troops, returned from a war against tyranny and for democracy, react to being treated as second-class citizens in their own country? Would there be a bloody summer of 1946 as there was in 1919 after World War I when black troops returned home to face repression?

The answers to the questions were contained in a book: *An American Dilemma* by Gunnar Myrdal. Myrdal, a Swedish social economist, had recruited a research team of over one hundred scholars to examine the role of race in America. The research they assembled through 1938–1943 was overwhelming in its completeness. Myrdal fixed the United States with an unblinking gaze, as the headlights of a car freeze a deer at night on the road, and his vision beheld a frightening sight. As Lafayette had done 110 years earlier, Myrdal took the concepts Americans deeply believed in—justice, equality, liberty—and discovered they only applied to white people. Blacks lived in an inferior, separate society and many had no vote, no protection of law, inadequate housing and jobs, and were surviving in quiet desperation.

Given the oppression of black people by the white majority, with all their grievances put on hold for the duration of the war, it was not a surprise there was a racial conflagration in 1943. Indeed, there were two hundred forty racial disturbances that year, with the largest in a major metropolitan city. The city was not Atlanta, Birmingham or another Southern city. Rather, the fire next time came to Detroit.

Gunnar Myrdal rendered his verdict through the written word, the black citizens of Detroit and other locales spoke through their actions. But the verdict was the same. The home of the free and the land of the brave was severely compromised by white racism.

The $50 billion infused into the Southern economy by defense-related industry in World War II ended the feudal era in the South. Since the end of Reconstruction, this feudalism had been enforced with lynching and a criminal justice system that featured the convict lease system and peonage. (See Douglas Blackmon's *Slavery by Another Name* for a detailed accounting of this period.)

The government created the Tennessee Valley Authority (TVA) through the New Deal in 1933. It generated cheap and abundant electrical power and controlled flooding in the upper South. The hydroelectric plants and dams brought safety from rampaging flood waters and provided electricity to much of the rural South. With the end of rationing and the conclusion of World War II, "citizens" became "consumers" in the South and across the nation.

If the Southern frontier was finally opened by the economic boom of World War II, how did the black minority fare? Did they benefit from the new interstate highway system that was begun in 1950, from air conditioning, and more appliances and automobiles than previously imagined? Was the white majority finally allowing black participation in the democratic process?

On February 25 and 26, 1946, there was a dispute in a department store in Columbia, Tennessee. Two blacks were arrested, including a recently discharged black soldier who felt his mother was harassed by a store clerk. The black community rallied in support of the two and whites organized and threatened a lynching. In the ensuring conflict, two blacks were killed, many businesses destroyed, and the state militia mobilized. In Monroe, Georgia, two black couples were murdered. Once again, returning black servicemen were involved. There were twenty-six lynchings in 1946 according to newspaper clippings, although Tuskegee Institute chronicled only six. The Segregation Regime was not yielding to change or aspirations of returning black veterans. Terror was once again a way of life for black people.

The Truman Administration

It was the irony of history that this cauldron of racial strife after World War II would be addressed by a President regarded by many as a Southerner. Harry Truman hailed from the border state of Missouri but he could tell a racist joke with the members of Congress that could draw a chortle from the Democrats from Dixie. So, it was much to the Southerners' surprise and horror that the little man from Missouri, a former lodge brother from the Senate, established a President's Commission on Civil Rights in December of 1946.

When the Committee on Civil Rights issued its report, *To Secure These Rights*, in October 1947, there were no surprises in the recommendations. The surprise came when President Truman initiated legislation based on the recommendation of the Commission on Civil Rights. The legislation called for an anti-lynching law, abolition of the poll tax, reviving the Fair Employment Practice Committee established by Roosevelt, outlawing segregation in interstate transportation, and other civil rights. Then in July 1948, President Truman desegregated the armed forces and all federal agencies.

For the Southern oligarchy, Harry Truman was their worst nightmare come true. Unlike Roosevelt, a Yankee they could never trust, Truman was one of their own. He had served in the Senate with them, supped with them and was a man they supposed they could count on. Now he was a traitor on race, advocating equal rights for black people.

The presidential election of 1948 would provide the Southerners with their opportunity for revenge. Abandoning the Democratic Party with its civil rights platform, Southern leaders created the States Rights Democratic Party and chose Senator Strom Thurmond of South Carolina to run for President. Although they knew they could not win, their fondest hope was to divert the electoral vote so Truman would not win and perhaps throw the election to the House of Representatives where the Dixiecrats power was supreme.

Despite being consigned to defeat by most political prognosticators, Harry Truman won the election. The Dixiecrats carried only four Deep South states and less than one fifth of the vote. Truman took all the remaining Southern states.

The Southerners returned to the congressional leadership after the election but they were not a chastened lot. The civil rights program of President Truman was defeated in Congress. Then the Korean War broke out and Truman, like Roosevelt, became preoccupied with the war and abandoned the civil rights fight with Congress.

Although the century of the whites was showing signs of unraveling by 1950, the South was still a segregated society. The Segregation Regime maintained its grip politically by disfranchisement and socially through terror. Between 1862 and 1950, Tuskegee Institute documented over 4700 lynchings. Eighty-five percent occurred in the South or a border state. The top fourteen states in lynchings, all with over 100, were Southern or border states. The pace of 150 lynchings a year from 1880 to 1890 dropped to 13 a year in the 1930s and 8 a year in the decade of the 1950s. But these statistics were more than supplanted by the incarceration and execution rates rising in the South. Judicial killing took the place of lynching but the racism behind each practice was documented clearly.

Section III. Penitentiaries

The leitmotif of white democratic America was the control of its minority population. We have seen how the Native Americans were pursued to near extermination. The slave population presented a different problem. Until the Civil War, the slave codes determined how slaves were treated. Punishment was meted out on the plantation by the slave master. Penitentiaries existed in the North and South, citadels with a grim visage and routine borne of a reform movement in the North to limit corporal and capital punishment. As Beaumont and Tocqueville reported on their investigations into penitentiaries in the New World, "the order of one day is that of the whole year." Edward Ayers describes a day inside a penitentiary in the nineteenth century:

> At dawn a trumpet awakened each numbered convict, when the trumpet sounded again all doors opened at once, the prisoner stepped out and instantly shut his door behind him. Taking one step toward the central yard, each prisoner waited with his night and water buckets in his hands until ordered by the turnkey to empty them. Prisoners marched to their workbenches, where they labored silently, until signaled to march to breakfast, where they ate silently. The rest of the day's labor was broken only by two other brief meals, also in silence. The convicts worked from dawn to dark six days a week. Sunday they might gather for a sermon and might get a chance to walk in the prison yard and chew the tobacco they had earned by their good behavior.

The prisoners in the penitentiaries were either poor or immigrant whites or freedmen. After 1818, only Louisiana allowed slaves to go to prison as an alternative to hanging. With that exception, slaves were universally punished on the plantation.

Despite the zeal of the reformers who created penitentiaries as a place an offender might go and be penitent through solitude, the ugly truth was there for all to see by the time of Beaumont and Tocqueville's visit in 1831–32. An official commented to Tocqueville in response to a question about prisoners reforming their behavior: "I am talking to you as a man who wants to know the truth. What the books say about the extent of reform is a fiction. I am certain no one here does." Prisons were punishment and despite the rhetoric of reformation, most people understood it.

Ayers points out that in the antebellum South, the prisons were no worse than the North:

> In virtually every facet of their antebellum history the penitentiaries of the North and South were far more similar than different. In 1850, for example, 5.8 percent of the nation's inmates died, with the highest death rates recorded in Ohio and Sing Sing; the average Southern figure was 5.5 percent.

Of course, the prisons were merely the tip of the proverbial iceberg when considering social control. All slaves were punished by their masters, so considering the slave population in each Southern state, it is clear the informal punishment of lash and rope provided the major means of social control in the South.

Although the South built penitentiaries, all Southern states except the Carolinas and Florida had prisons, their popularity was primarily among governors and legislators. The only two referendums taken on whether or not to build a penitentiary resulted in losses for those advocating such buildings. Alabama in 1834 and North Carolina in 1846 defeated efforts to build penitentiaries. A strong sense of Republicanism determined to limit the power of the state and maintain the freedom of the individual animated much of the opposition to prisons.

The Civil War ended the slave codes, although they were briefly reinstated as Black Codes in 1865, and a large free population of ex-slaves wandered about the South. The Freedmen's Bureau established courts to deal with legal problems of the freed slaves but as Ayers puts it, "The Freedmen's Bureau . . . was a well intentioned experiment that exerted only a temporary and limited influence on the fundamental patterns of postwar Southern crime and punishment." The power that dictated crime and punishment was white power after Reconstruction, or as the Greensboro, Georgia Herald put it: "The Organic Law of the Land." White men could still decide punishment for blacks, be it through the Ku Klux Klan or the judiciary.

To varying degrees blacks organized to protest. In the counties they banded together to oppose night riders, in the cities they rioted (Charleston and Norfolk in 1865, Memphis and New Orleans in 1866), but white tyranny exerted itself completely at the end of Reconstruction. As a result, by the mid 1870s, prison populations in the South increased dramatically. The white South responded to the challenge of free blacks with unofficial terror through lynching and judicial fear by increasing punishments for crimes most committed by blacks (vagrancy, a common charge against ex-slaves looking for work). The creation of all-white police forces in the cities (only Savannah had a police force before the Civil War) was another means of controlling blacks.

By 1850, every Southern state except the Carolinas and Florida had a penitentiary. Although small and solely for whites—Louisiana had 240 cells, Texas 225 cells, Alabama 208 cells, and Mississippi 150 cells—imprisonment was available on a limited scale. During and after Reconstruction, penitentiaries were built in the remaining Southern states. But the real form of punishment that emerged was the convict lease system.

The Convict Lease System

The convict lease system was initiated on a countywide basis where prisoners in the county jail would be hired out to work to private contractors. The various states began to see this as a means of supporting the penal system. Once begun it soon became a money maker rather than a mere sustainer of prisons. Alabama and Tennessee grossed $100,000 a year through mining while other Southern states garnered $25,000 to $50,000 from contractors interested in railroad work and turpentine collection. The modest effort of the South Carolina Reconstruction government was taken over and dramatically expanded by its successor government—the Redeemers—in 1877. Prison populations exploded as black labor provided the convict lease system with a means of making money and maintaining social subjugation of black people.

Sharecropping, what the ex-slave resorted to in order to survive, meant the freedman renting land from the white landowner and paying a portion of the crop for rent and "furnishings" needed to plant and harvest. Since the white landowners calculated the value of the crop, a state of peonage was created where freedmen were always beholding to the landowner after expenses were deducted. If their debt became too great or they abandoned the sharecropping process, the new vagrancy laws funneled them into county chain gangs or the convict lease system.

5. *Eugene Merrell (black hat), strike leader, with miners at Thistle Switch. Meeting before stopping Governor Buchanan's train. Photo: Courtesy of Boomer Winfrey.*

As in slavery, whippings were common for men and women under the convict lease system. Men and women were often confined in the same stockade and women worked in the fields with the men. Christopher Adamson comments: "As a result, black convicts through the South were starved, chained to each other at night in overcrowded, dirty stockades, overworked and forced to continue working while sick, and whipped, occasionally to death."

The Redeemers transformed the limited lease system of Reconstruction into a major supplier of labor for their business allies in the North. Prisoners were provided for railroads, mines, turpentine woods, factories, and every unskilled labor imaginable. No thought was given to providing prisoners for skilled jobs such as cabinetmaking.

A classic example of the white legislators' expanding the legal code in numbers of laws and length of punishment is found with the pig law. The Democrats in Mississippi made theft of property valued at more than a hundred dollars-including cattle and swine-grand larceny with a punishment of up to five years of hard labor. Georgia made stealing hogs a felony and North Carolina did not distinguish between petty and grand larceny. Hence a North Carolinian might receive ten years for stealing two chickens. The results in the imprisonment rate were impressive.

6. *Militia removing possessions and families of the miners from company housing prior to taking it apart to use in building a stockade for the convicts. Photo: Courtesy of Boomer Winfrey.*

In less than four years, Mississippi went from 272 convicts (1874) to 1,071 convicts (December 1877). In two years, Georgia went from 434 to 1, 441 convicts. Soon the leasing companies were getting a regular and stable pool of labor from convicts.

In the 1870s, 2,650 miles of railroad track were laid east of the Mississippi with over 14,000 miles added in the next decade. In 1884, more than 5,000 Southern convicts were leased to the railroads. In North Carolina, in a twenty-year period (1873–1893), prisoners built more than 1,800 miles of track.

"Penitentiary rings" of corruption were endemic in every Southern state where companies grew wealthy from convict labor. In Tennessee, Colonel Arthur Colyar, general counsel of the Tennessee Coal Iron and Railroad Company, leased the entire convict population for a year for $101,000.

The Southern states had a prison population over 95 percent black in most states. Georgia, in 1878, had 1,239 convicts of whom 1,122 were black. The few whites in the state system were kept in the penitentiary while blacks were leased out. No whites worked in the notorious mines of Tennessee on the convict lease system. Florida prisons rarely sent a white man to a prison camp. Mississippi sheriffs made sure whites did not work in chain gangs. As one camp overseer wrote: "It was possible to send a negro to prison on almost any pretext, but difficult to get a white man there unless he committed some very heinous crime."

Whereas the North built penitentiaries for rehabilitation (Pennsylvania built Cherry Hill in 1835 for $775,000, the most expensive building of any kind in the country), the South had a system built for race control and labor production. Adamson describes the camps:

> [They] consisted of make-shift huts [where] convicts slept chained together on wooden benches. Rolling cages were used on the railroads. Dogs and armed patrols, rather than granite and stone walls maintained security.

The conditions where the convicts worked were brutal, and disease and accidents rampant. No wonder, then, as Adamson reports, the death rate among convict laborers was quite high, fifty-three percent in the Greenwood and Augusta Railroad, for example . . ."Runaways were shot on sight, or brought back and punished by being strung up by the thumbs or shut in airtight boxes—a punishment known as sweating—which caused the body to swell and bleed."

As a result of the convict labor system, the South was developed for a market economy. The natural resources were exploited through almost free labor and the Southern economy grew at a rate commensurate with the rest of the country. It was a brutal and inhumane but it generated profits for companies.

"The convict lease system," he concludes, "was an economic substitute for slavery, but also a political replacement, insofar as it helped redefine the boundaries of the South on the basis of color . . . The convict lease system was the ultimate but very effective mechanism for keeping blacks politically and economically subservient."

In order to justify the increasing number of prisoners in the convict lease system, Southern governors assured their constituency that it was not the result of increased criminal activity. Rather, as a governor of North Carolina put it, it was "increased efficiency in the criminal justice system." The "increased efficiency" resulted in an all-black convict lease system with a lowering incarceration rate for whites. The decreased white incarceration in penitentiaries was paralleled by an increased black population at the end of the century. W.E.B. Du Bois analyzed this phenomenon in 1904: "There can be no doubt that crime among Negroes has sensibly increased in the last thirty years, and that there has appeared in the slums of great cities a distinct criminal class among the blacks." The reason was not black depravity but the response of whites after Reconstruction. Freedmen's crimes "were those of laziness, carelessness, and impulse, rather than of malignity or ungoverned viciousness. Such misdemeanors needed discriminating treatment, firm but reformatory, with no hint of injustice, and full proof of guilt." But the Redeemer governments "erred on the white side by undue leniency and the practical immunity of red-handed criminals, and erred on the black side by undue severity, injustice, and lack of discrimination . . . Negroes came to look upon courts as instruments of injustice and oppression, and upon those convicted in them as martyrs and victims." As a result of such invidious treatment, when more crimes were committed by blacks later on, Du Bois felt, "The greatest deterrent to crime, the public opinion of one's own social caste, was lost, and the criminal was looked upon as crucified rather than hanged."

The legacy of slavery carried over into the convict lease system with virtually every convict leasee being black. And they were so young. From two thirds to three quarters of the convict leasees were in their twenties or younger. About 7 percent of the population was women and almost all black. The color of the antebellum prison population and the post-Reconstruction prison population was completely reversed and it now included women. The convict lease system was a thriving profit venture and by 1890 there were twenty-seven thousand convicts leased to businesses in the South. But the brutality and horrors of the system had made it to public consciousness. The Northern press was particularly critical. However, it took rebellion to bring the convict lease system to an end in Tennessee, the first Southern state to abolish the practice.

A Note on Tennessee: The Coal Creek Rebellion

Tennessee, like all Southern states, passed draconian laws directed at free blacks after Reconstruction. These laws permitted the region's renewed power structure to prosecute blacks for more crimes and make those convicted serve their sentences by labor for private companies.

Colonel Arthur S. Colyar, general counsel to the Tennessee Coal, Iron and Railroad Company (TCIR) and prominent Democrat in state politics, described the effect of the convict lease system on free labor: For some years after we began the convict labor system, we found that we were right in calculating that free laborers would be loath to enter upon strikes when they saw that the company was amply provided with convict labor.

During the Civil War the coal seams in the mountains were noticed for the first time as a possible source of mining. And much of these lay along or near two railroad lines, the L and N and Southern. The Southern ran through Scott and Morgan counties, where after the war, the towns of Coal Creek and Oliver Springs became the first towns to be established around the new mining effort.

In the 1870s Coal Creek was served by a branch extending to the smaller communities of Briceville and Fraterville. It was there that mines developed. Free white miners worked most of the mines but black convicts worked some. The Knox Iron Company subleased the black convicts from TCIR. The state received $63 a year per convict and there were approximately 1,600 convicts in the state. The Black Diamond company led off the boom in coal sales, finding a strong customer in the Champion Paper Company mills over the mountains in Enka, North Carolina.

The key company in the mining effort, however, was TCIR. Its lobbyists were instrumental in passing the neo-slavery laws after Reconstruction in Tennessee and Alabama, thus providing free labor through the peonage of the convict lease system. The TCIR would develop into the second largest producer of steel in the United States, primarily through its industry near Birmingham, Alabama which devoured black convict labor. (See Douglas Blackmon's *Slavery by Another Name*.) What happened in the mountains of Tennessee can be termed their pilot program.

The mines in the mountains surrounding Coal Creek were mined by local men whose descendants still live in the area. They were not unionized in the late 1880s, but events transpired that brought the union to the mines as well as a challenge to the convict lease system. Although the mines were segregated, the circumstances the free white miners and the convict miners shared were similar. The white miners worked for the company, lived in company housing, used company 'scrip' for money and were treated by the company doctor. The black convicts were slaves of the company courtesy of a contract with the state, housed in a stockade outside the mine and totally dependent on the company for everything from food to medical care.

Where the fortunes of these two populations of miners—one free and white, one convict and black—eventually converged was on the occasion of two strikes by the miners in Briceville in the spring and summer of 1891. At issue was the dishonesty of the company's 'weighman' whose tallies of the miners' daily production were cheating the miners out of money rightfully earned. The miners struck and the company settled the strike, allowing the miners to elect their own 'weighman'. He lasted a week before he was fired by the company because the honest reckoning of what the miners were owed was too much for the company to accept. The miners went out of strike again.

On July 5, 1891, a train arrived in Coal Creek. The train unloaded and it was 40 black convicts brought into all white Morgan County with state militia. Under supervision of the militia, the convicts tore down the company housing the miners dwelled in and used the wood to construct a stockade for the convicts. The convicts then began working the mine and a short time later were reinforced with additional convict labor. This was an arrangement between TCIR and the state.

On July 15, recoiling from the loss of jobs and incomes, miners and local merchants, three hundred or so, converged at Briceville and surrounded the stockade. They forced the surrender of the guards and released the convicts on a train bound for Knoxville. The organized citizens forwarded a telegram to Governor Buchanan informing him they had taken "a necessary step in the defense of our families from starvation, and our property from ruin."

In response, Governor Buchanan made a visit to Coal Creek and his train was stopped at Thistle Switch with about 600 people blocking the track. The Governor had arrived with three companies of militia. (The Tennessee militia was comprised of three units—eastern, which were former Unionists and Union sympathizers—and middle and western, which were former Confederates or Confederate sympathizers.) The east Tennessee militia accompanied the Governor.

The Governor gave a speech about his hands being tied and he had to honor the contract between TCIR and the state of Tennessee. A number of miners spoke in response, outlining their plight and the conditions they labored under. The standoff ended that night and the Governor left the next day feeling "exceedingly rocky", after shots were fired outside the house in which he spent the night, in order to attend to "pressing business" in Nashville.

The east Tennessee militia would not use force against the miners since they held similar viewpoints. The Commissioner of Labor, George Ford, arrived and sought a compromise with the miners. After meeting with the leaders, the Commissioner offered the following settlement: If the miners would agree to not oppose the use of convict labor in a few mines, they could return to work in the mines TCIR had employed convict leasees.

It was worth pondering the possibility of returning to work. A general meeting was called. All the miners had to do was allow the black convicts to continue to work in neo-slavery conditions and they could work in their mines. However, by this time the free white miners were fully aware of the appalling conditions the convicts worked under. Those conditions were worse than the ones they labored under. They would not compromise. The convicts had to be set free.

The stand-off continued. For some time the miners had the upper hand in these communities. At one mine they surrounded the convicts stockade, forced the surrender of the guards and set the black convicts free. The miners even took over the company store and issued clothing to the convicts who left their striped uniforms along the track from Briceville all the way to Coal Creek four miles away.

It was at Coal Creek where the drama played out. The miners were counting on a special session of the legislature to address their grievances. The Governor convened the legislature but they concluded after a month with only one piece of legislation and that supported TCIR. The state militia arrived, this time composed of sizable units from the western part of the state who were former Confederates or Confederate supporters. The officer in charge, General Samuel Carnes, was a former Confederate soldier. He positioned artillery around Coal Creek and issued an ultimatum. Either the miners go back to work and release their captive, the commander of the previous militia unit, or the artillery would destroy Coal Creek in its entirety. The miners realized the rebellion was at an end and literally took to the hills. A reign of terror ensued with every male aged 15 to 75 arrested by the militia. The jail filled, a church was confiscated for a jail, box cars were full of men and trials ensued. Only two men of Coal Creek were convicted out of hundreds arrested.

Although General Carnes brought the Coal Creek rebellion to an end, its ramifications were felt throughout the state. The TCIR had lost thousands of dollars during the two year war with the miners. Their appetite for the convict lease system in Tennessee was gone, so their efforts redoubled outside the state in Birmingham, Alabama. The TCIR convict lease system expired in 1896 and the state did not renew the contract. A new prison, Brushy Mountain was built in nearby Petros, Tennessee and prisoners mined coal for the state there. Also, the Tennessee State Prison in Nashville opened in 1894.

Surveying the suppression of the Coal Creek rebellion, author and current resident Boomer Winfrey concludes: "And, so the Coal Creek Rebellion had ended in defeat for the miners, but although the men of the mountains lost the battle, they did not completely lose the war." Indeed, Tennessee became the first state in the South to abolish the convict lease system in 1896 and did so as a direct result of the Coal Creek war. (Boomer Winfrey recounts this struggle in *Coal Creek Lake City: Visions of the Past.*)

By the end of the century, Alabama, Georgia, the Carolinas, and Virginia had opted for the state farm system. But the convict lease system was only completely abolished in Tennessee and Louisiana at the end of the nineteenth century. By 1920, Alabama remained as the only Southern state still engaged in convict leasing.

Tragically, the appalling conditions in the mines that free miners and convict miners endured remained unchanged. This led to two of the worst mining disasters in United States history: The Fraterville mine explosion in 1902 at Coal Creek and the Cross Mountain mine explosion in 1911. Fraterville took at least 184 lives with some counts going as high as 220.

Cross Mountain killed 84 of the 89 miners who entered the mine. So it was that the highest casualty rate came not from the Coal Creek rebellion but the mines themselves who consumed many of those active at Coal Creek.

Section IV. The State Farm System

But the state-owned farms proved not to be much of an improvement. Convicts were now on chain gangs on state farms of thousands of acres. The picture of black convicts in prison stripes guarded by white armed guards spoke volumes as to how race continued to matter in crime control in the South.

In 1870, 41 percent of Alabama's convicts died. In Mississippi in the 1880s the death rate was nine times what it was in a Northern prison. As one convict leasee put it, "This place is nine kinds of hell. Am suffering death every day here."

What effect did this barbaric process have on the Redeemer governments throughout the South? C. Vann Woodward summarized it: "The convict lease system did greater violence to the moral authority of the Redeemers than did anything else. For it was upon the tradition of paternalism that the Redeemer regimes claimed authority to settle the race problem and 'deal with the Negro.'"

Edward Ayers describes Southern punishment at the beginning of the twentieth century:

> The fundamental patterns of institutionalized Southern justice and injustice established during the 1860s changed little for generations. Southern blacks in 1900 no less than in 1870 found themselves singled out for arrest, indictment, conviction, hanging, and long sentences to the chain gang or convict lease system. The punishment for whites remained as lenient as ever. One reason justice changed so little was that the machinery of the police and courts rested in the hands of a few white men, their offices secure in the absence of a vital two-party system.

The Southern Democratic oligarchy maintained the Segregation Regime through the criminal justice system of peonage that was slavery by another name, as well as sharecropping and lynching. The Segregation Regime maintained a legal, overt oppression through the legal system and the criminal justice system. Additionally, terror was maintained through lynching and vigilantism so that an informal form of social control over blacks was exercised.

By the beginning of the twentieth century, the Segregation Regime had utilized a system of punishment and terror to control the black population in the South. Although the convict lease system was on its way out, the

Regime had learned how to use a criminal justice system to achieve its goal of dominating the black minority. With no blacks on juries, no black judges, no black police, no black grand jurors, no black legislators and only rarely a black lawyer, whites effectively determined who was punished and how. The twentieth century saw the decline of lynchings but the increased utilization of incarceration and execution as a means of achieving the same end: intimidation and repression of the disfranchised black population.

Since the arrival of the first slave ship in 1619, white Southerners have led the way in deciding the fate of Africans and their descendants in America. The white oligarchy of the antebellum South was broken by the Civil War and Reconstruction. But during Redemption the Bourbon aristocracy reasserted itself. By utilizing the convict lease system it was able to restore the social order of post-bellum times so it resembled antebellum life: whites on top and blacks on the bottom. When the convict lease system proved too attractive for the state to ignore financially, the state-run prison farm/plantation came into being. Just as its predecessor's slavery and the convict lease system enabled the white control of the black, the prison farm accomplished the same end. An examination of one prison plantation provides understanding as to how the system of white control on the criminal justice system mechanism ensured the disfranchisement of blacks.

Brief History of Criminal Justice in Louisiana

The state of Louisiana was admitted to the Union in 1812. Edward Livingston, influenced by Enlightenment thought and Thomas Jefferson, wrote a Civil Code, a Code of Procedure, a Criminal Code and a System of Penal Law to bring coherence to the hodgepodge of laws in Louisiana. Livingston saw his purpose "to ameliorate punishment and not to avenge society; to reform the criminal and to prevent crime." His work prohibited capital punishment, felons were taught a trade, and first offenders were separated from repeat offenders. He also called for a separate prison for juvenile offenders under eighteen. The Louisiana Legislature, comprised of planters and slave owners, thought Livingston had gone too far. They adopted only the Civil Code and Code of Procedure.

The institution of slavery necessitated opposition to any prison reform effort. The philosophical notion of reforming a criminal, popular in the North in the 1830s, was incomprehensible to Southerners who maintained a slave society. The Abolition movement went hand in hand with prison reform. Neither would be tolerated in the South.

In 1831 Alexis de Tocqueville described the New Orleans jail: "We saw there [sic] men thrown in pell-mell with swine, in the midst of excrement and filth. In locking up criminals, no thought is given to making them better but simply to taming their wickedness; they are chained like wild beasts."

Louisiana opened its first penitentiary in Baton Rouge in 1835. Prisoners were put to work manufacturing cotton, leather, and woolen products. There were 300 convicts, of whom two thirds were white and one third immigrants.

By 1844 the legislature determined the manufacturing work was too costly and opted to lease the convicts out, following Kentucky's example some twenty years previous. The demands on the business leasing the convicts were minimal. The leasees simply assumed the burden of providing for the prisoners so there was no financial burden on the state. By 1850, the state decided to take one quarter of the profits upon negotiation of a new lease. In 1857, the state bargained for 50 percent of the profits from the lease. The Civil War interrupted leasing but, by 1868, convict leasing was resumed. The penitentiary officials submitted a detailed report before leasing the convicts and it would be the last report offered for thirty years.

On January 1, 1867, there were 228 convicts. During the year an additional 229 came to the penitentiary. Of them, 167 convicts were released, 11 pardoned, 41 escaped, and 16 died. As of June 14, 1868, the prison population consisted of 203 black males, 85 white males, and 9 black females. Prison officials, noting the increase in admissions, asked the legislature to "inquire into the reason why so many are sent to this institution for the term of three, four and six months upon the most trivial charge? Does there not lurk beneath, the law, mean motives of depriving them of the right(s) of citizenship?" Indeed, of the 229 prisoners admitted in 1867, 198 were convicted of property crimes of which 131 were for larceny. As of January 1, 1868, there were 116 convicts under the age of twenty-five; 73 between twenty and twenty-five, 40 between fifteen and twenty, and three between ten and fifteen.

In 1870, Major Samuel Lawrence James leased the convicts for twenty-one years. Historian Mark Carleton describes James as "the man who initiated and personally maintained for twenty-five years the most cynical, profit-oriented, and brutal prison regime in Louisiana history." A joint legislative committee visited the penitentiary in 1873 and reported: "Whipping was still used, also the dark cell."

There were two forms of convict leasing in the South. Under one method, a contract strictly applied left state officials responsible for feeding, clothing, and guarding the convicts who remained in the penitentiary. Through this system the labor, not the convicts themselves, was contracted for. South Carolina, Texas, and Virginia chose this method of convict leasing in the 1880s. The second form of leasing required the leasees to maintain the convicts but empowered them to work the prisoners outside the prison. All other Southern states plus the New Mexico territory and Nebraska utilized this system beginning in the 1870s.

Peonage: Blacks Under James

Under the Redeemer regime in the South, the convict lease system expanded. Disfranchisement reached a peak in Louisiana in the 1890s, the decade Populism bloomed in several Southern states. But in Louisiana the Bourbon Democrats squashed Populism and the oppression of blacks continued apace. Indeed, *Plessy v. Ferguson*, which was decided by the Supreme Court in 1896 was passed by the Louisiana legislature in 1890. Louisiana pioneered separate but unequal.

In 1881 Major James was opening new work camps and many were located near towns. Convicts were observed by citizens transported to their jobs and while at work. The press and citizens began to protest the abuses witnessed and a legislative investigation took place in 1886. The Clinton, Louisiana newspaper described the James convict lease system:

> Men on the [James] works are brutally treated and everybody knows it. They are worked, mostly in the swamps and plantations, from daylight to dark. Corporeal [sic] punishment is inflicted on the slightest provocation . . . Anyone who has travelled along the lines of railroads that run through Louisiana's swamps . . . in which the levees are built, has seen these poor devils almost to their waists, delving in the black and noxious mud . . . Theirs is a grievous lot a thousand times more grievous than the law ever contemplated they should endure in expiation of their sins.

The legislative committee investigating the work camps reported the case of Theophile Chevalier. Carleton states: " . . . a black convict who was observed to have no feet. Chevalier had been forced to work outdoors, without shoes, during the winter of 1884–85. Afflicted with frostbite, which soon led to gangrene, Chevalier endured the amputation of one of his feet by means of a penknife. (The other foot had meanwhile rotted off.) The committee was told Chevalier was serving a five-year sentence for the theft of five dollars."

In 1896, James submitted a report indicating there had been 216 convict deaths that year. The first such report in thirty years, the imagination is left to speculate how many deaths occurred in earlier years under the James lease. Finally, in 1894, the legislature abolished the convict lease system effective at the end of the current lease in 1901.

A rough estimate is that between 1870 and 1891 three thousand convicts died under the lease system in Louisiana. Virtually all were black. As Carleton notes, "This identity between blacks and criminals in the minds of many Louisianans not only helped to perpetuate the lease system but survived long afterward as an impediment to penal reform."

After Reconstruction the link between criminal and black became cemented in the Southern mind. It was maintained by the judiciary, which was all white, sending blacks to the penitentiary for various minor and imagined indiscretions while ignoring white crime. This dynamic allowed men like Major James to prosper. He obtained the lease again in 1890 with the help of legislators.

In 1892 Murphy J. Foster was elected Governor of Louisiana. His campaign pledge was to end the convict lease system and he persuaded the legislature not to renew the current lease when it expired in 1901.

On July 29, 1894, Major James suffered a stroke while on the verandah of his Angola home. He died within twenty minutes. A self-made millionaire originally from Clarksville, Tennessee, the Major had enriched himself through the brutal slavery of the convict lease system. His estate disbursed the $2.3 million in an economically depressed area.

When Samuel Lawrence James assumed control of the prisoners in 1869, blacks were a majority of the prison population. By 1900, blacks constituted 84 percent of the prison population. Black and criminal were synonymous in Louisiana.

Angola: The Plantation Prison

The state of Louisiana bought eight thousand acres of Major James' land and combined it with additional purchases of ten thousand acres in 1922. The Louisiana State Penitentiary at Angola became a prison farm of over 18,000 acres. It was built on the plantation model with various work camps constructed for prisoners. Camp D, for instance, housed 30 women in 1901.

In order to make the prison/plantation a viable economic enterprise, intensive labor was required. Cotton was the principal crop until 1912 when boll weevils attacked it. Sugar cane then became the dominant crop. The levee work James initiated continued under the auspices of the state. In 1912, six hundred twenty-five prisoners out of a population on one thousand nine hundred ninety-five worked the levees.

The attitude of those running Angola was revealed by a statement of the President of the Prison Board in 1914: "[Louisiana] where the vices and defects of the [N]egro race [were] well known." It would be foolish to apply "what are called the advanced system of treatment in use in some other states, where only white men are dealt with."

As under the James regime, blacks were good for one thing—labor. The race dynamic was clear in 1914 as it had been since Reconstruction. It was reflected in the classification of prisoners:

> First class men are . . . sound in every respect and accustomed to manual work. These men are sent to the levee camps where the work is most severe. Second-class men are . . . of moderate strength and capabilities, and are assigned to the sugar plantations . . . Third-class men are assigned to the cotton plantation (Angola), and fourth-class men are assigned the hospital.

Just as antebellum slave masters divided their work force according to physical strength, so did Angola and other prison plantations. Most of the prisoners sent to the levees and sugar cane fields were black. The whites, male and female, stayed on the plantation/farm doing clerical or hospital work.

On January 1, 1908, the ratio was 99 blacks to 1 white in the levee camps, 55:1 on the sugar plantations, and at Angola: 4:1. This meant, as Mark Carleton observed, "the largest slave-holder of post-bellum Louisiana was not Samuel L. James in the late nineteenth century, but Henry L. Fuqua in the early twentieth."

The end of the convict lease system and the establishing of the prison farm/plantation was the first prison reform of the twentieth century in Louisiana. It would not be until 1952 that the second prison reform era would commence.

Louisiana progressed in a lot of areas in the first forty years of the twentieth century. The penitentiary, however, was not one of the areas of improvement. Henry Fuqua, former manager at Angola, became Governor in 1924. "Marse Henry," as the black convicts called him, died in office after two years. Neither Fuqua, his predecessor, nor his successor, stressed the myriad problems at Angola. However, compared to the regression that took place from 1928 to 1935, benign neglect seemed a virtue.

Huey Long and Angola

Huey Long became Governor in 1928 and initiated a progressive period of free schools and textbooks, hospitals, paved roads, and billed himself a man of the people. But when it came to Angola, Long wanted it quiet and financially self-sufficient. The prison was to be run as a business, saving the taxpayer money and not embarrassing his administration. Profit was the motive and the prisoners worked long hours and suffered the lash. Prison records reveal the extent of the punishment of the prisoners. Between 1928 and 1940, the Huey Long-appointed guard captains recorded 10,000 floggings, some with as many as fifty lashes. These figures did not include beatings suffered by convicts in the cane fields, cotton fields, or elsewhere. Rather, these were the official whippings. As a result, the death rate climbed to an average of 41 a year, the most since the convict lease days.

The political appointments Governor Long made resulted in a good measure of official theft by diverting money designated for the prisoners. This left the prisoners to eat "grits, greens, sweet potatoes and black strap [molasses]." Carleton comments: "The result by the end of the era of Huey Long in 1940 was a penal system in a condition of physical wreckage and moral collapse similar to that handed Governor Heard by the James regime in 1901."

Although prison superintendent Henry Fuqua maintained a massive slave labor operation from 1901 through 1918, he was like many antebellum slave masters in that he wanted his slaves to survive in order to work. Keeping the slaves in good enough health resulted in better production so it was in the self-interest of the slave master to maintain the slaves at a level they were productive. "Marse Henry" utilized this philosophy and as a result treated prisoners better and the annual death rate lowered. This type of treatment was discarded by the Long appointees who drove the prisoners hard for a better profit margin. The whippings and killings escalated to the point prisoners merely sought a means of survival.

Angola: Brutality Made Public

In 1939, the "Louisiana scandals" erupted. Several of the late Huey Long's protégés were convicted of embezzlement, using the mails to defraud, and income tax evasion. Governor Leche went to federal prison and Louisiana State University President James M. Smith was sentenced and went to Angola to don the black-and-white-striped prison garb. Then World War II distracted everyone from Angola.

In 1951 Angola and public scandal were joined again. Thirty-seven convicts cut their heel tendons to protest "the system" of brutality, political appointees, over work, the utter lack of rehabilitation and decent food, and miserable housing. The prisoners' actions came to light in the local press as the story was smuggled out of Angola. Collier's magazine investigated and did a major story entitled "America's Worst Prison."

Governor Earl Long, no friend of prison reform, was embarrassed by the press coverage of Angola. He appointed a Citizens Committee to investigate the prisoners' charges. When the Committee interviewed one of the heel slashers, he was quoted: "We just couldn't stand it any longer. We'd rather be here [in the hospital] than take the beatings we have to take over there [in the prison camps].

Fortunately for the 37 who cut their Achilles tendon, they were treated by Nurse Mary Margaret Daugherty. Nurse Daugherty, a native of Ireland who had worked at Angola for six years, had tried to recruit a doctor for

Angola but funding was not available. An observer of surgeries done in Baton Rouge, she sewed the Achilles tendons back together.

> So I sewed them up and then I gave them a tetanus shot, and they all got well. The Achilles tendon, when you cut it, falls apart, so you have to reach down with the hemostat to hold one part so you can suture the rest of it. They may walk with a limp, but they are fortunate to walk at all.

What the Citizens Committee found at Angola in 1951 was twenty-seven hundred convicts crowded in unsanitary, wood-floored dormitories, in close rows of double bunks. (Conditions were very similar to Majdanek and Auschwitz concentration camps in Poland that the author has visited.) Clean clothes were issued once a week, hot water was available only when the sugar mill was working and, the meals were corn bread and vegetables. As one prisoner commented in response to a question about variety on the menu: "Some days we get white beans, some days it's red beans."

Wilbur "Blackie" Comeaux gave vivid testimony to life at Angola: Angola "ain't fit for hogs . . . in the long line we had to run out to the fields and run back, and a lot of us couldn't keep up with the [guards'] horses. Older men got whipped because they fell back. I saw men eat out of bloody plates; the blood came from their own heads." One prisoner who left his place in the long line to "attend to a necessary function" was shot in the arm.

As detailed and specific as the prisoner testimony was, Warden Rudolf Easterly and prison officials minimized the accusations stressing it was just convict talk. But when the prison administration learned Nurse Daugherty, who treated the "heel stringers," would be called to testify, they took action. Nurse Daugherty described Warden Easterly coming to her house one evening for a visit:

> He knew I was going to be called before the committee and all I would have to do would be to say that everything was OK and nothing was wrong. And he said, "You'll have a job, you'll have a job for the rest of your life and you can name your price." I told him, "Well, I'm looking at so many hundreds of inmates just looking at me to tell the truth, and I'm looking at a handful of politicians to tell me everything is OK. And I'm a registered nurse; I'm proud of my nursing, and I plan to keep it up. And I'm not going to lie for anyone."

When Nurse Daugherty testified before the Citizens Committee, she painted a portrait of brutality, political interference, and absence of rehabilitation. Angola was "a political football and dumping grounds for the state of Louisiana." She detailed rampant drug use and for her actions was threatened with prosecution by the local sheriff. Then Nurse Daugherty resigned on April 3, 1951, to keep from being fired.

The Citizens Committee report was released April 20, 1951. It found "conclusively that the 'heel slashing' was the result of physical brutality on convicts, the practice of brutality was established beyond any question on the 'physical, mental, emotional and moral [level].' Human lives and law enforcement cannot be measured in dollars and cents."

The conclusion that economics and prison labor were not to be equated struck at the *raison d'être* of Angola. It also totally contradicted what the Long regimes had fostered. Mark Carleton summarizes: "And if patronage had always effected Angola for the worse under any administration, Longite administrations with their patronage excesses, prior to 1952, produced Louisiana's most inept and brutal penal regimes since the turn of the century."

Reform at Angola

In 1952, Judge Robert F. Kennon defeated the Long candidate for governor. Angola was at the top of Kennon's reform list. Governor Kennon instructed the hospital board for the state, under whose authority Angola was placed, that "the employment of a competent penologist . . . is your No. 1 job." Governor Kennon informed the board he had suspended patronage at Angola and the board was to run the prison "free of strings."

Governor Kennon tapped legislative support for a $4 million bond issue for construction and improvements at Angola. Additionally, the 1952-53 operating budget was increased by seven hundred thousand dollars with a separate sum of two hundred fifty thousand dollars designated for additional civilian guards. Finally, some fifty years after its initial recommendation, a separate facility for first offenders was built.

Reed Cozort, director of the United States Correctional Institute at Seagoville, Texas, was brought in as the professional penologist Governor Kennon mandated. Subsequently, he hired Sam Anderson as warden and the process of turning an agricultural anachronism based on slavery into a modern, professional prison was underway. It would be a long and difficult struggle against the forces of reaction and tradition in Louisiana.

When Cozort left Angola in 1955, he reported the prisoner morale was improved and construction of new housing units underway. "Other types of penalties" rather than flogging were utilized as punishment and "university trained [staff] in special fields had been recruited." Cozort hoped politics would "stay away from the penitentiary" and give the beginning "of a real treatment and rehabilitation program" a chance to succeed.

So it was that the second era of reform in Louisiana prisons was underway as the Segregation Regime came to a close in May of 1954. This era of prison reform would share the struggles of the Second Reconstruction. Each period represented the radical proposition that black people were entitled to humane treatment and equal legal rights. Although each period would ultimately be overwhelmed by the white reaction of the tyranny of the majority, an alternative angle of vision was achieved that embraced the common humanity of us all.

Mark Carleton encapsulated prisons and politics in the South:

> Both the facilities and the philosophy of prison in the South, especially the Deep South, were tailor made for black convicts as viewed by their white former masters in the post-Civil War period. Today, despite gradual alterations and nominal progress, these institutions remain much as they were at the turn of the century, and are thus penologically, racially and economically two generations out of date.

Whether it be Angola in Louisiana, Parchman in Mississippi, Ft. Pillow prison farm in Tennessee, the eighty-three prison camps in North Carolina that made it "the good roads state," or the chain gangs throughout the South, the equation was the same. Black equals criminal equals labor. It would take the Second Reconstruction to shake the segregation foundations of a society to see if a new equation of mutual humanity could be forged.

In *Slavery by Another Name: The Re-Enslavement of Black Americans from the Civil War to World War II*, Douglas Blackmon describes the period post Reconstruction through World War II in the South as it manifested itself in the criminal justice system. We have reviewed one state in depth and dipped into several others but Blackmon provides an enveloping look at the entire machinery of punishment and how it pervaded the South:

> . . . In Alabama alone, hundreds of thousands of pages of public documents attest to the arrests, subsequent sale, and delivery of thousands of African Americans into mines, lumber camps, quarries, farms and factories. More than thirty thousand pages related to debt slavery cases sit in the files of the Department of Justice at the National Archives. Altogether, millions mostly obscure entries in the public record offer a view of a forced labor system of monotonous enormity.
>
> Instead of thousands of true thieves and thugs drawn into the system over decades, the records demonstrate the capture and imprisonment of thousands of random indigent citizens, almost always under the thinnest chimera of probable cause or judicial process. The total number of workers caught in this net had to have totaled more than a hundred thousand and perhaps more than twice that figure. Instead of evidence showing black crime waves the original records of county jails indicated thousands of arrests for [minor] charges or for violations of law specifically written to intimidate blacks— . . . vagrancy, riding freight cars without a ticket, engaging in sexual activity—or loud talk—with white women . . .

[H]undreds of forced labor camps . . . [were] scattered throughout the South, operated by state and county governments, large corporations, small-time entrepreneurs and provincial farmers. Repeatedly, the timing and scale of surges in arrests appeared more attuned to rises and dips in the need for cheap labor than any demonstrable acts of crime . . . Violence or the Ku Klux Klan terrorized black citizens periodically . . . the return of forced labor as a fixture in black life ground pervasively into the daily lives of far more African Americans. And the record is replete with episodes in which public leaders faced a true choice between a path toward complete racial repression or some degree of modest civil equality, and emphatically chose the former.

"By 1900, the South's judicial systems," Douglas Blackmon's book tells us, had been reconfigured to make one of its "primary purposes the coercion of African-Americans to comply with the social customs and labor demands of whites . . . Revenues from the neo-slavery poured the equivalent of tens of millions of dollars into the treasuries of Alabama, Mississippi, Louisiana, Georgia, Florida, Texas, North Carolina, and South Carolina—where more that 75 percent of the black population in the United States then lived."

And thus,

. . . a world in which the seizure and sale of a black man—even a black child—was viewed as neither criminal nor extraordinary had reemerged . . . . The practice would not fully recede from their lives until the dawn of World War II, when profound global forces began to touch the lives of black Americans for the first time since the era of the international abolition movement a century earlier, prior to the Civil War.

CHAPTER 10. THE BEAT GOES ON

From Angola, Louisiana to Huntsville, Texas

Awakening in the December predawn darkness, I gathered my things together for the trip to Texas. By catching the 5:00 a.m. flight out of the Nashville airport, I would be able to arrive in Austin, Texas in time to join Joel Berger of the NAACP Legal Defense Fund for the meeting with Governor Clement. The governor would decide whether or not to grant clemency to Charlie Brooks, the first Texas prisoner to exhaust his appeals in a death penalty case since the U.S. Supreme Court decisions reinstituting the death penalty in 1976.

The trip to Austin was uneventful, and upon arrival I rented a car and drove to the state capitol to meet Joel. Joel was one the indefatigable lawyers who had fought long and hard for his client, as well as other prisoners on death row. We greeted each other warmly and proceeded to wait. As time dragged on, I had the sinking feeling that sometimes seized me in these situations. The delay in seeing the governor meant this was not going to be a fruitful discussion. I had a long drive to Huntsville, the site of the execution, where I would rendezvous with colleagues coming over from Louisiana who would lead the protest outside the prison. Finally, exasperated by the delay, I told Joel I was going on to the prison.

Driving too fast, to make up for lost time, I was speeding through the Brazos River valley. It was dusk and I glanced in my rearview mirror to see a Texas state trooper with his lights on and siren wailing. I pulled over and the trooper came up to my car. He asked to see my driver's license and I showed it to him. I told the trooper I knew I was going too fast but that I was a minister and on my way to the execution in Huntsville. He looked at me and asked if I had a "preacher card." I realized I did not. So I reached into the back seat for the book I was reading and handed it to him. It was Dietrich Bonhoeffer's *Letters and Papers from Prison.*

He eyed the book, thumbed through it, sized me up in my rumpled suit and said: "Well, I'll let you go with a warning this time. I don't know of too many folks who aren't a preacher who would read something like this." I thanked him, took the book back, and we parted. I smiled to myself, thinking that Bonhoeffer would have enjoyed such a candid description of his work and feeling appreciative of the fact that his book sped me on my way to protest an execution.

Arriving in Huntsville in the early dark of a December evening, I drove out to the prison. Although the media were there in strength, none of my colleagues from Louisiana had arrived. I drove back into the town square and stopped at the Lonestar Café, which faced the courthouse on the town square. There were only two other folks in the café. I ordered a coffee and stood at the counter and drank it. My muscles were too tired to sit on the stool and I welcomed the hot, liquid caffeine on a cold December night. It had been a long, exhausting day.

As I stretched, I couldn't help but hear the good ol' boys talking, "They're gonna kill that nigger tonight." The other one nodded an assent. "Yup, I reckon they will. But you know what? He's gittin' off easy. They're givin' him the needle. They oughta fry the bastard."

I took a deep breath. I swallowed a large gulp of coffee. Then I turned and left the Lonestar Café. It was no time for dialogue. I drove back to the prison.

Unbeknownst to the good ol' boys in the eatery, it turned out Charlie Brooks' death wasn't a matter of "gittin' off easy." The warden mixed all three drugs together for the same syringe, rather than separately preparing and injecting them. This produced a viscous white goo. It did not kill Charlie Brooks immediately as advertised and the initial lethal injection in the United States was a gruesome and painful killing.

The Huntsville portion of the Texas gulag is called the Walls. The large, looming walls distinguished this prison from the prison camps spread throughout the state. Condemned prisoners were brought here from Ellis Unit I to be killed.

Greeting my friends, who had formed a protest line, we gazed at the illuminated concrete structure with the steps leading up to the main entrance. As we talked, awaiting the passage of time until midnight, the celebrators of the execution had begun gathering in force. As in prior generations when whites would gather around a lynching of a black man, these whites-inebriated and many students from nearby Sam Houston State

University—gathered to cheer the killing of another black man by the state of Texas.

Standing in the cold, the prison bathed in the white glare of television lights and security lights, I was struck by the contrast. The night was black as pitch. The prison gleamed with the whiteness of a San Francisco skyscraper. Suddenly, breaking the monotony of whiteness, three black people walked up the steps to the entrance of the prison. They were like black ink on a field of cotton. It was Charlie Brooks' family on their way for a final visit.

The Brooks family was a painful and symbolic reminder of what was going on here. Amid the sea of whiteness, characterized at its worst with yelling and chanting for a black man's killing, came these three for a final visit to a son and brother. Texas had seen a lot of this behavior through lynching and electrocution. Now the era of the poisoned needle was about to commence but the same machinery of death was still in place. White people were killing black people and only the method of extermination, along with a Potemkin display of due process, altered the proceedings. The style of things may have changed but the substance was grimly the same.

On a starry, windy, cold December night, the Lonestar State killed Charlie Brooks. The cheer from the drunken throng echoed off the white walls when the execution was announced by the Department of Corrections spokesperson. Although late resuming the execution business in 1982, in comparison with its sister Southern states, Texas history indicated a lust for this business which might well enable it to make up the tardy start. Charlie Brooks, like his family, was an ink blot on a field of Texas whiteness. He became the latest victim in a long line of people of color who the white majority in Texas eradicated using cowboy justice.

Charlie Brooks had come to this fateful end because he was convicted of killing someone he probably did not kill. His codefendant, the probable triggerman, cut a deal with prosecutors for forty years and testified against Charlie. Charlie received the death penalty. This was an all too frequent occurrence, under what is termed the felony murder rule, in the imposition of the death penalty. It guaranteed victims for the death chamber but made a mockery of justice. Indeed, in the *Brooks* case the prosecutor ultimately asked for clemency because he was not sure the right man received the sentence of death.

What really delivered Charlie Brooks to the Texas killing machinery was the color of his skin—black—and the color of the victim's skin—white. Charlie became the latest in a long line of blacks executed or lynched to keep the white tyranny of the majority in place. The scene of his family, black silhouettes illuminated by the glare of the light as they entered the Walls, was a vivid reminder of what Texas justice was about.

At first glance, it would seem the commission of a felony murder brought Charlie Brooks and his family to that cold December night in east Texas outside the Walls. Although Charlie Brooks was there when the crime was committed, it is doubtful that he killed anyone. As in many capital cases, the triggerman pled out for a lesser sentence and death is pinned on someone else. But there is so much more to the story than the mere commission of a crime. In the South, it is a matter of race. As W.E.B. Du Bois put it, at about the turn of the 20th century: "The problem of the twentieth century is the problem of the color line." The point is applicable to the 21st century as well.

My experience in the Lonestar Café the evening of the execution was an encounter with an honest expression of racial hatred: "The nigger is gittin' off easy. They oughta fry the bastard." The incident in the café and the mob outside the Walls provide a 'clue of a thread' to the lair of the Minotaur of race. These feelings have been manifest in a continuum since at least 1662, and albeit concealed in today's modern world, remain with us.

7. Bunk in holding cell near the execution machinery at R.M.S.I., Nashville, TN. Photo: Gigi Cohen.

In the 1890s, with the white majority firmly retrenched politically in the South, almost 1,700 lynchings were reported in the nation. Texas had over 500 lynchings recorded during that decade. It was a time of economic depression which brought hard times and the social dynamic was one of racial caste-the white elite bound the poor whites to them by appealing to skin color, thus obfuscating any social analysis as to who was making whom poor. To be white was a badge of honor and placed one above any black. As Lillian Smith described it in *Killers of the Dream*: "To be 'superior' because your sallow skin was white and you were 'Anglo Saxon' made you forget that you were eaten up with hookworms; made you forget that you lived in a shanty and ate pot-likker and corn bread, and worked long hours for nothing. Nobody could take away from you this whiteness that made you and your way of life 'superior.'"

The political movement of Populism, an attempt to unite the white poor and the black, began in the late 1880s and ran through 1896. In Texas, when Populism reached its peak in 1892, 162 blacks were lynched. The idea of joining poor white and black together for better job opportunities foundered on the shoals of race hatred.

Although lynchings had been common in Texas as it developed through various national identities—a frontier wilderness, the Texas Republic, a state in the Confederate States, a Reconstructed state and finally a state in the Union, five nations over a forty-year period—its white majority moved lynching to a public form of violence with 72 percent of the victims black. Indeed, between 1882 and 1942, a minimum of 468 lynchings took place; Texas was third in the nation in total lynchings, behind only Georgia and Mississippi (Ross, 2010). From 1889 to 1918, 319 lynchings occurred in east Texas, a cradle of the Confederacy, alone. (There is a thicket of unresearched information on Texas lynchings. I am grateful to Margaret Vandiver for helping me navigate my way through it.) The Equal Justice Initiative recently documented 3,959 lynchings in the South in the years 1877–1950.

The message of a lynching was directed not only at the black community but the white community as well. To appreciate that message, let us examine two of the more infamous lynchings: Ed Coy in 1892 and Henry Smith in 1893. The men were burned and the law assisted in their killings. A brief quote from each lynching reveals the visceral reality of the ritual and its formulaic nature.

Ed Coy, accused of the rape of a white woman, as were 30 percent of all black lynchings, had the pyre surrounding him lit by the woman who identified him as her rapist in Texarkana: "Burn him! Burn him!" was the cry and the terrified Negro was seized by the multitude. Someone placed a rope around his neck, and with this he was dragged more dead than alive to a level opening in the woods just outside the town limits. In the center of the opening was the stump of a large oak tree. To this Coy was secured with iron fastenings and a liberal quantity of kerosene poured over him. Some reports stated that "the flesh [was] cut from his body by men and boys.

On February 1, 1893, Henry Smith was lynched in Paris, Texas. In January, the body of the daughter of a white police officer, 3½ year old Myrtle Vance, was found in the woods. The white press reported she was sexually assaulted, but Ida Wells was told by witnesses, "There was no evidence of such an assault . . . only a slight abrasion and discoloration was noticeable and that mostly about the neck."

The entire town of Paris was consumed with the rape rumor. Bishop Haywood, a local clergyman luridly described the crime: "First outraged with demonical cruelty and then taken by her heels and torn asunder in the mad wantonness of gorilla ferocity."

Henry Smith was captured in Hope, Arkansas. The railroad had provided free transportation for his pursuers. Smith was brought back by way of Texarkana, where 5,000 people awaited, "anxious to see a man who received the fate of Ed Coy." However, Paris citizens prevailed upon the mob to allow them "to deliver him up to the outraged and indignant citizens of Paris."

When Smith arrived in Paris, 10,000 people gathered. The mayor had dismissed school for the day, whiskey shops were closed "so everything could be done in a businesslike manner."

Smith was taken to a ten foot high platform in a large clearing outside of Paris. The men of the Vance family 'tortured him for fifty minutes by red hot brands thrust against the quivering body.' Then he was drenched in kerosene and set ablaze. "Every groan from the fiend, every contortion of his body was cheered by the thickly packed crowd of 10,000 persons. The mass of beings was 600 yards in diameter, the scaffold being the center."

A local black minister described to Ida Wells the crowd's reaction:

> . . . when the father of the murdered child raised the hissing iron with which he was about to torture the helpless victim, the children became as frantic as the grown people and struggled forward to obtain places of advantage. It was terrible. One little tot scarcely older than little Myrtle Vance clapped her baby hands as her father held her up on his shoulders above the heads of the people. "For God's sake," I shouted, "send the children home." "No, no" shouted a hundred maddened voices, "let them learn a lesson." As the hot iron sank deep into poor Henry's flesh a hideous yell rent the air, and, with a shout as terrible as the cry of lost souls on judgment day, 20,000 maddened people took up the victim's cry of agony and a prolonged howl of maddened glee rent the air. No one was himself now. Every man, woman and child in that awful crowd was worked up to a greater frenzy than that which

actuated Smith's horrible crime. The people were capable of any new atrocity now, and as Smith's yells became more and more frequent, it was difficult to hold the crowd back, so anxious were the savages to participate in the sickening torture." (The minister who gave this account to Ida Wells was forced to leave town.)

Texas is a good example of a state where the matter of race needs to be examined, because there is an egregious pattern of discrimination manifested historically and currently in the treatment of blacks and Latinos. Although Texas may differ quantitatively in numbers of people executed and lynched, it is merely a difference in degree rather than kind. As the lynchings of Ed Coy and Henry Smith reveal, events touted and encouraged by the press, the white mob resembled a carnival of sadism. It was a common event throughout the South. (I am indebted to Danalynn Recer's unpublished study of the historical development of Texas with its utilization of lynching and capital punishment as a tool for oppressing the black minority for this discussion of Texas.)

As the events transpired outside of the Walls on the night of Charlie Brooks' execution in 1982, the drunken revelry and celebratory boisterousness of the white crowd fit the ritual of the mob at the scene of a lynching. The question remains: Is the formal judicial process leading to the antiseptic gurney and lethal injection significantly different from the informal process of lynching? As examination of who is chosen for execution in Texas, an example of the machinery of killing in the region, gives one pause for thought.

Although Texas came late to the state killing game—it was the next to last Southern state to resume executions since 1977—once it commenced, it did so with the passion and fury of the lynching era. As of July 10, 2013, Texas had executed 502 of 1,340 people killed by the state since the resumption of executions in 1977. Virginia was the second leading state with 110 executions. How did this phenomenon come to be in the late 20th and early 21st centuries? Each execution in Texas provides a glimpse through the keyhole of race relations in the South.

As of this writing, thirty-three percent of all murder victims are black men but only seven percent of death row prisoners are there for killing a black man in Texas. White women are 8 percent of the murder victims but thirty-six percent of persons on death row are there for killing white women. Eastern Texas, the region of the state which led in support for the Confederacy, also sends more people to death row than any other region of Texas while containing the highest black population in Texas. Black men constitute 44 percent of the murder victims but only 1.14 percent of the victims in which the death penalty is imposed. East Texas white women are 11 percent of the murder victims yet 47 percent of the victims for which people are sentenced to death.

This societal reality is rooted in a cultural viewpoint whereby the majority white population focuses its fear upon the black male and exalts the white female. Each role, however, is defined historically in relationship to their counterparts-white males. White males historically viewed blacks and white women as property and the laws were codified accordingly. Indeed, the cruelest state killing of all, burning, was reserved for two classes: Slaves and white women.

As Stuart Banner notes:

> Burning was reserved for two classes of offenders whose crimes were considered disruptive of the social order. The first of these classes was slaves convicted either of murdering their owners or of plotting revolt . . . the second and smaller class of offenders subject to being burned alive was women convicted of killing their husbands . . . What these claims have in common is the reversal of the traditional hierarchy of the household, the revolt by slave against master or wife against husband. The legal name for such crimes, petit treason, suggests the strength of the analogy contemporaries drew between the household and the state. Treason denoted "not only offences against the king and governments," explained William Blackstone, but crimes "proceeding from the same principle of treachery in private life."

The statistics of those who go to death row cited earlier, just as with lynchings, are part of a larger regional pattern. In *McCleskey v. Kemp*, a decision rendered by the U.S. Supreme Court in April of 1987, the majority (5-4) opinion, altered the constitutional standard of establishing racial discrimination. The majority did so to avoid the conclusions of the Baldus study which offered uncontroverted proof of a pattern of racial discrimination in the administration of the death penalty in Georgia.

Studying every murder case in Georgia and controlling for all factors, Professor David Baldus found a greater rate of discrimination in race, especially race of victim, than is demonstrated in linking lung cancer to smoking. Although the facts are not in dispute and now have been confirmed by the General Accounting Office of the United States Government in twelve other states, as well as other privately funded studies, a racist system in the administration of the death penalty remains intact, protected by the U.S. Supreme Court. This is simply because fear is too deeply rooted in the culture and the belief is prevalent that it is okay to discriminate, to even execute the innocent, as long as the myth of control of the black male through execution remains.

Although this discrimination in the death penalty is primarily a Southern phenomenon, it exists in other states. The Death Penalty Information Center has reviewed studies in 26 states that reveal race of defendant and/or race of victim racial discrimination. Yet the machinery of death keeps grinding along.

So one is left to wonder, what is at work here that keeps a demonstrably unfair and invidious practice ensconced in the heart of the judicial system? As W.E.B. Du Bois put it: "It is the problem of the color line."

Justice Lewis Powell, a courtly Virginian who cast the key vote in *McCleskey v. Kemp*, regretted that vote once he left the bench. Yet the institutional power of discrimination enshrined in our system is nurtured in the garden of race hatred that Lewis Powell, and I, grew up with in the South. We experienced an apartheid society, benefited from it, and family members instilled it, so it is hard to ignore its pervasive influence. However, that familiarity also brings recognition. It was late in coming to Justice Powell, but I have been cognizant of it since the first time I entered a prison in 1971 in the Bronx House of Detention in New York.

Race is the driving dynamic in our incarceration and execution machinery. We would have no death penalty, nor high incarceration rate, in America if it did not appease the white myth of maintaining safety from black people, especially black men. The numbers do not lie nor do the lives needlessly lost and damaged in this insane system. One need only recall the chants of "Fry the nigger" and "Kill the coon" that echo outside death houses around the South on execution night. Or remember the celebration in Huntsville, Texas, in 1982 when Charlie Brooks was poisoned to death.

W.E.B. Du Bois, would that you were with us in our hour of need.

Chapter 11. The Second Reconstruction

In the late spring of 1954, my mother moved us from Jonesville, North Carolina to Greenville. My father's sudden death of a heart attack in January left our family—Mom, my four-year-old sister Kay and me—bereft of emotional moorings. The move back to Greenville, home of my mothers' parents—Granddaddy and Ma-Ma, and my birthplace—was our attempt to reconnect and survive Daddy's death.

Greenville, a sleepy tobacco market town of 10,000 people, was inured to segregation as a way of life. There were "White" and "Colored" water fountains, rest rooms and a segregated movie house. East Carolina Teachers College, the local campus of the larger University of North Carolina system, was segregated as well. The white people of Greenville literally lived on one side of town and the blacks on the other side of the railroad tracks. The streets, sewer lines and other public amenities provided through taxation were woefully inadequate on the black side of town. And, of course, there were "separate but equal" public schools.

The Public Swimming Pool

This was the environment I experienced as a seven year old. Aside from my mother making it clear to me that white and black people were equal, no matter what I saw or heard my friends and relatives say, segregation seemed as normal as breathing air. Then, during the summer of 1954, an event occurred which grabbed even the attention of a seven-year-old. The city of Greenville closed the municipal swimming pool.

Summer in Greenville was hot and humid. Ninety degrees Fahrenheit and humidity were common. It was the clime which enabled the golden tobacco leaf to prosper so well in eastern North Carolina. In 1954, air conditioning was a reality for only a wealthy few and the fuzzy reception on the black and white television an item for fascination. Heat was a constant and oppressive reality.

For me, heat was handled by shade, lots of cold drinks and going swimming in the public pool. The pool was located on Fifth Street, only a few blocks' walk from my grandparents rented house on Jarvis Street. We could easily walk to the pool so it was readily available. Suddenly, it was closed and drained.

The reaction in Greenville to *Brown v. Board of Education* was traumatic throughout the South. The city fathers realized this could mean blacks would demand to swim in the public pool with whites. In order to prevent such an affront, they happily ordered the pool drained and turned into a parking lot. As Joni Mitchell would later write in a song: "They paved paradise and put up a parking lot."

Unbeknownst to me, I was living on a cusp of a remarkable historical period. The second great effort to enable black citizens to achieve equality under the law had been launched. My journey from childhood to manhood over the next twenty years would be in a milieu of change and struggle as the Second Reconstruction shook the foundations of the South and the country. The closing of the municipal swimming pool was my fateful introduction to the changing times.

School Desegregation

Brown v. Board of Education, Topeka, Kansas, was the United States Supreme Courts climactic response to the long campaign of Charles Houston, Thurgood Marshall and the NAACP for the equality of black people under the law. First graduate schools were integrated, then colleges and finally public schools. The twenty year legal campaign was unanimously (8-0) ordered by the Supreme Court on May 17, 1954. Taylor Branch describes the reaction:

> The earth shook, and then it did not. There were no street celebrations in Negro communities. At Spelman College in Atlanta, sophomore Barbara Johns continued her long-standing silence about her role in the case, sensing muted apprehension among her fellow students. They seemed to worry that the great vindication might mean the extinction of schools like Spelman.

In 1955, the Supreme Court articulated its doctrine of "all deliberate speed" for implementing *Brown*. By then, demagogic political leaders had emerged throughout the South to make sure the word emphasized in the phrase was deliberate and not speed.

When Americans elected Dwight Eisenhower President in 1952, they embraced a reassuring presence to lead them through the Cold War and the contumely peregrinations of Senator Joseph McCarthy. Eisenhower had no program or agenda for civil rights and was chagrined when his appointee as Chief Justice, Earl Warren, mustered the unanimous opinion in *Brown*, thus reversing the separate but equal doctrine articulated in *Plessy* in 1896.

Rosa Parks and the Montgomery Bus Boycott

In 1955, a tired employee of the Montgomery Fair Department store in Montgomery, Alabama, refused to give up her seat on the segregated city bus to a white man. As a result, Rosa Parks was arrested and jailed.

Rosa Parks's mother telephoned E.D. Nixon, a long-time champion of black equality in Montgomery. Nixon, unable to locate Fred Gray, a prominent black attorney, called Clifford Durr. Durr was a lawyer, and along with his wife Virginia, whites who were outspoken on the segregation issue. Nixon picked up the Durrs at their home and drove to the jail. They posted bond for Rosa Parks and took her home.

E.D. Nixon realized this could be the case to challenge segregation in Montgomery. Rosa Parks was well respected, with character beyond reproach. He asked her if she would be willing to pursue the case judicially. Despite her husband's fear—"The white folks will kill you, Rosa"— she determined to proceed. She had previously attended a workshop at Highlander Center in Tennessee and civil rights were on her mind. She responded to Nixon: "If you folks think it will mean something to Montgomery and do some good, I'll be happy to go along with it." Meanwhile, Fred Gray and E.D. Nixon spread the word through their networks of the arrest of Rosa Parks.

Jo Ann Robinson, of the Women's Political Council, who also belonged to Rev. Martin Luther King's Dexter Avenue Baptist Church, met with her friends at Alabama State at midnight to draft a letter of protest calling for a boycott of the segregated bus system in Montgomery. Robinson, a member of the English Department at Alabama State, knew the mimeographing of the call for a boycott on the Alabama State mimeograph machines could result in the white legislature shutting down the black university if her efforts were discovered.

Monday morning the buses rolled and they were empty of black people. Later Monday morning, at Rosa Parks' judicial hearing, over 500 people thronged the corridor. Although Rosa Parks was found guilty, Fred Gray gave notice of appeal. The turnout of support for Mrs. Parks was unprecedented in Montgomery for a civil rights matter. Monday afternoon a gathering of concerned people, including E.D. Nixon and many clergy, met and formed the Montgomery Improvement Association. The young minister at Dexter

Avenue Baptist Church had been in town less than a year. He was elected president of the new organization. His name was Martin Luther King, Jr.

Monday night at Holt Street Baptist Church, a large crowd assembled and overflowed outside the building. Several thousand, perhaps as many as five thousand people, surrounded the church. Loudspeakers broadcast the proceedings inside the church to those outside. Virginia and Clifford Durr could not get within three blocks of the church because of throng and the police.

The Rev. Martin Luther King, Jr. addressed the thousands gathered in and about the church that night. His speech electrified them, galvanized them to continue the bus boycott until Montgomery allowed open seating on its buses. A yearlong protest was underway in the initial capital of the Confederacy.

Through the cold of winter, the warmth of spring, the oppressive heat of a deep South summer and until the fall of 1956, the bus boycott remained intact. Dwight Eisenhower was reelected President of the United States. Then on November 13, 1956, the United States Supreme Court acted on the Rosa Parks case. Upholding a 2:1 appeals court decision which had struck the segregation law down, the Supreme Court issued the following order: "The motion to affirm is granted and the Judgment is affirmed." In one sentence Alabama's state and local laws regarding segregation on buses were nullified.

Brown v. *Board of Education, Topeka, Kansas* had provided the crack in the foundation of a segregated society. The Montgomery bus boycott supporting Rosa Parks shook the foundations of segregation. Although the Court reversed a policy of "separate but equal" extending back to the 1896 *Plessy v. Ferguson* decision, it was the victims of segregation in Montgomery, Alabama, who had organized to destroy apartheid on the bus lines of the city. In doing so, they launched a civil rights movement which would dismantle America's official policy of "separate but equal."

The first civil rights bill in 82 years emerged from the U.S. Senate on August, 2, 1957. It was a weak bill because the enforcement mechanism of utilizing the Justice Department to expedite school desegregation was deleted. The bill also permitted state officials to be tried in state court, which meant all white juries and judges would find white defendants innocent of civil rights violations. President Eisenhower, unable to deliver previously on voting rights, now found civil rights severely compromised.

Black Resistance: Little Rock, Greensboro and Nashville

On September 4, 1957, the governor of Arkansas, Orval Faubus, ordered the National Guard to stop nine black children from attending the segregated Central High School in Little Rock. In what became the first televised social confrontation centered on race, Faubus defied the federal government. For ten days, the mob of angry whites grew outside of Central High School as the nine black children were repeatedly turned away with threats and worse hurled at them. Tension mounted for another week as Faubus evaded court orders and broke agreements with the Eisenhower administration. Finally, after a near riot when the National Guard withdrew and the white mob almost captured the school building and the nine black children, Eisenhower acted. He ordered the 101st Airborne Division to move into Little Rock and secure Central High School. By nightfall of September 24, 1957, the 101st Airborne had restored order. The troops brought integration to Little Rock.

February 1, 1960, four black freshmen from North Carolina A and T college entered the Woolworth's store in downtown Greensboro, North Carolina. They sat on stools at the all white lunch counter. The afternoon passed without their being served and without incident. They promised to come back the next morning and returned to campus.

Upon returning to the college from the impromptu adventure, they were stunned to discover their colleagues excited about their action and volunteering to join the effort at desegregation. On February 2, 1960, nineteen students joined the four initiators at the Woolworth's lunch counter. By Wednesday, the number had risen to 85 students and the "sit-in" movement was launched, complete with rotating shifts of protesters.

A critical mass reacted in Greensboro, North Carolina to ignite the sit-in movement. Why Greensboro and why at that point in time is anybody's guess. Even though demonstrations had occurred in sixteen other cities during the last three years, none galvanized a people as this one did. A week after the initial Greensboro sit-in, other North Carolina cities—Raleigh, Durham and Winston-Salem—also experienced sit-ins.

In Nashville, Tennessee, 500 people turned out for the first mass meeting of the sit-in movement. Jim Lawson, a student of Gandhian philosophy who had been studying in India until he learned of the Montgomery bus boycott and hurried home, was enrolled at Vanderbilt Divinity School. Lawson trained SCLC members in nonviolence for Martin Luther King. He led the meeting that developed the plans for desegregating Nashville lunch counters.

Saturday morning, 500 black students marched into downtown Nashville from their base of operations at First Baptist Church Capitol Hill. The well-dressed, well-mannered students filled the downtown stores' lunch counters. The Nashville student movement, trained by Lawson in Christian/Gandhian non-violence, became the most cohesive group and a model of the sit-in movement.

The Nashville action demonstrated that the sit-in movement was igniting like a prairie fire cross the South. By the end of February, 31 cities in eight states witnessed the sit-in movement.

The Nashville sit-in movement reveals the dynamics of other sit-ins but it was the most disciplined in its commitment to nonviolence. Nashville, the Athens of the South, prided itself on its educational institutions: American Baptist College, Fisk, Meharry, Vanderbilt, Scarritt, Tennessee State University and Belmont were some of the colleges in the city. Secondly, there was strong leadership from black clergymen Kelly Miller Smith and Andrew White; as well as Will Campbell, a white, bootleg Baptist preacher. Civil rights lawyers Z. Alexander Looby and Avon Williams also provided support. But most of all it was Jim Lawson and the students, particularly Diane Nash and John Lewis, who sparked a formidable cadre of non-violent apostles determined to integrate Nashville. They began with lunch counters of the downtown stores but that would just be the opening salvo of the desegregation campaign.

The times met the man in Martin Luther King, Jr. Propelled into leadership by the Montgomery bus boycott, he began developing a network throughout the South which became the Southern Christian Leadership Conference. He moved from Montgomery to Atlanta, to co-pastor Ebenezer Baptist Church with his father, and finished organizing SCLC there.

The end of February of 1960 brought a fateful turn to the ongoing Nashville sit-ins. After two weeks of sit-ins, the police chief announced his tolerance was exhausted and arrests would commence. The students remained undeterred and filled the lunch counters once again. This time, the police allowed white bullies to attack the students with rocks, lighted cigarettes and fists. Seventy-seven black students and five whites persevered through the attacks and were arrested.

Monday, February 29, 1960, the students appeared for trial. Diane Nash told the judge she would do the time rather than pay the fine. She and 14 others, soon followed by 60 more inspired by her example, went back to jail.

The irony of the situation was apparent to all. The white hooligans who had beaten up the protesters were free and the non-violent apostles were in jail. Suddenly, support and commitment took on a deeper meaning in Nashville and throughout the South as word spread of the latest tactic of sacrifice.

On October 19, 1960, Martin Luther King was arrested trying to desegregate the Magnolia room of Rich's Department store in Atlanta. Unlike Nashville, which had yielded to the student sit-ins by desegregating the prior spring, Atlanta was still all white and only white when it came to dining facilities. King, aware of Diane Nash's example in Nashville, refused the $500 bond. He and 35 students went to jail and stayed in jail. It was Martin King's initial incarceration

A Telephone Call and a Presidential Election

The most prominent civil rights leader in America was imprisoned in an Atlanta jail as the country decided to choose a new president in November. The Democratic nominee John F. Kennedy and the Republican nominee Richard M. Nixon were faced with the quandary of how to respond to King's incarceration.

In the middle of the night, King was transferred to the Georgia State Prison in Reidsville. Over 200 miles south of Atlanta, located in rural southeastern Georgia, the prison was a daunting symbol of what awaited black people who transgressed the white man's law. King would remain there eight days until his release.

John Kennedy telephoned Coretta Scott King, Martin's wife, to offer his sympathies over her husband's imprisonment by Georgia authorities. The news of the telephone call was disseminated widely in the black community. It spread through the black churches nationally the Sunday prior to the election. On election day, John F. Kennedy won by two-tenths of one percent and his margin of victory in the heretofore Republican black community was an astonishing forty percent over Richard Nixon. In 1956 blacks had supported the party of Lincoln 60% to 40%, but in 1960 Kennedy won 70% to 30%. As President Eisenhower noted it was because of "a couple of phone calls" about the King case.

As the decade of the 1960s began, despite the *Brown* decision, desegregation of the Montgomery buses and lunch counters across the South, the white oligarchy that ran things since the end of Reconstruction remained in place. No one anticipated the revolution of American society, already underway, breaking forth in such a dramatic and consistent manner to redress the needs of the black minority.

The year 1961 brought the Nashville desegregation campaign to the movie theaters. In February, pickets were active in front of the segregated movie houses, learning from the Rock Hill, South Carolina, jail-in, where students from other cities joined protesters in jail by also sitting in. So, the Nashville students went to jail when arrested for picketing the movie establishments. The notion of the Freedom Ride began to evolve, the migrating of students throughout the South to desegregate facilities.

John Doar, a holdover from the Eisenhower administration because he was actively pursuing voting rights cases on behalf of blacks in the South, journeyed South to do research himself on how to effectively litigate voting rights cases. The F.B.I. was unreliable because the agents usually cooperated with the local, segregated, law enforcement officials. Doar and his colleagues developed their own methods for identifying witnesses and bringing lawsuits. A Southern litigation campaign for voter registration was launched by the Justice Department under Doar's leadership.

The Freedom Rides

On May 4, 1961, thirteen freedom riders left Washington, D.C. for points South. Sponsored by the Congress of Racial Equality (CORE), the Freedom Ride would take place on two buses; one a Greyhound and the other a Trailways. The riders' ultimate destination was New Orleans to celebrate the seventh anniversary of the *Brown* decision. Along the way, the seven black males and six whites-three females and three males-intended to desegregate bus terminal bathrooms, waiting rooms and lunch counters.

After traveling uneventfully through Virginia and North Carolina, the Greyhound bus arrived in Rock Hill, South Carolina. John Lewis, first off the bus, was struck and beaten by white youths when he tried to enter the white side of the bus station. Albert Bigelow, trying to protect Lewis from the beating, was the next Freedom Rider knocked down. Genevieve Hughes also went down. The police then broke up the attack and the bus terminal was closed. The first blood of the Freedom Ride had been spilled.

The Greyhound bus moved into Alabama, where word of its coming preceded the arrival. After stops in Tallapoosa and Heflin, the bus drove into Anniston. The mob awaiting the Freedom Riders was armed with knives, bricks, lead pipes and clubs. They were demonstrably angry, shouting at the passengers on the bus. When the mob tried to break open the front door of the bus, an undercover Alabama state investigator ran forward, held the door shut while revealing his status as an undercover policeman. The bus driver pulled out as the mob attacked the bus. But the mob pursued the bus with a caravan of some fifty cars. Finally, the bus pulled off the road on Highway 76, disabled by a slashed tire. Quickly, the crowd surrounded the bus again. This time, using bricks and axes, they smashed the rear bus window and tore open the baggage compartment. Then a fire bomb was hurled through the broken window. The Alabama agent pulled his pistol when he realized the mob was now sealing the door to keep them inside. He was able to open the door and get the passengers out of the bus. As individual Freedom Riders emerged from the vehicle, they were attacked by the mob. Finally, the Alabama State Police arrived. Firing shots into the air, the state troopers separated the mob from the Freedom Riders. A picture of the burning bus was taken by a photographer and the wire services sent it out nationally that evening.

Meanwhile, the second bus arrived in Anniston. The Freedom Riders disembarked and went into the terminal for sandwiches. They noticed how tense the white crowd appeared which observed them. Upon reboarding the bus, eight whites entered the bus and when the blacks refused to move to the back of the bus, the whites began their assault. Two white Freedom Riders sought to interpose their bodies between the attackers and their colleagues, thus drawing the fury of the beating to themselves. The "nigger lovers' " beaten bodies were thrown into a heap at the rear of the bus with the "niggers." The whites then sat down in the middle of the bus to insure no blacks left the rear of the bus. The bus driver, conveniently absent during the assault, climbed back onto the bus and drove out of Anniston.

The next stop on the Freedom Ride was Birmingham. Home of Police Commissioner Bull Connor, a large Ku Klux Klan klavern and a city adamant about segregation, Birmingham was a formidable objective.

By prearrangement, the bus terminal had been cleared by the Birmingham police, to allow the Klan fifteen minutes uninterrupted with the Freedom Riders. When Charles Person, black, and Jim Peck, white and still bloodied from the beating in Anniston, stepped off the bus and proceeded into the terminal, a sullen crowd of Klansmen awaited them. The fifteen-minute riot which ensued consisted of the Klan assaulting Freedom Riders, reporters and anyone who looked suspicious. It was fortunate that the carnage which took place did not kill someone. The Klan mob, including F.B.I. informant Gary Thomas Rowe, beat people senseless. When the police finally arrived after the fifteen minutes of mayhem, Person and Peck lay pummeled to the floor. Walter Bergman was crawling around trying to reach an exit while constantly attacked. Afterwards, the Freedom Riders made their way to the Rev. Fred Shuttlesworth's house. Shuttlesworth was the leading black minister in Birmingham in the desegregation campaign. Peck was immediately sent to a hospital where he was refused treatment because of who he was. Finally, in the Hillman Hospital emergency room, he received sutures for his six head wounds requiring 53 stitches.

Meanwhile, the other Freedom Riders were besieged by a mob at a hospital in Anniston. The Kennedy administration sought to assure safe passage for them, to uphold the interstate commerce law. The Freedom Riders remained determined to continue their journey.

Fred Shuttlesworth escorted the 18 Freedom Riders to the bus terminal for the 3:00 p.m. bus to Montgomery. By now, the entire country was watching the fate of the Freedom Ride.

The Freedom Riders, protected by police at the terminal but surrounded by another mob, began rethinking their position. Perhaps they should fly to New Orleans to get there in time for the anniversary celebration of the

Brown decision. No sooner did they begin moving to the airport than the mob reached it ahead of them. Attorney General Robert Kennedy sent a key aide, John Seigenthaler of Nashville, to be with the Freedom Riders in Alabama.

Simultaneously the Nashville sit-in group, alarmed at what had happened to their Freedom Ride colleagues, decided to go to Birmingham to replace them. Diane Nash pushed for her Nashville non-violent cohorts to go to support the Freedom Ride with their bodies.

Arriving in Birmingham, the nine new Freedom Riders were greeted by the police, who would not let them off the bus. A mob besieged the bus, and when the Freedom Riders finally left the bus to transfer to the Montgomery bus, Bull Connor ordered their arrest. When Fred Shuttlesworth inquired why they were being arrested, he too was arrested.

Bull Connor drove the Freedom Riders to the Tennessee state line and released them near the border town of Ardmore. When they phoned back to Nashville, they were informed that more volunteers were on their way to continue the Freedom Ride. The students caucused and decided to return to Birmingham.

The two groups of Freedom Riders came together at Fred Shuttlesworth's house. Proceeding to the bus terminal, determined to catch that Montgomery bus, they were soon surrounded by a milling mob of 3000 whites. Once again, Fred Shuttlesworth was arrested.

At 8:30 a.m., Saturday, May 20, the bus finally left Birmingham, with John Lewis and his Nashville colleagues aboard. John Seigenthaler went down to the bus station in Montgomery to meet the arriving Birmingham bus.

John Lewis, a native of nearby Troy, knew the look of the Montgomery bus station well. Stepping off the bus with his colleagues, he sensed something was wrong. The press gathered around for a statement and Lewis began to speak. But the terminal was deserted and eerily quiet. He soon realized why.

A group of twelve white men, armed with baseball bats, pipes and bottles, marched through the door straight for the Freedom Riders. Roughly parting the reporters, the men assaulted Lewis right after he told his colleagues: "Let's all stand together."

John Seigenthaler drove toward the bus terminal into the melee. Unaware that the bus had already arrived at the station, he saw the mob attacking a young black woman. He stopped the car to help her. As he urged the young woman to climb into his car, an angry white man pummeled Seigenthaler on the head with a lead pipe.

By the time the police arrived ten minutes after the mob attack commenced, the bodies on the ground were all Freedom Riders except for Seigenthaler. All the careful arrangements worked out between the Kennedy administration and Alabama officials were rendered impotent by the violence in Montgomery. John Lewis, Jim Zwerg, William Barbee and John Seigenthaler were all beaten senseless. The Kennedy administration had seen enough. Federal marshals were ordered into Alabama.

The Freedom Riders were taken to Ralph Abernathy's church in Montgomery. The congregation was packed as black Montgomery turned out to honor the courage of the Freedom Riders. Martin King had come to be the featured speaker of the evening.

The church was surrounded by a white mob. They overturned a car and burned it. Telephone connections were made to Attorney General Robert Kennedy, who spoke with King. He assured King the federal marshals were coming. Fortunately, the marshals arrived and were able to hold the mob at bay until the National Guard arrived on the scene.

The Freedom Riders, reinforced again from Nashville as well as from New Orleans and Washington, D.C., were determined to journey to Jackson, Mississippi. They were escorted to the bus in Montgomery and it pulled out for Jackson at 7:00 a.m.

The Kennedy administration worked with Alabama and Mississippi authorities to insure the safety of the Freedom Riders. The agreement was reached on the assumption it would be just this one bus and it would be humming at 70 m.p.h. without stopping until Jackson, Mississippi. Meanwhile, at 11:25 the new Freedom Ride volunteers boarded the bus to Jackson from Montgomery. The third bus of Freedom Riders headed out some four hours later. They would all end up in the Jackson, Mississippi, jail and then be shipped to the Mississippi State Penitentiary at Parchman, in the Mississippi delta.

Taylor Branch describes what the Freedom Ride did to the South:

> From the Montgomery Bus boycott to the confrontations of the sit-ins, then on to the Rock Hill jail-in and now to the mass assault on the Mississippi prisons, there was a "movement" in both senses of the word—a moving spiritual experience, and a steady expansion of scope. The theater was spreading through the entire South. One isolated battle had given way to many scattered ones, and now in the Mississippi jails they were moving from similar experiences to a common experience. Students began to think of the movement as a vocation in itself. From jail, John Lewis notified the Quakers by letter that he was withdrawing from the India program because he wanted to work full time in the South.

The Second Reconstruction was underway. A combination of federal court orders and the determination of black people was working to enfranchise a black citizenry which had been systematically denied their full rights of citizenship since 1877. It would be an arduous journey toward enfranchisement, one that was ultimately formally successful, but the direction was clear in the summer of 1961. One could hear the civil rights chant echoing through the South: "We're fed up! We ain't takin' no more! We're fed up! We ain't takin' no more!"

Perspective from High School

The spring of 1963 was my junior year in high school in Raleigh, North Carolina. The school, William G. Enloe, was newly opened and my class would be the first to graduate. The enthusiasm of the teachers and students in the new school was enjoyable. We were integrated from the beginning with a handful of black students. Almost ten years after *Brown*, integration was finally coming to the capital of North Carolina: "All deliberate speed," indeed.

The civil rights movement had not impacted me directly since the closing of the swimming pool in Greenville, North Carolina. I remembered the television coverage of the Greensboro sit-ins in 1960, but race was not really an issue in my life. Then came the events in Birmingham, Alabama, as I was preparing to end my junior year of high school.

The jails were full in Birmingham and the children were marching. Literally, school children were marching down the streets. On Friday, May 3, 1963, sixty singing students were confronted by the Fire Department of Birmingham. The firemen had orders to keep the children out of downtown Birmingham. A routine spraying from hoses escalated into a frightening display of reckless power as the monitor guns or water cannon, designed for long range fire fighting, were brought to bear on the children sitting drenched in the street. The power of the water cannons tossed the children around and down the street like rag dolls.

Other young marchers emerged from the Sixteenth Street Baptist Church and they went around the monitor guns, taking other routes toward downtown. The children were halted and arrested, but with the jails already full of protesters, the police brought out the K-9 teams. The German shepherds and their handlers menaced the children. Much to a watching nation's horror, images hurtled over the wire services and the television revealing the brutality of racism. One picture of a German shepherd with bared teeth next to a black child's stomach, restrained on a taut leash by a white policeman, burned into my consciousness. By 3:30 p.m. the Birmingham authorities were seeking to negotiate, but it would take more days of protesting to integrate Birmingham.

The civil rights movement was making a pilgrimage to Washington, D.C. in August of 1963. A. Phillip Randolph's long promised protest of the 1940s was being fulfilled in the summer of 1963. On August 28, 1963, 21 chartered buses and thousands of cars flooded into the District of Columbia for the

March on Washington. Over 250,000 people gathered beneath the Lincoln monument and around the reflecting pool and were galvanized by Martin King's "I Have A Dream" speech. This one speech cemented Martin King and the civil rights movement at the forefront of the national agenda. By articulating the biblical message of Amos and Isaiah, King lifted up his vision for the nation: "And when this happens . . . we will be able to speed that day when all God's children, black men and white men, Jews and Gentiles, Protestants and Catholics, will be able to join hands and sing in the words of the old Negro spiritual: 'Free at last! Free at last! Thank God Almighty, we are free at last.' "

On November 22, 1963, I was sitting in my senior English class at Enloe High School in Raleigh, North Carolina. The principal interrupted the class with an announcement on the school intercom: "President Kennedy has been shot. I will play the radio broadcast so we can determine how serious this is." The news broadcast from Dallas was piped over the intercom throughout the school.

We were stunned in our seats, straining to hear the news report. Was President Kennedy dead? Who could have done it? These thoughts raced through my mind. But in some classes in the school, and elsewhere across the South, spontaneous applause burst out when students heard the announcement. President Kennedy and his brother Robert, the Attorney General, were vilified by many Southern whites for their stance on racial integration. When the tyranny of the white majority was threatened, in this instance the white Southern oligarchy, life became extraordinarily difficult for the black minority and those perceived as their allies. Hence civil rights workers and presidents became victims of violence.

The irony of the situation was that President Kennedy had moved extremely cautiously on civil rights. A tepid civil rights act was meandering through Congress because Kennedy did not want to antagonize the Southern Democratic oligarchy. He needed their support in the re-election campaign, so he had moved reluctantly on the integration front. His federal judge appointments in the South were deferential to white Democrats as well. In appointing Judge Harold Cox to the federal bench in Mississippi, he placed a notorious segregationist on the bench.

President Lyndon Johnson

The swearing in of Lyndon Baines Johnson, the Vice-President, as President of the United States of America, took place on Air Force One on the tarmac at the Dallas airport. The nation was reeling and stunned by President Kennedy's assassination. As a veteran of Congressional wars and the former majority leader in the Senate, Lyndon Johnson knew he had to move quickly to enact legislation that under ordinary circumstances was unlikely to pass. Mobilizing his troops and organizing a full scale legislative attack, President Johnston introduced more programs than any other administration since the New Deal of Franklin Delano Roosevelt. In so doing, Lyndon Johnson of Texas came to be regarded as a traitor to the white South, just as did Harry Truman when he introduced civil rights initiatives twenty years previously. By embracing civil rights and having it legislatively mandated through his considerable skill and persuasion, Johnson ensured that the white Southern oligarchy would regard him as a turncoat.

President Johnson moved the Senate to invoke cloture on the Southern filibuster of the Civil Rights Bill. In signing the bill into law, Johnson drew upon the Kennedy legacy, and in January of 1965, the Justice Department filed suits for school desegregation in Louisiana and Tennessee under the 1964 Civil Rights Act.

On February 26, 1965, a young black man in Selma, Alabama, was shot and clubbed to death. The civil rights community mobilized a march from Selma to Montgomery. On March 7, 1965, the Alabama state troopers used tear gas, clubs and whips to halt the march. On March 9, a white minister from Boston was severely beaten and died two days later.

Lyndon Johnson had seen enough. On March 15, 1965, he addressed the nation on television. His speech unveiled the Voting Rights Act, which would eliminate literacy tests and poll taxes. President Johnson was determined to enfranchise black Americans in the South and he left no doubt of his intentions when he closed his speech with the refrain from the anthem of the Civil Rights Movement: "We shall overcome."

On August 12, 1965, the Los Angeles ghetto of Watts exploded. It was a rude awakening for those who thought race a Southern problem.

August also saw the reorganization of governmental civil rights litigation under one authority—the Attorney General. In September, Congress responded to President Johnson's prodding by passing a one-billion-dollar Elementary and Secondary School Act. This legislation financially enticed schools to desegregate. By the fall of 1965, when school was underway, the number of blacks in desegregated schools had tripled over the previous high.

President Johnson also got Congress to appropriate $2.3 billion for Model Cities, an attempt to remedy the decades of neglect in urban areas for poor people. By the end of the 89th Congress, of the 200 measures proposed by the Johnson administration, 180 had been enacted. In addition to those mentioned previously, other significant items included the War on Poverty, health care for the elderly and poor (Medicare and Medicaid), urban mass transit money and Head Start Programs.

Lyndon Johnson, the Texas politician who had stolen his first election to the Senate and voted against civil rights as a Senator, put the muscle and flesh on the bones of Abraham Lincoln's Emancipation Proclamation of January 1, 1863. Johnson, a terribly flawed man, mustered all his wiliness and cunning to implement the most far-reaching social agenda in thirty years. In terms of actions on behalf of black people, Johnson accomplished more than any administration since Reconstruction.

Although Johnson's Great Society program was not perfect by any means, it secured the rights of black Americans in a way which had been wanting for over one hundred years. This commitment also led to his appointment of Thurgood Marshall, the black civil rights litigator, to the U.S. Supreme Court. He was the first black justice on the Court.

Tragically, Lyndon Johnson insisted on fighting the Vietnam "war" (Congress never declared war, only giving the President "power to use military force") even as he waged the battle for the Great Society. Personally intimidated by the glamour and elite air that surrounded John and Robert Kennedy, he was unable to transfer the enormous self-confidence he displayed in the legislative arena to his encounters with the Kennedy clan. The Kennedys brought "the best and the brightest" with them into power, and Johnson relied upon them after John Kennedy's death. Hence people like Defense Secretary Robert McNamara, a brilliant man and tireless worker, would (with all of President Johnson's advisers, except George Ball), remain blinded by American technical and military superiority. The misplaced hubris of the Best and the Brightest went unrecognized by Johnson. His failure to recognize such hubris, within himself and his advisers, would finally drive him from office. (See David Halberstam's *The Best and the Brightest*.)

The Tet offensive which the Viet Cong launched beginning the lunar new year in 1968 demonstrated the tenuous grip of the Thieu regime backed by the U.S. in South Vietnam. It also revealed to Americans that despite assurances of victory, and increased body counts, the war was a long way from being concluded. The antiwar candidate in the New Hampshire primary, Senator Eugene McCarthy, went from single digits in the polls to garnering 42 percent of the vote in the March 12 primary. It was a stunning refutation of Lyndon Johnson's policy in Vietnam.

The author of much of the Second Reconstruction had been defeated by a war in Southeast Asia. Yet Johnson's own prideful stubbornness would not allow him to admit defeat of a policy, and he kept the war going when it could not be won. President Lyndon Baines Johnson, on March 31st, announced to the American people he would not run for re-election.

April 4, 1968. The tumultuous spring of 1968 became ugly and violent. Martin Luther King, Jr. was shot and killed in Memphis, Tennessee. He had journeyed to Memphis to work with Jim Lawson on behalf of a strike by sanitation workers. Riots shook the country as urban areas exploded in response to King's assassination. In the week after April 4, there was violence in 125 cities in 29 states and the District of Columbia.

Presidential Politics

By winning the April 2 Democratic primary in Wisconsin, Eugene McCarthy demonstrated he was a serious candidate for President. Robert Kennedy announced he too was running for President as a Democrat. For the first time since the grim war in Vietnam had come to the nation's attention, it looked as though it might be possible to elect a president who would end the war.

June 5, 1968, the fatal spring took yet another victim. Robert Kennedy was shot and killed as he left the ballroom of a Los Angeles hotel in the wake of his 46% to 41% victory in the California primary over Eugene McCarthy. Another Kennedy had fallen to a gunman.

An historic event occurred in Chicago, Illinois, on August 26, 1968. The Democrats, a Party divided and embittered over Vietnam, gathered to nominate a presidential candidate to oppose Richard Nixon. The 'peace with Vietnam' wing of the party—still strong despite Robert Kennedy's murder—was opposing Vice President Hubert Humphrey, who led the delegate count for the nomination and espoused the administration's pro war position.

A police riot broke out in the streets of Chicago, courtesy of Mayor Richard Daley and the Chicago police. The anti-war protesters, who had come to Chicago to protest President Johnson's bankrupt policy on Vietnam, were attacked by the Chicago police on the night of August 28. As the television cameras recorded the nomination of Hubert Humphrey inside the convention center, outside the cameras revealed the police brutally beating peaceful protesters. Blood was flowing. It was reminiscent of the police in the South attacking civil rights protesters for integration, and the alacrity with which the police moved was astonishing and appalling.

The Democratic Party nominated Hubert Humphrey on a Vietnam War plank identical to Lyndon Johnson's. Such a decision was unacceptable to millions of Americans who had rallied strongly against the war. In addition, the Republican nominee, Richard Nixon, had courted the white vote with racist code phrases as well as supporting the war in Vietnam. Where would the peace wing of the Democratic Party turn in this election?

The election was won by Richard Nixon by 500,000 votes over Vice President Hubert Humphrey. Although it was difficult to tell where the peace votes went, or whether they stayed home in protest, the election ensured one thing. It was a death warrant for thousands of American troops (ultimately some 27,000) because Nixon was committed to "winning the war," which meant no negotiated peace until four long years later.

The Nixon Administration

By January of 1969, Nixon's promised continuance of the war assured the truth of the antiwar slogan: "Ho, Ho, Ho Chi Minh, the NLF is gonna win." For millions of Americans, it was clear the war was futile and the National Liberation Front was going to win. They felt the United States should declare victory and withdraw from the quagmire of Vietnam. Indeed, the peace terms announced four years later could have been accomplished in 1969 if President Nixon and his National Security Adviser Henry Kissinger had been willing to agree to them. Unfortunately, their ascendance to the top of the power structure meant their chance to try to achieve victory. In seeking to win the "honorable peace," they ensured that thousands of American soldiers as well as Vietnamese were killed. Cambodia was destroyed as a country since the war was widened into its territory, thus assuring the rise of the genocidal Khmer Rouge regime. It also meant thousands more Vietnamese people had their lives destroyed. However, Henry Kissinger was awarded the Nobel Peace Prize in one of the more ironic twists of the twentieth century.

The question of what W.E.B. Du Bois termed "the problem of the color line" was on the minds of Americans in 1969. President Nixon inaugurated a revenue sharing program which sent federal dollars back to the cities and states, thus aiding minorities significantly, as 80 percent of them lived in the cities. In upholding *Brown v. Board of Education*, Nixon inherited a meager legacy from his predecessors. In 1968, fifteen years after the *Brown* decision, the Supreme Court's "Deliberate speed" doctrine had resulted in only 5.2 percent of black children finding their way to desegregated school systems. The federal courts had begun ordering busing as a means of achieving integration. Nixon, on record as opposing busing, supported the laws that enabled busing to work. Like President Eisenhower, he would see the law enforced. This placed him in opposition to the policies of governors such as George Wallace of Alabama and Ross Barnett of Mississippi.

On June 24, 1970, the first of President Nixon's state advisory boards composed of local citizens was invited for lunch at the White House. The purpose of the committee was to achieve desegregation in the school systems. This luncheon brought together black and white Mississippians to see if they could agree to serve on the President's advisory board. Administration staff worked the parties and President Nixon appeared for a brief period. None of the Mississippi congressional delegation deigned to attend. As one Mississippi congressman stated to a White House aide: "You've been around long enough to know I'm against desegregation, and most of all against eating with niggers." So it was with the Southern oligarchy in 1970.

The Mississippi group agreed to serve as did other advisory committees in Alabama, Georgia, Louisiana, North and South Carolina. In 1970, the South ended its separate but equal school system. Under Richard Nixon's administration, desegregation was accomplished at a greater rate than the sixteen previous years since *Brown*.

In reviewing the anti-busing rhetoric of Richard Nixon's presidential campaign and contrasting it with the success of the advisory committee's and federal courts in dismantling segregation in the South, Tom Wicker observes of Nixon:

> The indisputable fact is that he got the job done—the dismantling of dual schools—when no one else had been able to do it. Nixon's reliance on persuasion rather than coercion, his willingness to work with Southern whites instead of denouncing them, his insistence that segregation was national, not just a Southern problem, the careful distance he maintained between himself and the "liberal establishment," the huge political credit he earned in the South with his Supreme Court nominations and his other gestures to Southern sensibility—particularly local leadership—all resulted in a formula that worked.

At the same time, Nixon launched an assault on the programs that made up Johnson's "Great Society." John Ehrlichman, aide to President Nixon, called the strategy of dismantling the programs the "zig-zag" approach. Publicly, concern would be articulated for the poor and keeping the programs that benefited them. Simultaneously, those programs would be taken apart.

The hatchet man chosen for this job was Donald Rumsfeld. Rumsfeld was a congressman from Illinois. Nixon described him thus: "He's a ruthless little bastard, be sure of that." He was appointed to serve as Director of the Office of Economic Opportunity (OEO). He had voted against the Economic Opportunity Act as a congressman.

Robert Korstadt and James Leloudis describe the Nixon Administration in *To Right These Wrongs*:

> Rumsfeld's actions reflected a broader desire within the Nixon administration to curtail Washington's role as a broker among competing economic and political interests. The federal government had taken on that responsibility during the New Deal, and in Lyndon Johnson's Great Society the mandate for an activist state was enlarged many times over. Federal agencies became for the dispossessed and disfranchised a forceful lever for dislodging local and private power. They removed segregationists from the schoolhouse door, enforced fairness in the voting booth, and demanded justice in court of law.

Nixon aimed to restrain that intrusion into local affairs with what he called a "new federalism." The idea was to decentralize control over social welfare programs, either by moving administrative authority out of Washington, as Rumsfeld had done with Legal Services, or by allocating federal funds in the form of block grants awarded directly to states and municipalities with few strings attached.

This is precisely what the Nixon administration did and the Watergate crisis was the event that slowed down this process. However, Nixon's successor Gerald Ford, delivered the *coup de grâce* when he abolished OEO, which he had opposed since 1964. Hence the War on Poverty was stopped in its tracks.

8. *Light filtering into holding cell, RMSI. Photo: Gigi Cohen.*

Of course, race and poverty are twins of the dispossessed. Destroying a poverty program has a significant impact on African Americans. This was the intent and was the result of the Southern Strategy campaign that Nixon used to win election (with the assistance of Kevin Phillips). By signaling to whites his antipathy to blacks, in code, Nixon overcame the threats of Hubert Humphrey and independent candidate George Wallace and won the White House with a margin of less than one percent of the popular vote. His attitude toward blacks, which was not unique to white Americans at the time, was basically: "blacks are genetically inferior to whites . . . all the federal money and programs could never achieve parity—in intelligence, economic success or social qualities; but ... we should still do what we could for them, within reasonable limits, because it is 'right' to do so."

The beginning of the end of the Second Reconstruction was at hand.

The Spring of 1970

Two events in the spring of 1970 were profound in their impact on the American political landscape. In April, the first Earth Day event kicked off as people expressed their concern about the environment. The scope of this initial event was surprising: 10,000 schools, 2,000 colleges and universities, and virtually every community in America took part.

President Nixon, acting upon the popular groundswell for the environment, proposed the Environmental Protection Agency two months later. The agency's stated purpose was to defend the environment. Congress approved the legislation, and by December 2, 1970, the EPA opened its doors.

The second event of the spring of 1970 was President Nixon's expansion of the Vietnam Conflict into Cambodia. On April 30, Nixon told the nation in a televised address that American and South Vietnamese troops had extended their campaign into Cambodia.

When Richard Nixon assumed the Presidency in January of 1969, 200 Americans were being killed a week in Vietnam—for a total of 31,000 to that date—and the war had cost about $30 billion a year. This new theater of the war in Cambodia would mean more losses and more costs to a country that was increasingly sick of war.

President Nixon had promised a "Vietnamization" of the war. This meant the gradual turning over to the war to the South Vietnamese to fight. But the body count had remained as high on his watch as it was under President Johnson. Now, Nixon was escalating the war.

Nixon's announcement shot a bolt of electricity through the anti-war community. Protests blossomed on campuses, and at Kent State University in Ohio on May 4 and Jackson State University in Mississippi on May 15, protesting students were killed by National Guard and state police.

A national mobilization was planned in D.C. to protest the Cambodian invasion. The Communist headquarters Nixon promised to capture in Cambodia proved elusive; the "incursion" into the Communist sanctuaries did not deter future attacks from those places and it contributed to the destruction of the fragile political structure of Cambodia. As mentioned, the nation later became a victim of the genocidal campaign of the Khmer Rouge who literally destroyed the people in a supposed quest for a utopian society.

The War in Vietnam

President Nixon had promised to "end the war and win the peace." Cambodia revealed that this translated into expanding the war and to what end, no one knew. The Cambodia campaign seemed like sheer hypocrisy to many. The reaction was so strong against it that the Senate voted 58 to 37 to prohibit use of government funds for the military operation in Cambodia after July 1.

Finally, in the fall of 1970, President Nixon authorized Henry Kissinger to tell the North Vietnamese that he would agree "to a cease-fire in place in South Vietnam without first requiring that the North Vietnamese agree to withdraw their forces." Given the inability of the South Vietnamese army to defend themselves despite years of American training, weapons and soldiers, this meant the end of the war was guaranteed. The North Vietnamese would conquer the South Vietnamese army without American troops opposing them. Nixon promised America that 150,000 of its troops would be home by April 20, 1971, and 40,000 home by Christmas.

The North Vietnamese, in the words of a Bob Dylan song, didn't "need a weatherman to see which way the wind blows." They launched a major offensive on March 30, 1972. Nixon responded with intense air bombardment to support the South Vietnamese troops since all American troops had left.

On May 8, Nixon told the nation he would mine North Vietnamese harbors and bomb Vietnamese cities. The subsequent air campaign stopped the North Vietnamese offensive and prevented the city of Hue from falling. The bombing supplemented an effective diplomatic campaign which had resulted in China and the Soviet Union, the major benefactors of North Vietnam, entering into diplomatic exchange and a SALT treaty with the Americans. North Vietnam began to consider a negotiated peace.

On October 12, merely a month before his re-election campaign would conclude, Nixon announced that the United States and Hanoi had agreed to a "negotiated settlement." Although North Vietnam permitted President Thieu of South Vietnam to remain in power, the United States agreed to a Provisional Revolutionary Government comprised of the Vietcong as well as South Vietnamese. And, fatally for the future of President Thieu and South Vietnam, the North Vietnamese army remained in South Vietnam.

President Thieu was justifiably upset by this arrangement. He knew his government was doomed. He angrily confronted Kissinger, to no avail. In a national press conference on October 26, Kissinger announced, "Peace is at hand." In order to placate Thieu, Nixon ordered the Christmas bombings of 1972. The North Vietnamese leaders in Hanoi, anticipating Nixon's action, evacuated women and children from the city. B-52 bombers flew 116 missions on Hanoi. On January 15, 1973, the bombing of the city and mining of the harbor ceased. President Thieu remained worried about the future, despite continued American assurances. But he had no choice. The deal was done and he had to go along.

On January 23, 1973, the agreement ending the war in Vietnam was signed and a cease fire scheduled for January 27. The "peace with honor" left the North Vietnamese army in place in the South thus assuring the demise of the Thieu regime. All parties to this agreement realized it was the end of South Vietnam.

April 30, 1975, two years after Lyndon Johnson died of a heart attack and eight months after President Richard Nixon resigned in disgrace because of the Watergate scandal, the Vietnamese government of President Thieu fell to North Vietnamese offensive. Perhaps Jerry Garcia and The Grateful Dead said it best in one of their songs: "What a long, strange trip it's been."

We have spent a significant time analyzing the Vietnam Conflict for two reasons: (1) The opposition to the Vietnam Conflict along with the marches in the Civil Rights Movement, led thousands of Americans into the streets to protest the tyranny of their government, and (2) The Vietnam Conflict resulted in the eclipse of the Civil Rights Movement. When Dr. Martin Luther King, Jr. linked opposition to the war with civil rights in his speech at Riverside Church in New York, thus earning the enmity of President Johnson, he articulated the power of violence on society. He knew that as the war grew, it drained resources from the civil rights agenda. Just as with F.D.R. and World War II, Harry Truman and the Korean War, Lyndon Johnson found the war in Vietnam overtook and ultimately led to the demise of his Great Society. The fighting of a war abroad meant the neglect of civil rights at home.

Vice President Gerald Ford succeeded Richard Nixon, presiding over an essentially caretaking government. He did make one appointment to the U.S. Supreme Court: Justice John Paul Stephens.

In evaluating the Nixon/Ford years of the presidency, we see them as the end of the Second Reconstruction. As we have seen, despite rhetoric to the contrary, busing proceeded to bring integration to the country in conjunction with the state advisory committees and court orders. The commitment of the federal government to the cities and the states continued through revenue sharing. Affirmative action was a policy followed by the government. The Vietnam Conflict had finally wound down.

But Richard Nixon had brought disrepute to the White House through the Watergate crisis and his impeachment shook the Republican Party. In the 1976 election, Gerald Ford was the nominee of the Republicans and a Southerner, the former governor of Georgia, Jimmy Carter, was the

Democratic nominee. After eight years in power, the Republicans lost the White House to the peanut farmer from Georgia.

The End of the Second Reconstruction

In reviewing the executive, legislative and judicial branches of government as they existed in 1976, it is clear that despite strides toward enfranchisement, the representative process of government was still overwhelmingly white. Reforms had resulted in an increase in black elected officials throughout the South, but the legislatures, governors' offices, not to mention the U.S. Congress, remained overwhelmingly white. The judiciary, a bastion of whiteness since Reconstruction, remained so throughout the country. Despite the success of the Second Reconstruction, including the dramatic growth of the black middle class, the tyranny of the racial majority remained intact with only 13 of 292 judicial appointments made by Nixon and Ford coming from minority populations. All five of the appointees to the Supreme Court were white men.

The white majority wearied of the policies of Reconstruction, just as it had done in the 1870s. Resentment built, and phrases like reverse discrimination (an oxymoron) began to be bandied about in public conversation. Just like the initial Reconstruction, whites began to feel that the blacks were receiving too much, too fast. At least the onerous days of lynching, segregation and disfranchisement had passed. So, a more subtle but equally effective means of dealing with the black minority emerged in the policies to come from 1976 onward. With the election of Jimmy Carter as President, the nation embarked on the Era of Disfranchisement.

The Republican legacy for Jimmy Carter contained 292 federal judges appointed, including five Supreme Court justices. The balance of the Court had been shifted to the right through these appointments. Two issues illuminated the changing judicial landscape: the death penalty and discrimination in hiring.

In 1972, the Supreme Court struck down capital punishment by a 5–4 vote in *Furman v. Georgia*. The plurality opinion found the administration of the death penalty in Georgia was "freakish," "arbitrary" and "random." It noted the discrimination in the utilization of judicial killing; especially egregious was the fact that 377 men had been executed for rape in Georgia and all but three were black.

In 1971, in *Griggs v. Duke Power Company*, the Supreme Court established that demonstrating a pattern of discrimination was the standard for determining whether or not one was discriminated against. The opinion, written by Chief Justice Warren Burger, elucidated the doctrine that if a pattern of discrimination in hiring decisions could be established, the individual did not have to prove per se the intent to discriminate against him or her. This would remain constitutional law until 1987, when *McCleskey v. Kemp* established the more difficult, virtually impossible standard, of proving individual racial intent in discrimination.

The crest of the Second Reconstruction was reached in 1976. The Supreme Court decisions restoring the death penalty on the eve of the bicentennial birthday, not unlike the reaction of the white majority learning of the loss of the Seventh Cavalry and George Custer during the centennial celebration, served as a compass orienting the country back to the old familiar territory of the racial tyranny of the majority. Along with Jimmy Carter's election as President, the course was charted for the shift from a strong, central government back to the states control of more programs and resources. As we have seen after the First Reconstruction, when a similar reversal occurred, the minority would be left to the mercy of the states without firm intervention from the government in Washington.

CHAPTER 12. THE REGIME OF DISFRANCHISEMENT I (1980–92)

Ronald Reagan, a former movie actor, mounted a successful campaign for the presidency against the incumbent Jimmy Carter in 1980. Carter, mired in the hostage crisis in Iran and plagued with a general perception of a failure of leadership, lost to Reagan in a campaign that found a dramatic shift in the white vote in the South from a Southern incumbent president to a feel-good Republican from California. The white Southern vote fled the Democratic Party, as it would increasingly in future elections. The white South continued to turn Republican. Exploiting the ground Richard Nixon had tilled in 1968, Reagan clearly signaled he was in opposition to programs for minorities and a staunch proponent of the tyranny of the white majority. His election also fulfilled President Lyndon Johnson's prediction when he signed the Voting Rights Act: "This will be the end of the Democratic party in the South."

Although posturing as a conservative, Ronald Reagan ran up the largest budget deficit in the history of the United States in his eight years as president. Indeed, the national debt skyrocketed from $909 billion in 1980 to over $4 trillion in 1992. The percentage of debt rose from 34.4 percent to 67.6 percent. Despite the Soviet Union's entropy, Reagan led the United States into its largest peacetime military buildup as a means of countering "the evil empire" of Soviet aggression. What his exorbitant expenditure of funds really accomplished was the gutting of social programs. In order to fund the Star Wars program and other defense boondoggles, the Reagan administration cut social programs in the name of maintaining an austere budget. David Stockman, the manager of the Office of Management and Budget, gave a candid interview to *The Atlantic* magazine detailing the success of the strategy. The legislature happily cooperated in the feel-good scenario Reagan projected in television ads as "morning in America."

Funding to cities, states and minority programs shriveled and died in the Reagan years.

The Reagan administration assault on the poor and minorities was cloaked with the benign title of the Omnibus Budget Reconciliation Act of 1981 (OBRA). Regulatory changes imposed lower income ceilings on working women and their children as a criterion for eligibility for AFDC (Aid to Families with Dependent Children). Hence there was, in effect, a punishment for working. Millions of partially dependent families were removed from welfare rolls or endured dramatic declines in their living standards. Dr. Julius Wilson points out that: "average disposable income of working AFDC families [including net earnings, benefits, and food stamps] for the nation went from 101 percent of the poverty line to 81 percent. And average AFDC benefits were reduced from $186 to only $20 monthly." The conclusion was inescapable: "the rise in official poverty; between 1979 and 1982 is not simply due to macroeconomic conditions [mild recession of 1980, high inflation, then deep recession], but is also a function of fundamental changes in the federal government's response to conditions of poverty."

As deleterious to the minority population as the executive and legislative branches of government were under President Reagan, his judicial appointments placed an ideological stamp on federal judges unmatched by previous presidents, including President Nixon. Reagan appointed 356 white men to the bench, 7 African Americans, 13 Latinos and 2 Asian Americans. Once again, the U.S. judiciary shifted dramatically to the right, entrenching judges committed to an agenda hostile to individual rights and minorities. Reagan also appointed William Rehnquist Chief Justice of the U.S. Supreme Court, elevating him from associate justice. Additionally, Reagan placed Anthony Kennedy, Sandra Day O'Connor and Antonin Scalia on the Court. This completed the unity of the three branches of government being implacably hostile to the rights of minorities. Hence we term it the Regime of Disfranchisement.

McCleskey v. Kemp

Although there are several court cases decided by the Rehnquist Supreme Court which undergirded the tyranny of the white majority, there is perhaps none as singular in import as *McCleskey v. Kemp*, decided April 22, 1987. At first glance, it is a case about the death penalty in the state of Georgia, but a careful reading of the decision finds constitutional law reversed in a manner that affects a broad range of cases.

As previously noted, *Griggs v. Duke Power*, a decision authored by Chief Justice Warren Burger in 1971, created criteria for proving discrimination in hiring which relied on establishing a pattern of discrimination by the employer. Warren McCleskey's lawyers utilized this accepted manner of determining discrimination by examining all murders in the state of Georgia in a five-year period. The study, undertaken by Professor David Baldus, revealed a pattern of racial discrimination existed to a significant degree in the administration of the death penalty in Georgia. Indeed, Professor Baldus mulitregression analysis, later awarded the outstanding achievement in sociology by colleagues in the field, showed that blacks who killed whites were far more likely to receive the death penalty than whites who killed whites; from 11 to 22 times more likely!

Warren McCleskey, a black man convicted of killing a white police officer, was clearly the victim of racial bias which Baldus demonstrated throughout the Georgia criminal justice system. If all variables were controlled, the study revealed, killing a white person was 4.3 times more likely to result in the death penalty than killing a black person. This level of statistical proof is more than twice the linkage of smoking to lung cancer. Additionally, and not part of the case, the prosecutor withheld exculpatory evidence from the defense and jury before, during and after the trial.

Unable to overcome the level of proof mounted by McCleskey's lawyers through the Baldus study, the State of Georgia could not prevail. Neither could the Supreme Court when the case reached that body. What Justice Lewis Powell authored, in the 5–4 majority opinion of the Court, rewrote the accepted standard of constitutional law in existence since *Griggs v. Duke Power*. Justice Powell stated that McCleskey had failed to prove individual intent to discriminate against him personally. Of course, this was not the constitutional threshold, so McCleskey's lawyers had not addressed the issue from this perspective. Rather, they established, under settled constitutional law, that their client was a victim of a documented pattern of racial discrimination. Justice Powell wondered in his opinion if the lawyers for McCleskey wanted the Court to declare the Georgia criminal justice system unconstitutional because of demonstrated racial discrimination. He was unwilling to take the Court in that direction—though the evidence required it.

Thus with the *McCleskey* case the Supreme Court established a new level of constitutional proof for discrimination. The individual had to establish intent within the court to discriminate against him or her personally, thus creating a level of proof virtually unattainable. (Especially when the Court specifically instructed that the jurors were not to be contacted.) Did the Court expect Warren McCleskey to document a juror or judge calling him a "nigger" to prove personal intent? By turning its back at this juncture, the Supreme Court signaled it would tolerate discrimination in the criminal justice system, specifically in the administration of the death penalty, despite the fact the criminal justice system remained untouched by the Civil Rights Movement and was a bastion of discrimination. Federalism, whether it was the old version counteracting the First Reconstruction, or the New Federalism ending the Second Reconstruction, successfully removed the federal government as a guarantor of rights of minorities. The recent version manifested in *McCleskey* meant discrimination would continue to hold sway in the criminal justice system, not only unchecked by the judiciary but encouraged in its efforts to discriminate.

Years later after retiring from the bench, Lewis Powell admitted he would change his vote in *McCleskey* if he could. That was too late for Warren McCleskey. He was electrocuted by the state of Georgia on September 25, 1991. It was also too late for the 3000 on death row who resided there courtesy of an invidious system of racial discrimination—documented by David Baldus in his *McCleskey* study that remained unchallenged.

The Code

The Civil Rights Movement changed laws and attitudes. It also changed language. In Ronald Reagan's successful run against the Southern incumbent Jimmy Carter, one of the chief architects of the campaign was Lee Atwater of South Carolina. Atwater realized it was not good to still be talking against blacks in a national campaign, and the key was to use code words. Anti-black sentiment had to be cloaked in words a candidate could use that would telegraph his position on civil rights without appearing racist. One such classic phrase was states' rights. He admitted the use of this strategy after Reagan's election to the presidency. Although a plethora of examples could be quoted which illustrate this tactic, one in particular conveys the message clearly.

On June 21, 1964, three college age civil rights workers, Michael Schwerner, James Chaney and Andrew Goodman, were arrested on their way from Meridian to investigate the arson of Mt. Zion Baptist Church in Neshoba County, Mississippi. Later that night they were killed by the Ku Klux Klan in Neshoba County. It is significant that Ronald Reagan kicked off his election campaign for the presidency in 1980 at the Neshoba County Fair, and it serves as a primary example of the use of code in language and place to convey an anti-black position obliquely. Journalist Bob Herbert describes the scene and the political messaging:

> They [the murders of the civil rights workers] constituted Neshoba County's primary claim to fame when Ronald Reagan was the Republican Party's nominee for President in 1980. The case was still a festering sore at that time. Some of the conspirators were still

being protected by the local community. And white supremacy was still the order of the day.

That was the atmosphere and that was the place Reagan chose as the first stop in his general election campaign. The campaign debuted at the Neshoba County Fair in front of a white and at times, raucous crowd of perhaps 10,000, chanting: "We want Reagan! We want Reagan!"

Reagan was the first presidential candidate ever to appear at the fair, and he knew exactly what he was doing when he told the crowd, "I believe in states' rights."

Everybody watching the 1980 campaign knew what Reagan was signaling at the fair. Whites and blacks, Democrats and Republicans— they all knew. The news media knew. The race haters and the people appalled by racial hatred knew. And Reagan knew.

He was tapping out the code. It was understood that when politicians started chirping about "states' rights" to white people in places like Neshoba County they were saying that "when it comes down to you and the blacks, we're with you." (*The New York Times*, November 13, 2007)

The Reagan administration, succeeded by Vice President George Bush in the 1988 election, shifted the burden of poverty to the poor. In demonizing "welfare queens," Reagan racialized poverty as a black issue. Ignoring systemic changes and decades of black immigration from the South into Northern cities, the Reagan/Bush regime utilized the judiciary, the legislature and the executive branch of government to fully oppress the poor and minorities. Harsher policies on welfare and sentencing laws, including the death penalty for federal crimes, emanated from Washington as well as from statehouses around the country.

The South, as usual, led the way with the most people incarcerated and on death row. President Reagan's judicial appointees, including the four Supreme Court appointees, were joined by the 192 appointees of President Bush: 172 white, 11 African American, 8 Latino and 1 Asian American— including two appointees to the Supreme Court-David Souter and Clarence Thomas. The tyranny of the majority was cemented for a generation to come due to the number and ideological commitment of these appointees. The interlocking of all three branches of the federal government was reminiscent of the government after Reconstruction. White people felt enough had been done for minorities and the poor. The latest boot heel of the white majority after the Second Reconstruction fell upon those Jesus of Nazareth termed "the least of these my brothers and sisters" and is aptly labeled as the Regime of Disfranchisement.

Events of 1975–1995

In order to appreciate the role the criminal justice has played in the wake of the Second Reconstruction, the key to black disfranchisement just as it was after the initial Reconstruction, an examination of the time period of 1975 to 1995 is revealing. During this era of Disfranchisement, the crime rate either declined or held steady. This is simply due to the aging of the baby boom generation beyond the period of life when a person is most likely to engage in criminal activity—16 to 25 years of age. Despite this fact, the state and federal governments, assisted through media distortion of the crime issue, embarked on a campaign of incarceration unprecedented in American history.

This was a political decision rooted in response to the gains of the Second Reconstruction and not one rooted in the reality of what was happening with crime in America. Indeed, in 1975, 23.4 million households reported crime or about 32 percent of all households. Despite public perception to the contrary (an understanding created by politicians and the media), in 1992 some 22.1 million households were affected by crime or just under 23 percent of all households. Over that time period, unprecedented numbers of prisons were built (one opened every ten days) and death sentences handed out—despite the lower crime rate. Thus a thriving business in imprisonment and political careers undergirds the political reality in state and federal policymaking. This has resulted in the United States leading the world in per capita incarceration, with 2.2 million people locked up in 2013 which is a 500 percent increase in the last thirty years. (These and further data available from The Sentencing Project.)

Of course, such a policy disproportionately affects the black population. Black males in the United States in our twenty-year time period were incarcerated at more than four times the rate of black males incarcerated under the apartheid regime in South Africa, 3,822 per 100,000 to 851 per 100,000. Not surprisingly, there are more African American males in prison than in college—583,000 in prison and 537,000 in college. Indeed, one out of ten African American males in their thirties in the United States is in prison.

One of the clearest examples of the impact of sentencing in a discriminatory manner is found in the federal sentencing laws governing cocaine usage. Powder cocaine, a very expensive form of the drug, is available only to people of means. Crack cocaine, the street version which is not as pure or expensive, is readily available to poor people. Yet the sentencing disparity regarding the drug in its two manifestations is remarkable.

Congress enacted legislation in 1986 that punished the first-time offender with five years in prison for possessing five grams of crack cocaine. With powdered cocaine, a person would have to possess 500 grams, more than a pound, to receive an equivalent punishment.

As a result of this policy, by 1993, 88.3 percent of federal defendants convicted of selling crack cocaine were African American. For powder cocaine, only 27 percent convicted were black. By 1995 the discrimination was so blatant the U.S. Sentencing Commission described the crack sentences as "a primary cause of the growing disparity between sentences for black and white Federal defendants."

The commission recommended basically the eradication of the sentencing disparity but Congress, along with President Bill Clinton, rejected the recommendation. Since the Sentencing Commission's recommendations were routinely followed by Congress this failure to act could be attributed to one motive: Congress and the President wanted to continue the racialization of the perception of crime being black and were willing to countenance gross discrimination in sentencing for crack cocaine because it successfully imprisoned large numbers of black people.

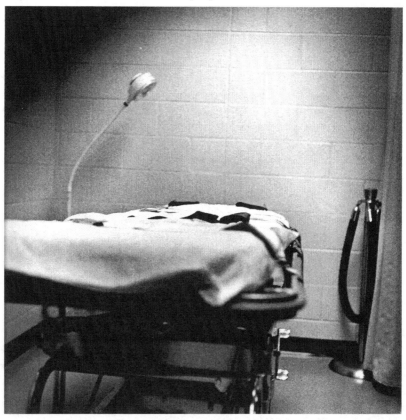

9. The execution gurney, RMSI. Photo: Gigi Cohen.

In 1976, the incarceration rate in the United States was 123 people per 100,000 per capita of the population. The death row population, newly sanctioned by the U.S. Supreme Court on July 2, 1976, stood at 437. It must be remembered at this juncture in time the crime rate was level or falling, a pattern continued for the next twenty years.

What happened over the next decades was the complete transformation of the crime issue into an issue of race. Just as we saw Louisiana do, the white majority came to perceive crime as black crime. In accomplishing this recasting of the issue, politicians led the way—just as they did after Reconstruction by codifying harsher sentences that would have a disproportionate impact on blacks (after Reconstruction, vagrancy was one outstanding example of such a "crime"). The politicians of the 1980s responded similarly. Crime became the issue by which to disfranchise the black minority. Although the policy made no fiscal or social sense, and was exorbitantly expensive and had no effect on the crime rate, it made excellent political sense. By posturing as being tough on crime, politicians could play an elaborate charade which accomplished nothing in terms of effecting crime but it decimated the black male population, thus bringing the threatening prospect of a continued civil rights movement to a halt by severely impairing the black community.

The salient point to remember about this "War on Crime" is that it came with the removal of social support from the inner city. Jobs dried up as manufacturing closed down, AFDC was slashed to the bone, and revenue sharing evaporated, so the black community suffered out of proportion to the white community. As a result, crime did increase within the black community—but it infrequently manifested itself as black on white crime.

But the white majoritarian response was one of frustration and resentment with the policies of the Second Reconstruction. The white majority felt that too much was done for the black minority and although blatant racism was no longer possible as social policy, subtle racism through the development of an enormous criminal justice machinery enabled the majority to keep the minority oppressed.

Let us examine what happened from 1973, with the passage of the Rockefeller drug law in New York, when the incarceration rate began to rise until 1995.

Although the criminal justice system underscored the determination of the white majority to remain in control after the Second Reconstruction, the engine driving the machine was initially established by President Nixon in 1969—The War on Drugs. Historically, illicit drugs were more readily available in the black community of the United States. The counter-culture movement of the 1960s made them accessible to white middle class youth.

Richard Nixon's response was cultural and visceral, directed at blacks and the protesting white youth. Neither group was one he cared for, and he campaigned vociferously against them. The Nixon White House seized upon the "get tough on drugs" approach as a cheap political fix to establish Nixon's credentials as being tough on crime.

The War on Drugs

The drug situation in 1969 could hardly be deemed a crisis. (Only 1,601 people died from drugs, legal or illegal, that year)—unless one counted the over 200,000 people who died from smoking tobacco and 50,000 from alcohol related deaths. But cigarettes and alcohol did not fit the cultural war President Nixon wanted to wage with American blacks and youth, who were leading the campaign against the war in Vietnam and for Civil Rights. By 1970, 1,899 people died from illegal drug use while 3,707 died from the flu. Nonetheless, the Drug War was launched.

Beside alcoholism and tobacco addiction, the only significant drug problem in American in 1970 was the drug addiction of returning servicemen from Vietnam. The military had become alarmed by the number of disillusioned or traumatized soldiers who were smoking pot and using heroin. So, the military cracked down to dry up the supply in Vietnam, thus driving up the price. In order to avoid cooking the heroin, soldiers began to inject it, which enabled them to get higher using smaller quantities. Soon the military had a serious heroin addiction problem and created a drug testing program to which every soldier was subjected upon returning from Vietnam.

In 1969, the Drug War cost just $65,000,000 to get underway. Five years later, the cheap and quick Drug War had assumed a life of its own. The budget was $719,000,000 in 1974, and what was actually a medical problem, and treated as such by many European countries, was converted into a law-enforcement matter.

On May 8, 1973, the State of New York, under the aegis of Governor Nelson Rockefeller, enacted the most punitive drug laws in the land. One ounce of marijuana would land one in prison for 15 years. One could receive life in prison for an ounce of heroin. Plea bargaining was prohibited in drug cases. The net result, despite a dramatic expansion of the courts, was a backlog of cases, a boom in prison construction and a lot of people of color going to prison. In 1973, New York incarcerated 71.4 people per 100,000. By 1983 the number was 172 per 100,000. In 1993, New York was locking up 354 people a year per 100,000. The vast majority were blacks.

John Walters, the deputy drug czar from 1988–93, stated: "Between 1977 and 1992 a conservative cultural revolution occurred in America. It was called the drug war." It is an accurate but minimalist description of the engine that drove the Disfranchisement Era.

Douglas Blackmon, in *Slavery by Another Name: The Re-Enslavement of Black Americans from the Civil War to World War II*, chronicles the response of the white majority to Reconstruction. The criminal code was manipulated and charges such as vagrancy, which could be applied to any black person looking for work in the devastated frontier South after the Civil War, resulted in the creation of a vast peonage system which was another form of slavery. After the Second Reconstruction, the white majority manipulated the criminal code again, particularly with drugs, to engage in mass incarceration of black people. The result in each era was the same: the oppression of black people through a criminal justice system that resulted in the stopping and the dismantling of gains made through the First and Second Reconstruction.

Michelle Alexander, in *The New Jim Crow: Mass Incarceration in the Age of Colorblindness*, documents in detail the utilization of the War on Drugs to create a racial caste system in America. She accurately describes the milieu that made the transformation of the criminal justice system possible:

> In the 1968 election, race eclipsed class as the organizing principle of American politics, and by 1972, attitudes on racial issues rather than socioeconomic status were the primary determinant of voters' self-identification. The late 1960s and early 1970s marked the dramatic erosion in the belief among working-class whites that the condition of the poor, or those who fail to prosper, was the result of a faulty economic system that needed to be challenged. As the Edsalls explain: "the pitting of white and blacks at the low end of the income distribution against each other intensified the view among many whites that the condition of life for the disadvantaged—particularly for the disadvantaged blacks—is the responsibility of those afflicted, and not the responsibility of larger society.

If the above quote sounds a familiar note, it should. It is reminiscent of the period that defeated Populism in the 1890s and also helped unwind the gains of the First Reconstruction. Now it would come into play once again to counteract the progress of the Second Reconstruction. As Alexander describes the situation: "The War on Drugs, cloaked in race-neutral language, offered whites opposed to racial reforms a unique opportunity to express their hostility toward blacks and black progress, without being exposed to the charge of racism."

After Jimmy Carter's defeat, Ronald Reagan as president launched his War on Drugs in late 1982. Although less than two percent of Americans viewed drugs as a significant problem, the federal dollars exploded in the amount directed to the War on Drugs. Alexander documents the dramatic increase under Reagan: "Between 1980 and 1984, FBI antidrug funding increased from $8 million to $95 million. Department of Defense antidrug allocations increased from $33 million in 1981 to $1,042 million in 1991. During that same period, DEA antidrug spending grew from $86 million to $1,026 million, and FBI antidrug allocations from $38 to $181 million. "

Key to spreading fear of drugs and molding public opinion through media was the utilization of the spread of crack cocaine in the black community. A sophisticated media campaign inflamed fear of crack cocaine in 1986. In response, the House of Representatives passed legislation for $2 billion for the War on Drugs while requiring the military to participate in the drug war; suspect evidence became admissible in trials, and the death penalty came into play. This became the Anti-Drug Abuse Act of 1986 which included mandatory minimum sentences and the establishment of dramatic sentencing disparities between crack and powder cocaine.

The legislation was expanded in 1988. Alexander explains:

> The resulting legislation was once again extraordinarily punitive, this time extending far beyond traditional criminal punishments and including new "civil penalties" for drug offenders. The new Anti-Drug Abuse Act authorized public housing authorities to evict any tenant who allows any form of drug-related criminal activity to occur on or near public housing premises and eliminated many federal benefits, including student loans, for anyone convicted of a drug offense. The act also expanded the use of the death penalty for some drug-related offenses and imposed new mandatory minimums for drug offenses, including a five-year mandatory minimum for simple possession of cocaine base—with no evidence of intent to sell.

In 1992, with the elaborate Drug War mechanism consuming billions of dollars, the Regime of Disfranchisement came to an end after twelve years with the election of the Democrat Bill Clinton as president. Clinton, a former Southern governor, revealed his social policies to be in line with the Republican administrations of the Disfranchisement Era. However, Clinton's judicial appointments, as with Jimmy Carter's, were the defining reason his administration would not be classified as part of the regime of the previous twelve years. He appointed two Supreme Court justices, Ruth Bader Ginsberg and Stephen Breyer, and a total of 378 judicial appointments (267 white males, 111 females, 62 African Americans, 5 Asian/Pacific Americans and one Native American). Hence Bill Clinton continued the Era of Disfranchisement, and the War on Drugs continued to grow.

President Clinton, like his Southern predecessor Carter, wanted less federal government and more state government. This tried and true formula of Southern politicians since Reconstruction effectively removed the programs for the poor and racial minorities (public assistance and public housing) to prevent the "legislative despotism" Thomas Jefferson warned of two hundred and fifty years ago. There are three examples of President Clinton abandoning the poor and working class black minority, ironically while being a proponent of the middle class black agenda by supporting affirmative action, that illustrate the total retreat from the gains of the Second Reconstruction: The Welfare Reform Act of 1996, escalation of the War on Drugs and the expanded application of the death penalty.

The old Southern standby of imprisonment and killing, whether by judiciary or lynch mob, was taken to a new level by Bill Clinton and done so with a master stroke of public posturing. The man who championed the Anti-Terrorist and Effective Death Penalty Act, dramatically expanding the use of the death penalty and limiting death penalty appeals, then made a grand gesture in the opposite direction by inviting a former prisoner convicted of murder, Ruben "Hurricane" Carter, to the White House to preview the film about Carter's frame-up for a crime he did not commit. But aside from his judicial appointments, President Clinton was all style and negative impact regarding the fate of the poor, black community.

The Personal Responsibility and Work Opportunity Reconciliation Act (the Welfare Reform bill) substituted the federal AFDC (Aid to Families with Dependent Children) with the Temporary Assistance to Need Families (TANF), which would limit welfare assistance to a five-year period in a person's lifetime. Also, if someone was convicted of a felony drug offense, he would be prohibited for life from receiving food stamps or welfare. Remember, possession of marijuana was such an offense under the new punitive state and federal drug laws.

Alexander observes that although all of this "reform" was done in the name of fiscal responsibility and reining in big government—the old Southern strategy of transferring it from the federal government to the states, where minority protection ceases to exist—what really was happening

> . . . was radically altering what the funds would be used for. The dramatic shift toward punitiveness resulted in a massive reallocation of public resources. By 1996, the penal budget doubled the amount that had been allocated to AFDC or food stamps. Similarly, funding that had once been used for public housing was being redirected to prison construction. During Clinton's tenure, Washington slashed funding for public housing by $17 billion (a reduction of 61 percent) and boosted corrections by $19 billion (an increase of 171 percent), effectively making the construction of prisons the nation's main housing program for the urban poor."

When Bill Clinton became president in 1992, he brought a routine he had mastered as Governor of Arkansas. It was the routine of increased incarceration and execution while maintaining a patina of racial moderation. This was a public policy akin to the old black-face routine of white comedians supposedly representing the actions of blacks. Indeed, it was a well-practiced role by all "moderate" Southern governors. So, it was no surprise that in 1994 he brought the idea of "three strikes and you're out" to federal sentencing policy. This was part of a larger bill that created many new capital crimes, made life sentences mandatory for certain three-time offenders and granted $16 billion for state prison grants and expanding local and state police.

The $30 billion crime bill was hailed by both Parties as an antidote to the crime epidemic. Of course, there was no crime epidemic. Rather the epidemic consisted of increasing rates of incarceration and execution. As the Justice Policy Institute noted, "the Clinton Administration's 'tough on crime' policies resulted in the largest increases in federal and state prison inmates of any president in American history."

Michelle Alexander sums up Clinton. "In so doing, Clinton—more than any other president—created the current racial undercaste."

Perhaps an argument could be made that creating a new racial undercaste was worth it to protect citizens from truly dangerous people. Nothing could be further from the truth. As of 2005, four out of five drug arrests were for simple possession, not sale. The so-called drug kingpins, though the subject of occasional media report, are not the ones going to prison. As a matter of fact, the majority of people in prison on drug offenses had no prior history of violence or selling drugs. In the Drug War, the law enforcement authorities by and large arrest the minnows and let the sharks go free. The confiscation of property, and federal financial rewards to local law enforcement based on the number of arrests, not the degree of danger, makes this a self-perpetuating policy.

Finally, it is worth examining the Act that was the precursor of what was to come in the Clinton presidency. This one Act was a defining moment in the character of the man, and from it one could have predicted the future should he be elected president.

The Politics of Killing

In January of 1992, Bill Clinton was campaigning for president in New Hampshire. He was embroiled in a scandal about a sexual liaison with Gennifer Flowers. As Governor of Arkansas, he was facing a decision of whether to grant clemency to a condemned African American prisoner. He returned to Arkansas to determine the fate of the prisoner, Rickey Ray Rector.

Rector faced execution for the killing of a white policeman. After shooting the policeman, Rector felt so terrible about the deed that he turned the weapon on himself and shot himself in the head. An emergency operation saved his life but left him essentially lobotomized. Rickey Ray Rector was no longer a functioning human being in the normal sense of the term. Yet the State of Arkansas prosecuted him, sentenced him to death, and incarcerated him on death row. Governor Clinton would decide Rector's future since the courts had turned down the prisoner's appeals.

Marshall Frady records Rectors' situation at Cummins prison:

> Rector, a ponderous two-hundred-and-ninety-eight pound heap—far from the lithe youth he had once been—was alternately "dancing around the cell singing and laughing" in his T-shirt, boxer shorts, and socks, according to the prison's sedulously kept death-watch log, and "howling and barking like a dog." He kept on at this, as indeed he had for most of his ten years in prison—intermittent bursts of barking, baying, then blaring laughter and little gleeful shuffles of dancing, fingers snapping through Friday. That afternoon, after Clinton refused all final entreaties for clemency, Rector sat with one of his attorneys, watching on a TV outside his cell, news reports of his impending execution, two hours away . . . and he abruptly announced, in a thick mumble, "I'm gonna vote for him. Gonna vote for Clinton." It had always been his habit to put aside his dessert until bedtime, and after eating his last meal of steak and fried chicken in gravy, with cherry Kool-Aid, he carefully set aside his helping of pecan pie, to finish later. One of his attorneys had earlier stated that Rector "thinks he'll be back in his cell on Saturday morning. (*The New Yorker*)

Rickey Ray Rector did not return to his cell for his pecan pie. Despite documentation of mental impairment from the surgery, over three inches of the brain was removed, Governor Bill Clinton refused to reverse the jury's decision to impose death and Rickey Ray Rector was executed. In reflecting on the event after the execution, Clinton revealed his priorities: "I can be nicked a lot, but no one can say I'm soft on crime."

The practice of the politics of killing was not unusual for Governor Clinton. He joined a host of Southern governors who participated in state-sanctioned killing since John Spenkelink was electrocuted by the state of Florida on May 25, 1979. Indeed, Clinton had allowed four other executions in Arkansas prior to Rector. Although the diminished capacity of Rickey Ray Rector raised troubling moral considerations for Clinton, he was running for president and fundamentally a calculating politician. The calculation in this instance being executing Rector demonstrated he was tough on crime.

As disturbing as Clinton's participation in killing Rickey Ray Rector was, it was equally chilling that the press and all involved expected precisely that. By 1992, the Disfranchisement Regime had reached the point it had made the taking of black life acceptable and even expected, as long as certain perfunctory procedures were followed. It mattered not that Rickey

Rector had at best an I.Q. of 63 or that the prison chaplain found him utterly mad. Nor was it of concern that killing a human being would become just a matter of political calculus in the presidential race. There was not even consideration, much less discussion, of these and other pertinent points. Rather, any news of the execution was set in the context of "how killing Rector would enhance Clinton's political career."

The Sea Change

In 1993, when Clinton was inaugurated president, there were 350 prisoners per 100,000 citizens in the United States. In 1973, the ratio had been 97.8 per 100,000. Death row had gone from zero in 1973 to almost 3,000 by 1993. President Clinton would work to see these figures augmented. Indeed, in urging the passage of the Anti-Terrorism and Effective Death Penalty Act of 1996, Clinton provided for the removal of appeals so executions could proceed at a faster pace. The Clinton administration, building upon Carter, Reagan and Bush policies, propelled the greatest growth in prison population in the nation's history.

The incarceration and execution policies of these administrations constitute the Era of Disfranchisement. As a result of the manipulation of the criminal justice system, the black population was shattered, especially urban men, and the black minority struggled to survive, leaving such matters as civil rights in the background while striving to make ends meet. (The exception was the growth of the black middle class, which benefited from the gains of the Civil Rights Movement.)

In 25 years, a sea change had occurred. In 1968, a national consensus had emerged which led to a moratorium on executions, culminating in 1972 when the Supreme Court struck down the death penalty in *Furman v. Georgia*. In 1993 a politician who executed a mentally deficient African American during his presidential campaign would be inaugurated. The intervening years from 1973 to 1993 had actually seen the crime rate decline, except when black on black crime was examined in the inner city. Yet the perception, indeed, the fear created amongst the citizenry by the media and politicians, allowed for unprecedented incarceration and death sentences from 1968 to 1993. This policy with its subsequent deleterious effect on black America revealed that the Disfranchisement Era was in full swing.

One woman's account of the phenomenon of fear of crime despite the lowered levels of criminal behavior provides insight into how many Americans felt at the end of the twentieth century. She lived in a "mid-size Pacific Coast city" and experienced some unknown person throwing a rock through her window in the middle of the night.

The expectation of violence—personal, lethal, unpredictable violence—forms a part of the daily outlook of everyone I know. Certainly it's part of mine, I feel as if I've been expecting attack my whole life, believing that times have changed, that random violence is a new invention. I'm sure there are various psychological cul-de-sacs in how such a belief develops, but I need only channel-surf past the network news to know where it really comes from. The anchors with their pliably dour mouths report in racy undertones on one person's misfortune. Congress members intone dire predictions of terror in the city and the point doesn't need to be made out loud—this is your city, your misfortune. This is your future . . . The fear of violence is a national shiver of anticipation, so intense, talked about so much, it is as though the things we fear have already happened to us.

But I got curious, and looked up crime statistics. Violence of the kind the ratings-hungry nightly ratings news prepares us for is actually quite rare in the United States. Any one of us is far more likely to die of pneumonia than to be killed by another person—that's as true in Manhattan as it is in supposedly calmer, smaller cities. What violence occurs is terribly maldistributed, focused tightly on the urban poor and occurring largely among people who know each other, who are victims of sociological and economical circumstances rarely mentioned by news anchors and Congress. Random violence is nothing more than the new American myth, and one has to wonder whom that myth is really serving.

. . . It came to me quite abruptly. After all, it had taken me an absurdly long time to realize what had happened . . . I have been safe all along—but that's not news. (Sallie Tisdale, *The New York Times Magazine*, November 17, 1976)

Marshall McLuhan wrote, "The medium is the message," as a way of describing the impact of television on people. TV creates the illusion of reality in what it presents, whether it is a cartoon or the evening news. By projecting an aura of objectivity, the medium presents only the slice of reality which it believes will win ratings and hence attract advertisers. In this manner, television has focused on crime in the last half of the 20th century, and into the 21st century, and is directly responsible, along with politicians, for the fear Sallie Tisdale so cogently names. In the continual and constant bombardment of images of murders, usually involving black people, with black suspects in custody, there is no consideration of the context of the situation. Rather, the impression is this could happen to you and probably will happen to you, as the images repeat night after night, year after year, decade after decade.

Such a repeated bombardment creates a fear of black men in the white populace and results in such aberrations as the Harvard University police routinely stopping black men at night on the campus. If the student cannot produce an I.D., he is in trouble. If this is happening at Harvard, it takes no leap of imagination to consider what the local police department profile of a criminal suspect looks like. The culture is inculcated with a fear of crime, i.e., of black crime, and especially fear of black men. Thus the receptivity to tougher sentences, more prisons, more executions, which becomes the way to deal with black people.

This culture of fear has been fostered and exploited by every administration since Richard Nixon, the latest version being the War on Terror (more on that later), and there appears to be no end in sight. As Sallie Tisdale notes: "I have been safe all along—but that's not news." This information will not be provided by television because it is not "sexy"; it doesn't sell.

Coupled with politicians shamelessly using crime or terror to pander to voters fears, the tyranny of the majority marches on in ways Tocqueville could never imagine but which serve to illustrate the profundity of his observation of the fear of the tyranny of the majority against the racial minorities as the greatest danger to democracy in the United States of America.

Michelle Alexander states:

> Once again, in response to a major disruption in the prevailing social order—this time the civil rights gains of the 1960s—a new system of racialized social control was created by exploiting the vulnerabilities and racial resentments of poor and working class whites. More than two million people found themselves behind bars at the turn of the twenty-first century, and millions more were relegated to the margins of mainstream society, banished to a political and social space not unlike Jim Crow, where discrimination in employment, housing and access to education was perfectly legal and where they could be denied the right to vote. The system functioned relatively automatically, and the prevailing system of racial meanings, identities, and ideologies already seemed natural. Ninety percent of those admitted to prison for drug offenses in many states were black or Latino, yet the mass incarceration of communities of color was explained in race-neutral terms, an adaptation to the needs and demands of the current political climate. The New Jim Crow was born.

CHAPTER 13. WILLIE DARDEN

"Hey, home boy!" The greeting came out of the cage where the prisoners were waiting to be called in for my visit in the Colonel's room at the Florida State Prison. My friend, Willie Darden, ebony skin glistening with the sweat of F.S.P. in the spring, face alight with a big smile despite the cramped confines of the cage with the other prisoners, brought a chuckle to my heart. I grasped him on his shoulder through the bars and told the guards to bring him inside the Colonel's room.

Willie understood that I usually saved him for my last visit of the morning or the afternoon on those marathon days at F.S.P. It was a totally selfish act on my part. He was so much fun and we shared so much from our North Carolina upbringing; I was revived by his presence. The more difficult cases I visited initially knowing that Willie was the end of the visits.

So, how had I, a white man, become Willie Darden's homeboy? Willie and I hailed from eastern North Carolina. I was born in Pitt County, Willie in the adjacent Greene County. Willie was born in 1933 and I in 1946. I was born into the white segregated world and Willie the black segregated world. It is difficult to portray just how separate and unequal our lives were in that society but the Rev. Leon White, an African-American born in Franklin County in 1932, gives a picture of eastern North Carolina: "In 1860, slaves constituted half the total population of Greene County; in 1930, blacks constituted half the population. (In the entire state) blacks owned only 4%of taxable wealth and the average black income was less than $1,000 annually. Four out of five black families were tenant farmers or sharecroppers."

Willie Darden's mother gave birth to Willie in a state where infant mortality was fifth highest in the United States, with 9 out of every 1,000 infants perishing.

Willie's mother, who was fifteen when she birthed Willie, died in childbirth two years later.

Willie's maternal grandfather, with whom Willie was very close, was the son of a slave and ran a "two horse" farm. Of course, the horses were utilized to plow the fields, and as soon as Willie was old enough to help he was assisting his grandfather in the field.

In a segregated world with no money, education was hard to come by. However, Willie persevered at the Zechariah School for the Colored through the eighth grade. The average age of completed education for blacks was the second grade. But with his grandfathers' death, school became a luxury and he had to be the man of the family. His aunt recalled him as child: "Because I spent so much time with Willie, Jr. . . . I was as close to him as if he were my own. He went to Sunday School every week with my children, and I know for a fact that that child was always a solid rock."

The aunt described the family as a "first-class colored family in Greene County. The white families would hire our husbands and children to work in the tobacco factories during the season because (we) were known to be a hard-working and religious family."

Within his aunt's words lay the reality of life in rural Greene County. The white people ruled through ownership of land and what little industry there was, dominated and controlled the political process and determined what tax money was spent for whom. It was the classic separate and unequal system throughout the state and the region.

In neighboring Pitt County, where I was born in 1946, it was very much the same. Greenville, although barely a town of 10,000 souls, was a veritable metropolis compared to the isolated farming life Willie endured. Yet I observed the "white" and "colored" drinking fountains. I went to segregated schools from the first through the tenth grade when *Brown v. Board of Education* finally began to take hold. I knew of the epithet "nigger" because it was commonly used by almost every white person I encountered except for Mom and her mother, my Ma-Ma.

But despite the vast racial divide that separated Willie Darden and me, we were also kindred spirits. We were of the same culture. Despite the twisted, inverted, apartheid state our lives endured growing up, we had experienced it in the same part of the world. As Willie put it: We were "homeboys."

For me, this was an easy and natural relationship despite the walls and bars that separated us. Maybe my two years living in East Harlem, as well as my ongoing relationships with black people growing up in the South despite segregation, explained my comfort with different races. Maybe it was my Mom's stern early instruction in the area of race. I really didn't know. I just felt completely at ease with Willie and proud to be his homeboy.

I first came to know Willie in the spring of 1979 when his initial death warrant was signed simultaneously with John Spenkelink's. In the years that followed that fateful spring, Willie had survived several more death warrants and Governor Bob Graham's tenure in the state capitol. (Bob Graham, the first and foremost practitioner of the politics of killing in the New South, rode his record number of death warrant signings into the U.S. Senate.) Graham was succeeded by a Republican Governor Bob Martinez and there was no hope that he would do anything different than Bob Graham. In the spring of 1988, Willie Darden faced a seventh death warrant. ABC featured him on a news program and coined the term "The Dean of Death Row" to describe Willie's situation.

The 1987 U.S. Supreme Court decision in *McCleskey v. Kemp* made it abundantly clear that two facts prevailed in the administration of the death penalty: 1) The law was demonstrably racially discriminatory. 2) The Court would not redress the issue. Justice Lewis Powell authored the majority opinion (5–4), a decision in retirement he would publicly regret, and I thoroughly enjoyed Gail Rowland, a paralegal, donning her black robed hand puppet doing her "Mr. Justice Powell" mimicry, as she so often did around Florida execution crises. Unfortunately, that was no longer possible because Gail, along with justice in the *McCleskey* case, moved elsewhere by the time of Willie's final death warrant.

Race was the theme of Willie Darden's life that led to death row at F.S.P. After his grandfather's death in Greene County, Willie's stepmother deserted the family. He was placed in foster care. In a virtual state of slavery with his foster family, worked like a beast in the field, Willie began to steal to obtain food and clothing. Eventually caught stealing from a farmer's mailbox, he was sent to the National School for Boys at the age of 16. A segregated facility in North Carolina, it served as Willie's apprenticeship in how criminal behavior enables one to survive in an apartheid society.

After his release Willie began a series of odd jobs. In 1953 he met his future wife. They dated for two years before marrying in 1955. In January of 1956, Willie was arrested for cashing a forged check for $48.00. He was sentenced to four years in prison. His wife at the time recalls: "It broke my heart that they put him away so long because I knew that he had done it to buy us some food."

When Willie and I were growing up, white people in the South divided black people into distinct categories: "good niggers" and "bad niggers." The law was the arbiter under which category a black person might fall. Of course, the law was merely an instrument of social control by an apartheid society as it had been since the 1600s in the colony of Virginia. When Willie and I grew up, the judges were white, the jurors were white, the lawyers were white, the prosecutors were white (today 98% of prosecutors in death penalty cases are white) and black people were under the boot heel of a segregated regime. The law kept them that way.

So, it was no surprise that when Willie walked into the courtroom in 1974, facing a murder charge in rural Florida, everyone except Willie was white. The trial, transferred from the murder site in Lakeland to Inverness, had Willie as the only black person in the courtroom. As Willie told me: "Joe, I looked around at all those white faces and I knew how it was gonna come out. I was like a raisin in a bowl of milk."

It was a classic recipe for the death penalty in the South. A black man accused of killing a white man. It was white justice v. black bestiality—the prosecutor described Willie as subhuman throughout the trial with such stereotypical portrayals as: "Willie Darden is an animal who should be placed on a leash . . .As far as I'm concerned, this animal . . . " The prosecutors expressed the desire that Willie be seated at counsel table "with no face, blown away by a shotgun."

A savage attack by the prosecutor was unchallenged by defense counsel. A court-appointed lawyer, as is true in 9 out of 10 death penalty cases, he was worse than inept. He refused to call an eyewitness who vouched for Willie's whereabouts near the time the crime occurred.

The trial took place in January of 1974. Christine Bass, a white woman from Lakeland, came to the courthouse with information exonerating Willie Darden. She spoke to his lawyer and told him the information. It established a clear alibi for Willie.

Christine Bass was at her home in Lakeland when a black man, Willie Darden, rang her doorbell. He explained his car had broken down and he would like to call a tow truck. She allowed him to make the call and he went back outside to be with his car. She estimated the timeframe to have been from 4:00 to 5:30 p.m. on September 8, 1973.

The police estimate of the time of the crime at a furniture store in Lakeland wavered from 6:00 to 6:30 p.m. There was no way Willie could have been at Christine Bass's home with a broken down car and made it to the furniture store for a robbery/murder.

The defense lawyer did no investigation. He assumed his client was guilty. After all, all the other white people were telling him Willie Darden committed the crime. Then there was Christine Bass. He did not allow her to testify or investigate her story.

The only testimony that linked Willie to the crime was eyewitness testimony. Although laymen think eyewitness testimony is a sure thing, those familiar with such testimony know it can be highly suspect. This is especially true in a cross-racial crime. As the old Southern saying goes about black people: "They all look alike anyway." The eyewitnesses in Willie's case were white.

When "they all look alike" combines with a criminal justice system that is actually discriminatory in the application of the death penalty, justice is a rare commodity. In Willie's case the eyewitness testimony was most suspect.

The widow, Mrs. Turman, and her husband operated a furniture store in Lakeland, Florida. Mrs. Turman initially informed police she could not remember what the subject looked like or what he was wearing. After some time discussing things with the police, and on the day after her husband's funeral, she was led into a small courtroom where only one black person was present. The black man sat at the defense table and the prosecutor asked Mrs. Turman if "this man sitting here" was "the man who shot your husband." Willie Darden was the only black man in the room and since the assailant was identified as a black person, Willie was identified by Mrs. Turman as the murderer.

The prosecution had one other eyewitness, a neighbor who came over when he heard shots and was shot himself. This young man was in a hospital bed and was shown six photographs. Willie Darden's picture was among them and it was the only one labeled with "Sheriff's Department, Bartow, Florida." He chose Willie as the man who had shot him.

The police airbrushed major discrepancies in the eyewitness accounts in order to identify Willie. The color of the assailant's shirt, whether he had a moustache, his height—5'6, 5'8" and 5'10" and finally 6'. All that really seemed to matter, however, was the unanimous identification that the assailant was "colored." If they all look alike, and this one was a bad nigger according to his criminal record, what difference does it really make as long as you get one of them off the streets?

On January 23, 1974, Willie Darden, forty-four years old, was sentenced to death by electrocution. The white people in that courtroom never dreamed they would hear anymore about this uppity nigger until he was electrocuted at the Florida State Prison. Little did they know they had launched a high profile death case.

The reason Willie's case would not go away was the dedication of Christine Bass. She could not keep from talking about the case and finally in a 1979 post-trial hearing, her testimony was given for the record. Unfortunately, her story was not corroborated and there the matter remained as the case wound through the courts until 1986.

Governor Graham made a point of mentioning Willie's case as he campaigned across the state for re-election in 1983. He had signed two death warrants on Willie and the courts had stopped each one for further consideration. He was making Willie into a poster boy for the death penalty in Florida. After re-election, Governor Graham signed Willie's third death warrant, setting the execution for September 2, 1985.

This warrant brought me to Starke for what I feared would be a final visit with Willie. The U.S. Supreme Court was considering Willie's case. Given the rightward march of the justices under the coffin builder, Chief Justice William Rehnquist, it was not a hopeful scenario.

In the emotional visit that is deathwatch, the most difficult aspect is often the pain experienced by the family and loved ones of the condemned. As the emotional vise is tightened with each passing minute, the pressure often becomes excruciating. Given that reality, I was most concerned for Felicia, Willie's girl friend. She was a middle-aged Hispanic woman with an incomplete grasp of the English language. The legal mechanism of the killing machinery totally eluded her; she just loved Willie.

The first day of September found Margaret Vandiver, Felicia and I in our friend Mike Radelet's house in Gainesville, Florida. We were waiting to hear from the U.S. Supreme Court before driving over to our scheduled visit with Willie at the prison in Starke, about an hour's drive away. We were almost twelve hours from the electrocution that would be at 7:00 a.m. on September 2.

Margaret, Mike and I were arranging who would drive whom to the prison while Felicia watched television. The local news was full of Willie's pending execution. Suddenly, a piercing wail slammed into us. Felicia grabbed her purse and ran out the door. We turned to catch the last of the broadcast. Willie had been turned down by the Supreme Court. I bolted out the door to catch Felicia because I didn't want her driving, as distraught as she was.

I slid into the front seat of the car and grabbed Felicia's hand, which was turning the keys in the ignition. "Felicia, don't drive this car. You're too upset. You won't do Willie any good if you wreck this car trying to drive to the prison."

Felicia broke down, sobbing in my arms, moaning: "They're going to kill Willie." I sought to comfort her. I told her we had not heard from the lawyers yet, so we needed to hang on and make a plan.

Although I was seeking to provide comfort, I was despairing as well. Felicia's wail had been an outward manifestation of the desperation we all felt about this decision. "Sweet Jesus, have mercy upon us," I muttered.

I drove us to the prison and we waited for Margaret Vandiver to bring the confirming news from the lawyers so we would be able to explain to Willie all we knew.

The Supreme Court vote had been 5–4 against Willie. It had come around 6:00 p.m. There was nothing left, legally. We entered the prison to be with Willie.

As was customary under deathwatch, this visit would last until midnight. It would be a non-contact visit, through the glass partition. Then Willie would have a one-hour contact visit with Felicia. At 1:00 a.m., I would accompany Willie back to his cell and spend the night with him outside his cell as his spiritual adviser.

We had brought a tape player with us and played songs from Sweet Honey in the Rock. Their songs of oppression and liberation, of freedom and joy, echoed through the non-contact visitation room. Willie could have been one of their songs given his life and impending killing.

Willie tried to keep things upbeat. Margaret and I migrated to the end of the partition so he and Felicia could have as much time as they needed. He summoned us all back together after a long visit with Felicia. He wanted us to "be keeping up the struggle. Not letting these people defeat us."

A few minutes before midnight, our parting time, I eased out the door and sat in one of the ubiquitous plastic chairs of deathwatch. I shut my eyes, prayed and tried to make this nightmare go away.

Suddenly, I heard the sound of rapid footsteps. A lawyer came running down the hallway. She was saying something about a stay of execution. I was incredulous. How could this be?

Margaret came out of the non-contact area and we heard the incredible story. Although they had been denied 5–4 on the request for a stay of execution, the lawyers realized they had the four votes needed for the case to be accepted as a *certiorari* petition, which meant the Court would hear oral argument. Justice Lewis Powell, realizing four of his colleagues felt very strongly about this case, switched his vote to grant the stay of execution upon petition of the lawyers. The courtly Virginian saved Willie's life as courtesy to his fellow justices. Willie would survive Governor Graham's repeated efforts to kill him.

Governor Bob was about to become Senator Bob, in large measure due to his relentless signing of death warrants. He initialed 155 in eight years and electrocuted 18 people. Some political observers saw him as a possible presidential candidate. It appeared the political reward for killing citizens, especially black citizens, was a continued political career at a higher level.

Unfortunately, barring an unexpected change of judicial heart, the votes were not there for Willie Darden to prevail in the Supreme Court. The case was briefed and argued. Governor Bob Martinez, a Republican former mayor of Tampa, had succeeded Bob Graham. There was no hope of clemency from Martinez, as he embarked on an even brisker pace of signing death warrants than his predecessor.

With all political and legal avenues foreclosed, none of us were hopeful. When the Supreme Court ruled 5–4 against Willie, Justice Harry Blackmun penned a bitter dissent:

> Thus, at bottom, this case rests on the jury's determination of the credibility of three witnesses . . . I cannot conclude that McDaniels' [the prosecutor] sustained attack on Darden's very humanity did not affect the jury's ability to judge the credibility question on the real evidence before it. Because I believe that he did not have a trial that was fair, I would reverse Darden's conviction; I would not allow him to go to his death until he has been convicted at a fair trial. I believe this Court must do more than wring its hands when a state uses improper legal standard to select juries in capital cases and permits prosecutors to pervert the adversary process. I therefore dissent.

10. *The Florida electric chair. Photo: Scharlette Holdman.*

Justice Blackmun clearly had Willie's case on his mind in the summer of 1987. He spoke at a judicial conference of the Eighth Circuit Court of Appeals: "If ever a man received an unfair trial, it was Darden. He may be guilty, I don't know, but he got a runaround in that courtroom."

The public campaign on Willie's behalf intensified. Thousands of petitions flooded Governor Martinez' office in Tallahassee. ABC's program

"20/20" and CBS on its "W. 57th Street" did news magazine stories on Willie, which aired in January of 1988.

The problem was the inability to overcome the trial court record. Willie was a lone black man in a sea of white in the courtroom. His own lawyer referred to him as a "nigger." The prosecutor pictured him as inhuman. Christine Bass was not put on the stand. It was an all white jury. It was a historic Southern recipe for a modern lynching.

Christine Bass, having been haunted by this case for years, one day mentioned it to the Rev. Sam Sparks, a chaplain she knew at a local hospital. Rev. Sparks was startled to hear what Christine Bass had to say because he had rushed to the scene of the crime as the minister to the victim and his widow. He had a clear recollection of the time sequence and the trauma of the widow. He had assumed Willie was guilty and not paid any attention to the facts of the case. When Ms. Bass explained the time Willie was at her house and Rev. Sparks recalled the time he was at the victims' furniture store, he realized Willie could not have been in two places at once. So, Rev. Sparks and Ms. Bass, whose stories corroborated each other, filed affidavits on the record indicating verification of Willie's alibi story. But we could never get a hearing to put the evidence on record, and the trial court record remained the engine driving the train to the electric chair.

Among those contacting Governor Martinez was Andrei Sakharov, the 1975 winner of the Nobel Peace Prize. His message came to the heart of the matter:

> I ask you to intervene in the affair of Willie Darden. I am convinced that capital punishment is an inhuman institution for which there can be no room in a civilized, democratic society.

> Injustice, a mistake in relation to an innocent person, cannot be set right. Moreover, capital punishment may not be applied in cases' where there's at least a shadow of doubt of the legality of the sentence, or the unbiased nature of the legal system for racial or other reasons. I asked that the death sentence for Willie Darden be revoked.

The torrent of words, deeds, protests, crashed upon the Florida ship of state killing. But it was to no avail because Governor Martinez signed Willie Darden's seventh death warrant and set the execution for the Ides of March, 1988.

***

Becca and I had brought our newborn baby Amelia home after her birth on March 5, 1988. After Governor Martinez signed Willie's death warrant on March 8, I received a call from one of Willie's lawyers. He conveyed Willie's request that I not come down there to be with him the night of his execution.

He knew how much our newborn daughter meant to us and did not want me leaving Becca and Amelia to come to deathwatch.

I certainly did not want to leave my family. But my homeboy was about to be electrocuted and I could not remain with Becca and Amelia no matter how much I wanted to do so. I flew down to Starke, bringing my communion kit and legal pad, joining Willie on death watch on Q-wing.

The evening of March 14 found me ensconced in the all too familiar noncontact visiting area at the Florida State Prison. Willie had a final visit with Felicia. We had communion for a final time. After the visit, I accompanied him back to Q-wing. A last ditch round of appeals had been denied by the U.S. Supreme Court and we knew this time there would be no stopping the killing machinery.

Willie's cell was full of correspondence from around the world. He sorted through it, handing me some to respond to and giving instructions about others. Since this death warrant was signed for a week period, rather that the customary 30 days, it was impossible for Willie to respond to everyone as he wished.

It was past two a.m. He had about five hours left to live. He started calling me Dad, asking me how I liked the sound of it. He was joyful for Becca and me as new parents. We shared a couple of Jamaican cigars, smoking and visiting down the hall from the death chamber. Reminiscing about North Carolina, his children, and the struggle for justice, there was neither dearth of conversation nor any hurry to say anything. The night moved on toward morning.

Willie had requested I witness the execution. Now, I had a cardinal rule in ministering to the condemned, and that was not watching them be killed. But Willie really wanted me there. I felt my insides turn over as I agreed to honor his request. We discussed where I would be so he could find me when he entered the death chamber. I told him I would be holding out my pendant, a gold symbol of the equal marks in the world under the cross (the symbol of the Committee of Southern Churchmen given to me by Will Campbell) for him to focus on. He liked that and asked me to be standing, not sitting in the witness chair, so I would be easier to see.

Although I was exhausted, my adrenaline had kicked in and I was quite alert. I noticed the light creeping through the window at the top of the wall and realized it would soon be time for me to go. We held hands and had a final prayer.

At 5:30, the guard arrived with the gray briefcase that contained the tools of barbering for Willie's electrocution. Willie had already shaved his head but they would do it again and also shave the hair off his right calf. This would allow the electricity to flow cleanly into the body from the attachments.

I told Willie I loved him. We embraced through the bars. I turned and walked down the hall, escorted to the cafeteria.

All the witnesses to the execution were fed breakfast in the prison cafeteria, a nice Southern amenity to the process of slaughtering a human being, compliments of the state of Florida.

I had no desire to eat. I sat alone, sipped an orange juice, ignored the chitchat of the other witnesses. The flag of the state of Florida and the flag of the United States hung high on the walls. So this is what those flags symbolized? An institution of killing citizens overlaid with a patina of due process. Complete with breakfast before the witnesses observed a cold-blooded state murder. As the death certificate always recorded after an execution, "cause of death—homicide." And, irony of ironies, the Florida flag had inscribed upon it "In God We Trust."

Oh, yeah, I thought, let's bring God into this unholy proceeding. The state-promulgated killing was the opposite of trusting in God. It was the exercise of the power of taking life, an act of idolatry. Or as the Gospel of John put it, in describing Satan as the murderer from the beginning, that is what the death penalty was: it was an evil process, conceived solely to murder from the beginning. It usurped the sovereignty of God.

As I thought of all those I worked with on death row, not a single person was a murderer from the beginning. No one on death row was born a killer. Each had a unique story and only the State was barbaric enough to be a murderer from the beginning.

At 6:45 we were summoned and led outside to two white vans. It was a gorgeous morning. We clambered into the vans and were driven to Q-wing. I had witnessed this scene from across the road in the cow pasture many times as a protester. Now I was in the belly of the beast.

We exited the vans when they stopped outside the death chamber, and proceeded through the door into the witness room. There were three rows of white, high backed chairs facing the window. Everyone filed in and found a seat. I remained standing in the rear, as I had arranged with Willie.

The clock on the wall behind the electric chair read 6:58. Promptly at 7:00, the door opened and Willie was escorted into the death chamber. He was manacled at his ankles and his arms were handcuffed to a chain around his waist. His bearing was erect and proud. The light glistened off his bald ebony head. He looked like an African king.

The guards removed the shackles and waist chain. He was put in the electric chair and strapped down: arms, chest and legs fastened with big leather straps. Willie looked for me as they fastened him down to the chair. He met my gaze and smiled. Willie then met the eyes of each witness, surveying each one individually.

Willie Darden was asked if he had a final statement. He said, "Yes." The voice came out clearly and firmly:

> I tell you that I am not guilty of the charge for which I am about to be executed. I bear no guilt or ill will for any of you. I am at peace with myself, with the world, with each of you. I say to my friends and supporters around the world, I love each and every one of you. Your love and support have been a great comfort to me in my struggle for justice and freedom.

Willie found me and fixed his vision on the gold symbol of the C.O.S.C. I held out before me. The symbol of God in the world, for all of us equally, united us in life and would do so in death.

The guards roughly pushed Willie's head back and he winced with pain. They strapped his chin. Still maintaining eye contact with me, he winked at me. Then he lifted his thumb on his left hand upward, the "it's all right" sign. Then, as the black mask was dropped over his face, Willie waved good-bye with his left hand. I thought I would break down on the spot.

Three charges of electricity went surging though Willie's body. A voice announced: "The sentence of the court against Willie Darden has been carried out. He was pronounced dead at 7:12 a.m."

When I emerged from the witness van into the bright morning sunlight, Margaret Vandiver was waiting for me. It was so good to see a dear friend. She asked if I was all right and I said yes. I grasped the cross Willie had bequeathed to Felicia, and my last mission was to deliver it.

Margaret and I drove back to the airport and visited. She was heading to Boston and I to home. I was stunned by the events I had gone through. Not just the last twenty-four hours but the cumulative effect of all the executions from John Spenkelink in 1979 through Willie in 1988. From Florida to Alabama, to Virginia, to North Carolina, to Louisiana, to Mississippi, to Texas, to South Carolina, to Georgia, I had visited death rows, come to love the individuals condemned there and beheld their extermination by the state killing machinery.

In 1979 John and Willie had their death warrants signed together. John was the victim of electrocution that spring. Willie went through six more death warrants until he was destroyed in the spring of 1988. They had served as bookends supporting me as I worked among the condemned that were the books on death rows throughout the South.

Now both my bookends were gone and I was falling into a vortex, without the support of my home boy and my brother.

* * *

He is free today, free at last as he was free at First
Black as the Bluemen of the Nubian Desert
Teeth snow white and not a one missing at 60 years old
   A smile as broad as Satchmo's and
A deep inner Strength that allowed the younger
   Ones to look to
     Shango
The African name that Willie Jasper Darden
   Claimed
The name of the Electric Lord of the Storm
Known far and around as a Poet/writer
Someone to draw flowers and hearts and Dragons
On a letter to you girl
In his youth, he was a fighter for prizes, too
In the ring
Such a body, such hands, indeed
Are dangerous and knock men dumb
Smart ones on the row and cons at large
Gave this old man respect
He said that he had lived well: home, wife, children, car
Before he came to hell
The death house, Florida State Prison
He said that he did not do the crime
Time and time and time again, he asked for a
Friend . . . (of the court?) he cried
Innocence, he cried foul but the minions of
Death
Howl and howled for his blood and screamed for
his life
and now he is free at last as he was free at first
and the worst is yet to come.
The Bible says that the Jasper stone is precious
And Beautiful, too.

—Delbert Tibbs, March 15, 1988

(Delbert Tibbs resided on death row with Willie Darden in the mid-1970s. Delbert had made the mistake of hitchhiking through Florida while he was seeking to discover himself. As a result, this young African American was sent to death row for a crime he did not commit. He was finally exonerated and returned to Chicago to live and write poetry. This poem originally appeared in *Hospitality*, the newsletter of The Open Door in May of 1988. It is reprinted with permission.)

11. Willie Darden. Photo: Doug Magee

CHAPTER 14. THE REGIME OF DISFRANCHISEMENT II (2000–2008)

George W. Bush, the Republican candidate, came into office having lost the popular vote but winning a 5–4 vote of the Supreme Court that provided his appointment to the Presidency by five Republican appointees on the Court (*Bush v. Gore*). The decision was so beyond the pale that the majority instructed that the opinion not be used in the future as a precedent. But just as with Bill Clinton, a look at the death penalty record of this former Southern governor provides a glimpse of what we should have expected from a new President Bush.

As Governor of Texas, George W. Bush executed 152 people in a five-year period. This is more than thirty killings a year. It is also more than any other modern governor had done at the time. He was unstinting in his support of the death penalty. "I'm confident that every person that has been put to death in Texas under my watch has been guilty of the crime charged, and has had full access to the courts." What he did not discuss, however, was how he made the decisions on granting clemency.

Perhaps there was a reason George Bush was not candid about the decision making process. When a death row prisoner's clemency petition was filed with Governor Bush, it was reviewed by Alberto Gonzalez, his legal counsel. Gonzalez then provided a précis of the case to Bush. The précis consisted solely of the prosecutions position regarding the case.

Without discussion of any position but the prosecutor's, there would be no concern about the following facts found in some of the 152 cases. A *Chicago Tribune* study revealed that in about a third of the cases the defendant's lawyer was subsequently disbarred or otherwise sanctioned. In at least forty cases lawyers presented no defense evidence or only one witness at the sentencing phase of the trial. And then there were the psychiatrists, known in the trade as Doctors of Death. These doctors provided expert testimony, based on the examination of a defendant's record but not the defendant, that the defendant was a "future danger" to society and would commit another violent crime. Although this practice is condemned by the national professional psychiatric organization, these Doctors of Death testified in at least 29 cases and continue do so.

In response to this information, Governor Bush had this to say: "We've adequately answered innocence or guilt in every case," as well as the defendants having had "full access to a fair trial."

And on that note, courtesy of the U.S. Supreme Court, the governor of Texas became president of the United States. Hence the Regime of the Disfranchisement resumed with the Republicans controlling the Congress, judiciary and executive branches of government for the next eight years.

Section I. The War on Drugs

Any consideration of the administration of President George W. Bush must take account of September 11, 2001. The criminal attacks upon the World Trade Center and the Pentagon were publicized as the work of zealots for a cause. Yet it was not the warped fundamentalist interpretation of the Koran by a terrorist group that George Bush focused upon in the wake of the attacks. It was how to augment executive power to respond to such an attack and of course that meant raising the banner of war. In this case, the War on Terror would do.

We find a similar dissonance between Governor Bush's statements and the reality of the death penalty in Texas, and the statements versus the reality on the ground when discussing the "War on Terror" (a phrase Bush brought into existence during a speech on September 20, 2001). Indeed, we need to use a reality seine, much like casting for gold in a creek, to find the nuggets of truth around and under the words of President Bush. Although there are many examples, we illustrate the point with this public remark on October 5, 2007, responding to questions about the United States torturing "unlawful enemy combatants" captured during the War on Terror: "This government does not torture people. You know, we stick to U.S. law and our international obligations." On December 6, 2007, the CIA admitted it destroyed videotapes which detailed torture going back to 2002.

The Open Society, an organization concerned with human rights, issued a report on the practice of "extraordinary rendition and detention." The report, published in March of 2013, documented 136 individuals who were tortured under the Bush Administration. Of course, since the program was secret, there is no telling what the total might be.

The "unlawful enemy combatant" would be arrested, transported to a "black site" and tortured. Fifty four countries cooperated with the United States in this program. Some of those involved in transporting prisoners to the black sites were Thailand, Poland, Romania, Spain, Portugal, Afghanistan, Australia, Canada, the United Kingdom and even Sweden. The process was known as "extraordinary rendition."

It is important to clarify the intentionally vague bureaucratic language of the War on Terror. "Extraordinary rendition" is a euphemism for kidnapping someone, transporting him to a black site—a place of torture—and torturing him. The person designated as an "unlawful enemy combatant" has no due process, no court hearing, no chance for anything but "enhanced interrogation techniques." Needless to say, this process leads to mistakes. Here are three of the "unlawful enemy combatants" and their stories.

- Muhammed al-Zery taught chemistry and physics at Cairo University. He was leafleting, protesting excesses of the Egyptian government. Persecuted by authorities, he sought asylum in Sweden. His asylum petition was dismissed by the Swedish government and he was turned over to the C.I.A. He was "extraordinarily rendered" back to Egypt where he suffered "enhanced interrogation techniques" that included being manacled to an electrified bed and also his genitals were shocked. After two years he was released.
- Ahmed Agiza was also seeking asylum in Sweden. His request was denied and the C.I.A. "rendered" him back to Egypt. Again, "enhanced interrogation techniques" which included shocks to the genitals were administered.
- Maher Arar, a Canadian and Syrian citizen, was stopped at JFK Airport in New York City and held for interrogation for two weeks. He was then "extraordinarily rendered" back to Jordan, where he was beaten, and then on to Syria to a "black site." There he experienced "enhanced interrogation techniques."

All of the above horrors were authorized in a "Memo of Notification," which the government refuses to release but is referenced in several C.I.A. documents. President Bush directed the "MON" to the CIA on September 17, 2001. The C.I.A. was following orders from the self-described no torture President.

The central lock up for terrorist suspects became the prison at Guantanamo Bay, Cuba. The Bush administration obtained legal authorization from itself to ignore the Geneva Conventions in terms of Guantanamo but this was reversed by the U.S. Supreme Court in 2006. As of March 2013, there were 166 prisoners subject to "advanced interrogation techniques."

As for the effectiveness of a program that was in violation of the Geneva Convention and international treaties, a CIA official had this to say to *The Washington Post*: "They picked up the wrong people, who had no information. In many, many cases, there was only some vague association" with terrorism.

On September 16, 2001, Vice President Dick Cheney commented on "Meet the Press": "We have to work the dark side, if you will. Spend time in the shadows of the intelligence world. A lot of what needs to be done here will have to done quietly, without any discussion." And so it was.

Joining Cheney in the cabal of darkness was Defense Secretary Donald Rumsfeld. In November of 2002 he flew to Santiago, Chile, to meet with South American leaders. He was selling the War on Terror. He sought to recruit South American countries to engage in extraordinary rendition and black sites. He advocated a Patriot Act for South American countries. Rumsfeld: "The kind of fears we face are global . . . These new threats must be countered with new capabilities."

Although South American countries refused to join the United States in the War on Terror, the head of the Argentine army was echoing Rumsfeld's theme after the Defense Secretary departed: "Defense must be treated as an integral matter," which means no distinction between "internal and external security." The army would be involved in crime fighting, which means complete militarization of society. Of course, this takes a country perilously close to a totalitarian state.

The Patriot Act was passed in the wake of the September 11th attacks. It ceded civil liberties to an alarming degree and dramatically expanded the power of the state in surveillance. In the mass hysteria after 9/11, the patriotic theme was exploited to pass the Patriot Act and achieve stunning access to the private information of U.S. citizens. Only the unauthorized disclosure of this program by Eric Snowden in 2013, a program administered by the National Security Agency (NSA), gave us a clue of the depth of the NSA's penetration into billions of bits of data from ordinary Americans.

In addition to the War on Terror, there was the matter of two other wars: Operation Enduring Freedom, launched on October 7, 2001, against Afghanistan and the invasion of Iraq on March 20, 2003. Although these wars cost thousands of U.S. soldiers' lives, with thousands maimed as well, not to mention the thousands of civilian casualties, neither accomplished the stated goal. Although the brutal Taliban government was taken down in Afghanistan, Osama bin Laden and his network fled the country and continued to operate for another ten years from a base in adjoining Pakistan. And the rationale given for invading Iraq, that there were weapons of mass destruction and Saddam Hussein was providing support to Osama bin Laden, proved to be false. The public was misled into a war which toppled Hussein. Perhaps one of the real reasons for the war was that he had tried to have George Bush's father killed, but all this achieved nothing except exacerbate the relations with Muslims throughout the world.

With the three wars going on simultaneously, Terror, Afghanistan and Iraq, it was easy to forget the War on Drugs was also in high gear within the United States. The incarceration rate continued to rise until it reached two million. This made the United States the leader in imprisonment, in terms of absolute number of prisoners as well as per capita, in the world.

The Patriot Act provided increased surveillance capacity on American citizens so that the reality of a police state, as advocated by Defense Secretary Rumsfeld in his trip to Chile, became more of a possibility than at any previous time in the nation's history. The ability to disfranchise the citizenry had reached new heights.

Section II. The Courts

As we have noted in earlier historical periods of government in the United States, what separates a classification of a regime from an era is the appointment of judges. President George W. Bush appointed 327 judges, 256 of them male, 71 female, 30 Latino and 4 Asian/Pacific Islander. He also appointed John Roberts as Chief Justice and Samuel Alito as Associate Justice to the Supreme Court. This took place with the Republicans in control of Congress and the Executive, as well as the Judiciary, interlocking the three branches of government in a continued effort to disfranchise citizens.

A classic example of the Regime in action is the role of the FISA Court in determining who gets picked up for extraordinary rendition and detention. This court supposedly serves as a check against terror in the issuance of an order to apprehend an enemy combatant. In reality, the FISA court simply rubber stamps whatever request is brought before it. Indeed, it functions more like Governor of Texas George Bush deciding clemency in a death penalty case than any true deliberative body. As we noted earlier, Bush was given a précis of the case which contained only the prosecution's position. The FISA Court is presented an argument with only the prosecution's version as to why to pick someone up. As with Governor Bush and the death penalty, the rate at which extraordinary rendition is blocked is about 1%.

The FISA Court is chosen by the Chief Justice of the Supreme Court, and since 1954 that office has been held by a Republican. As noted earlier, Republicans tend to favor the prosecution's presentation; and especially when it is the only side represented, one's chances of avoiding apprehension, extraordinary rendition and detention are miniscule. Chief Justice John Roberts routinely appoints Republicans to the FISA Court and they almost invariably grant the government's request for extraordinary rendition.

Of course, we are not merely discussing the FISA Court. Rather, we are discussing the entire federal judiciary. Two Tennessee death penalty cases, with which the author was intimately involved, reveal the impact of the

Bush appointees in death penalty cases. (For a detailed examination of the entire machinery of killing in these cases see *The Inferno: A Southern Morality Tale* by this author.)

The Sixth Circuit Court of Appeals

The cases of Paul House and Philip Workman provide insight into the impact of the judiciary under the Disfranchisement Regime. Paul House was convicted of a murder he did not commit in Union County, east Tennessee. Philip Workman experienced the same fate in Memphis, west Tennessee. Each man was convicted of killing a white person, which places them squarely within the calculus of *McCleskey v. Kemp* which reveals heightened likelihood of the death penalty for killers of whites. For Philip, convicted of shooting a policeman, the echoes of McCleskey's case are particularly haunting because Warren did not slay the policeman he was convicted of killing, either. Rather, Philip Workman, Warren McCleskey and Troy Davis (another Georgia death penalty case) were assisted in their convictions by police and prosecutors using unscrupulous tactics to obtain convictions for murders that involved policemen. It did not matter that Philip, Warren and Troy did not kill the policemen. Someone had to be condemned, and they would do as well as anyone else.

Paul House was prosecuted in Union County, Tennessee, for rape and murder. He maintained his innocence. He received the usual poor defense representation and was sentenced to death. As his case was on appeal, a good defense lawyer took over at the federal level and discovered DNA evidence that indicated House was not the rapist. The state's theory was that the case was a rape/murder, so if he did not commit the rape, he did not commit the murder.

The appeal wound its way to the Sixth Circuit Court of Appeals, the federal appellate court with jurisdiction over Tennessee. In 2002, the Sixth Circuit was persuaded that a new trial was in order based on the DNA evidence which exonerated Paul. It sent the case back to the Tennessee Supreme Court to see if they would remedy the situation. The TSC refused to do so. So after procedural twists and turns, the case came back before the Sixth Circuit once again in 2004. The entire Sixth Circuit court heard the case. Four new Republican Bush appointees were on the Court. The case before them was the exact same case in terms of law and facts in which the court granted relief in 2002. This time, Paul House was denied relief. The recent Republican appointees opted to side with the prosecution side despite the evidence and the previous position of the court.

Paul House, stricken with multiple sclerosis while on death row and receiving no treatment for it, watched helplessly as his case moved on to the U.S. Supreme Court. The Supreme Court ruled in Paul's favor and issued a decision that said, in part, "any reasonable juror would have found Mr. House not guilty."

Paul's case was sent back to the federal district court and a hearing was held in Nashville to determine if he should be released from prison while awaiting a new trial. At this point, Paul was confined to a wheel chair as a result of the multiple sclerosis, and unable to walk.

The hearing before Judge Mattice found the State of Tennessee, represented by the Attorney General's office, arguing that Paul House was a flight risk and should not be released from prison. As I sat with his mother, Joyce, listening to the state's argument, I experienced the proceeding as completely surreal. A wheelchair-bound man, on death row for over twenty years for a crime he did not commit, was being told by the state of Tennessee he was a flight risk. The state would have Paul sit in prison until his new trial, without medical care, because he was liable to flee. I gazed at Paul in his wheelchair. I had seen this man deteriorate from a healthy, poker-loving guy to a helpless man. I had the feeling of being in cloud cuckoo land.

Finally, Judge Mattice leaned forward on the bench and asked the State: "How, Ms. Smith, might Mr. House be a flight risk?" Indeed, this was the question. He was innocent, he had a new trial, he was physically impaired and there was actually evidence pointing to the person who did kill the victim (not that the authorities in Union County had any interest in pursuing that line of inquiry when they had Paul House for a scapegoat).

Paul was allowed to go home to his mother's and await a new trial. The prosecutor in Union County decided not to try him again, and Paul House is a free man today, cared for by his mother.

***

The saying amongst defense lawyers representing death row clients in the Sixth Circuit Court of Appeals is that you know the result of your argument as soon as you know the composition of the panel. This was certainly true of Philip Workman.

Post-trial evidence produced the recantation of the only "eye witness" to Lt. Oliver's being shot. Forensic evidence also established it was not a bullet from Philip Workman's gun that killed Lt. Oliver. Despite a "colorable claim of innocence" which entitled him to a hearing in federal court, the Republican appointed judge, who was married to the prosecutor whose office manufactured the case against Workman, denied the request for a hearing. This sent him off to the thicket of the Sixth Circuit Court of Appeals.

Workman drew three Republicans on his panel. They would vote unanimously against him despite the exculpatory evidence. It was appealed to the entire Sixth Circuit, fourteen judges. Workman lost by a 7-7 vote.

Seven Republicans voted against him and seven Democratic appointees voted for relief. The tie vote meant that procedurally the case reverted to the panel decision which was 3-0 against him. Hence the seven to seven split vote was a "tie, you die" decision.

As Philip Workman's spiritual adviser, I have to restrain myself as I describe his case. Hence I am focusing only on the most egregious legal issues involving the federal courts. The complete story of this miscarriage of justice is in my prior book, *The Inferno: A Southern Morality Tale.*

In order to underscore the political dynamics of the Sixth Circuit Court of Appeals, consider an article that Dan Horn, a journalist for the *Cincinnati Enquirer*, wrote and published on April 15, 2007. It offers corroboration of the politics of the Sixth Circuit Court of Appeals: "*The Politics of Life and Death: An Inmate's Fate Often Hinges on Luck of the Draw.*"In reviewing death penalty cases decided by the Sixth Circuit Court of Appeals from 2000 until 2007, Horn discovered the following voting patterns: Republican appointees to the Court voted to deny appeals in death penalty cases 85 percent of the time and Democratic appointees voted to provide at least partial relief 75 percent of the time. As the title of the article indicated, the outcome of the cases depended not so much on matters of fact and law as on which political party appointees composed the majority of the panel hearing the capital appeal. (Although no formal study has been done since 2007, as of 2014 anecdotal instances indicate the voting rate is roughly the same.)

Philip Workman never received a Republican appointee's vote in federal court in twenty-five years of litigation. Even at his last appeal, based upon the flawed lethal injection protocol utilized in Tennessee, he was turned down 2–1. Two Republican appointees voted against him and the Democratic appointee voted for him. After his execution, the lethal injection case that Philip had brought was later heard in conjunction with another Tennessee death row case. Although he was already gone, he prevailed in federal district court.

It is easy to be mesmerized by cases, statistics and numbers when reviewing the death penalty record in the South. I included the stories Paul House and Philip Workman to bring home the point that the tyranny of the majority is not an abstract concept; it is one that disfranchises and kills citizens under the Disfranchisement Regime. It has taken a new shape and language after the Second Reconstruction but its intent is deadly clear just as it was after the initial Reconstruction.

Chapter 15. President Barack Obama and the Era of Disfranchisement

After eight years of Republican rule, the citizens of the United States elected a Democrat for president. Barack Obama, an African American, was elected in 2008 and then reelected in 2012. An examination of his record places him firmly in the Disfranchisement Era but his judicial appointments, the passage of the Affordable Care Act and the winding down of the wars in Afghanistan and Iraq prevent his administration from meeting my criteria for being categorized as a regime.

Perhaps the reader is thinking, "Wait a minute! How can an African American president be part of the Disfranchisement Era?" The answer is found in a statement made years ago by Gloria Steinem in response to a question about how excited she was to have a woman finally appointed to the U.S. Supreme Court: "It is not gender alone that is important but where she stands on the issues." So although there is understandable racial pride in having an African American president, the question is, how do his policies affect black and poor people? In particular, our concern is how Obama's policies utilizing the criminal justice system, as has been done post First and Second Reconstruction, impact those who were trying to be fully enfranchised through Reconstruction.

The War on Drugs provides a focus for analysis. It provided a systematic means of attack on the black community with the corresponding soaring incarceration rate. All of this occurred at a time when the crime rate was either stable or dropping. How would an African American president address this problem?

The answer is in the federal budget. Michelle Alexander, in *The New Jim Crow*, explains: "Obama has revived President Clinton's Community Oriented Policing Services (COPS) program and increased funding for the Byrne grant program—two of the worst federal Drug Programs of the Clinton era. These programs, despite their benign names, are responsible for the militarization of policing, SWAT teams, pipeline drug task forces and the laundry list of drug-war horrors described in chapter 2." Alexander concludes, "Obama, who is celebrated as evidence of America's triumph over race, is proposing nothing less than revving up the drug war through the same failed policies and programs that have systematically locked young men of color into a permanent undercaste."

Indeed, taking President Clinton as an example to follow, the president under whose watch more Americans were incarcerated than ever before, not to mention his appalling record on supporting the death penalty, puts President Obama in the ironic position of being the first African American president but one who helps perpetuate mass incarceration that creates a "permanent undercaste" of African Americans.

Perhaps it was awareness of this dynamic, or the shock of the Trayvon Martin trial with the acquittal of the man who shot an unarmed black teenager in July of 2013, which moved President Obama to some action. After the acquittal in the Martin trial in Florida, Obama stated, "there is a history of racial disparities in the application of our criminal laws, everything from the death penalty to enforcement of our drug laws." Previously, in 2010, President Obama had worked for the passage of the Fair Sentencing Act that reduced the disparity in sentencing between powder cocaine and crack cocaine. But his public remarks after the Trayvon Martin case were the first acknowledgement of "a history of racial disparities in the application of our criminal laws, everything from the death penalty to enforcement of our drug laws."

On August 12, 2013 the Attorney General of the United States, Eric Holder, gave a speech to the American Bar Association. The speech spoke of the need to reduce mass incarceration and other racial disparities in the criminal justice system. Clearly, his thoughts echoed those of his boss, President Obama.

Attorney General Holder instructed his federal prosecutors to recalculate how to pursue drug offenses. The point is to not charge low level drug offenders with crimes that would result in mandatory minimum sentences. This was part of his being "smart," rather than "tough," about crime pitch.

> As the so-called "war on drugs" enters its fifth decade, we need to ask whether it, and the approaches that comprise it, have been truly effective—and build on the Administration's efforts led by the Office of National Drug Policy, to usher in a new approach. And with an outsized, unnecessarily large prison population, we need to ensure that incarceration is used to punish, deter and rehabilitate—not merely to warehouse and forget.

It's clear, as we come together today—that too many Americans go to too many prisons for too long, and no truly good law enforcement reason . . . .widespread incarceration at the federal, state and local levels is both ineffective and unsustainable. It imposes a significant economic burden—totaling $80 billion in 2010 alone—and it comes with human and moral costs that are impossible to calculate.

Then Holder gets to the heart of the matter:

We must confront the reality that—once they're in the system— people of color often face harsher punishments than their peers. One deeply troubling report, released in February, indicates that—in recent years—black male offenders have received sentences nearly 20 percent longer than those imposed on white males convicted of similar offenses.

The speech is remarkable for an Attorney General in many ways and there has not been one with this tone and content from a high level governmental official since the War on Crime began in the 1960s. Yet what is striking is the unwillingness to name the beast and try to address it. Indeed, elsewhere in the speech he indicates more money for the COPS program which, as Michelle Alexander points out, is not the direction money needs to be going. Rather, we should acknowledge that illicit drugs are a medical problem and act accordingly: Treatment programs for drug addiction, legalize drugs, dismantle the huge infrastructure that currently exists that punishes drug users and move to a rehabilitative model. Now that would impact the high rate of incarceration with its disproportionate effect on black people.

Attorney General Holder gave his speech in San Francisco on August 12, 2013. On the same day on the east coast, in New York City, federal judge Shira Scheindlin issued a 195-page opinion finding that the New York City police policy of "stop and frisk" was unconstitutional.

Judge Scheindlin examined the aggressive "stop and frisk" effort and found it intimidated inner city communities, engaged in "indirect racial profiling" and was humiliating to thousands of innocent people. The case, *Floyd v. City of New York*, is a rebuke to the harassment by the New York City police of citizens which has grown dramatically in the last decade even as crime remained low. As the judge stated: "No one should live in fear of being stopped whenever he leaves his home to go about the activities of daily life."

The number of "stop and frisk" stops by New York police from January 2002 until June of 2012 was 4. 4 million. The people targeted were overwhelmingly black and Latino but were not criminals. They were ordinary citizens going about their business until some policeman intuited they were somehow a criminal suspect. One such signal was "furtive" behavior, a subjective and expansive category. Although Mayor Bloomberg and Police Commissioner Kelly repeatedly tried to rationalize this policy as an effective crime fighting tool there was no evidence to support it. As Judge Scheindlin found: " I also conclude that the city's highest officials have turned a blind eye to the evidence that officers are conducting stops in a racially discriminatory manner."

The Fourth Amendment to the U.S. Constitution prevents illegal search and seizure and was the legal branch Judge Scheindlin hung her decision upon. The problem is that the Fourth Amendment has been so weakened by a series of decisions by the U.S. Supreme Court, from the ascension of William Rehnquist as Chief Justice to the current Roberts court, it is quite possible five justices on that court will have no problem with citizen harassment and racial profiling. Indeed, as was seen with *McCleskey v. Kemp*, the Court seems to implicitly endorse discrimination in the criminal justice system. (Fortunately, with the election of Mayor De Blasio, a consent agreement was reached between the parties and Judge Scheindlin's order is being implemented.)

So, although August 12, 2013 was a noteworthy day in the Era of Disfranchisement, it is still the Era of Disfranchisement. The Attorney General and Judge have laid out the beginning of a reversal of the War on Crime which has animated the creation of the racial undercaste. But it is merely a beginning and we have yet to address the foundations of the invidious discrimination that has resulted in mass incarceration in the United States. It is an open question as to whether or not this country will entertain a discussion about racism and mass incarceration.

Another mechanism for remedying malfunctions in the criminal justice system is executive clemency. Of course, the argument of this work has been that the system is not malfunctioning but doing precisely what it was designed to do after the First and Second Reconstructions: Create a system of controlling black males to an extraordinary degree so that the gains of the two Reconstructions are halted and limited, if not reversed.

But for the sake of argument, let us accept the Attorney General and President at their word. They want to redress a system in which "there is a history of racial disparities in the application of our criminal laws, everything from the death penalty to drug laws ."(Obama) And from Eric Holder, the Attorney General: " . . . that too many Americans go to too many prison for too long with no truly good law enforcement reason."And "We must confront the reality that-once they are in the system- that people of color often face harsher punishment than their peers."

A Possible Administrative Response to the War on Drugs

Given the above description of reality, we should recall Jesus of Nazareth from his inaugural teaching in his home town. He quoted Isaiah, calling for us to "Proclaim liberty to the captives." (Luke 4:18–21, Isaiah 61:1–3). Indeed, as Jesus suggests, let's set some prisoners free. (This is never an easy thing to do. Just recall what happened to Jesus after he gave this proclamation in Luke.) Not only free some prisoners but thousands of them. For starters, since the Attorney General is providing new guidelines in prosecuting non-violent drug offenses, let's apply those same guidelines to people already sentenced. If they meet those guidelines, set them free with executive clemency. I would argue much more is needed because the reality of the incarceration rate is that it is so tied to race that we need a wholesale clemency for thousands of people in order to obtain a modicum of justice.

Unfortunately, executive clemency has become a relatively little used relic. It has reached a historical low under Obama. The original intent, to rectify errors in the system, has given way to pardons for covering up: from George H.W. Bush's pardoning of Caspar Weinberger in order to keep the cover-up of the Iran–Contra scandal intact—to Bill Clinton pardoning wealthy donors or people with connections to wealth. The original intent of making right a wrong done by the criminal justice system seems to have fallen by the wayside.

President Obama could take the bold and much needed step to translate his analysis of a racially discriminatory system into action by freeing victims of this invidious discrimination through executive clemency. Of course, Democrats have taken to being "tough" on crime, until Holder's reformulation of being "smart" not "tough" on crime, so the Republicans could not demonize them with the crime issue. (See George H.W. Bush's skewering of presidential rival Michael Dukakis with the Willie Horton ads.) Hence we get the callous but accurate statement from Bill Clinton after participating, Pontius-Pilate-like, in the execution of the black, mentally impaired Rickey Ray Rector. "They can nick me on the crime issue. But they won't be able to get me on it." Or President Obama's obligatory statements of support for a limited death penalty. Due to the fear of Republican attacks on anyone who advocates a reasonable position on crime or the death penalty issue, Democrats often seem to be in a rush to preempt the Republicans with the result of proclaiming support for the very programs that have created the racial undercaste. Thus the system just marches on unimpeded as it sucks up thousands of lives in its maw on an annual basis.

Section III. The U.S. Supreme Court

If the executive branch indicated through President Obama and Attorney General Eric Holder that this branch of government was beginning to grasp the disfranchisement that characterized the criminal justice system, the Supreme Court showed no such inclination. The end of its term in

June of 2013 found the Court playing the role it starred in after the First Reconstruction: Disfranchising the gains of Reconstruction, this time the Second Reconstruction.

The two cases involved affirmative action and voting rights. In *Fisher v. the University of Texas*, the Court sent the case back to the Fifth Circuit Court of Appeals for "strict scrutiny." This left affirmative action hanging by a thread which will most certainly be cut by the Fifth Circuit Court of Appeals. The end of affirmative action in higher education is nigh.

The second case was the Voting Rights Act of 1965. The Supreme Court gutted the Voting Rights Act in this decision—*Shelby v. Holder*, and the irony of such action taking place on the fifty year anniversary of Martin Luther King's "I Have a Dream" speech was chilling. (It was also the 50th anniversary of the Birmingham bombings of the 16th Avenue Baptist Church that killed four African American children going to Sunday School.) This decision reveals the dynamics of the Court in a way that allows us to see the determination to undo the gains of the Second Reconstruction.

Chief Justice John Roberts wrote for the majority in the 5–4 opinion. "Our country has changed. While any racial discrimination is too much, Congress must ensure that the legislation it passes to remedy that problem speaks to current conditions." The Chief Justice referred to the data Congress relied upon in its most recent reauthorizing of the Voting Rights Act. The study was the same used in the prior reauthorization of the Act. He also thought the Voting Rights Act could be passed in an updated form by Congress once again.

These two reasons are disingenuousness at best. In the South voter photo I.D.s are required, gerrymandering has occurred, as well as other obstacles to limit minority voting. The Chief Justice really thinks things have "changed" when state governments are doing all in their power to limit minority ballot access? And the thought that Congress would pass another Voting Rights Act when the House of Representatives is controlled by Republicans who have no interest in such an effort is a mere throwaway line to obscure the reality of what this decision permits.

In her dissent, read from the bench to demonstrate her strong objections to the majority opinion, Justice Ruth Bader Ginsberg comes to the heart of the matter: "The great man who led the march from Selma to Montgomery and there called for the passage of the Voting Rights Act, foresaw progress, even in Alabama. 'The arc of the moral universe is long,' he said, but 'it bends toward justice,' if there is a steadfast commitment to see the task through to completion."

Justice Ginsberg stated that Congress was the appropriate body to decide whether the law was needed and she noted it was reauthorized by a unanimous vote in the Senate and a 390 to 33 vote in the House in 2006.

"Beyond question, the V.R.A. is no ordinary legislation. It is extraordinary because Congress embarked on a mission long delayed and of extraordinary importance: to realize the purpose and promise of the Fourteenth Amendment . . . For half a century a concerted effort has been made to end racial discrimination in voting. Thanks to the Voting Rights Act, progress once the subject of a dream has been achieved and continues to be made. The court errs egregiously by overriding Congress's decision."

"The nation's commitment to justice has been disserviced by today's decision," Ginsberg wrote. The current focus of the V.R.A. was now on racial gerrymandering and laws requiring at large voting in places with a sizable black minority. The law had developed from simple access to these appropriate safeguards. From "first generation" barriers to ballot access to "second generation barriers." The law was effective in preventing such efforts and that's why those nine states and scores of counties and municipalities still needed to seek clearance before changing their voting laws.

It was because the law was effective that it was struck down by the majority. Even Chief Justice Roberts had to acknowledge that "any racial discrimination was too much." He was just unwilling to do anything about it. After all, we are speaking of a Republican dominated white South and he would not want that reality to change by enfranchising black people.

A Dream Deferred

We conclude our look at the national dilemma of race with a consideration of the economy. Thomas Edsall (August 19, 2014, *The New York Times*) delineates the economic effect on race that has taken place under the tyranny of the majority. He notes that with the passage of the Voting Rights Act in 1965 and the Civil Rights Act of 1964, launched thirty years of economic improvement for black Americans:

> The percentage of blacks over the age 25 with a high school degree more than tripled, going from just under 20 percent, or less than half the white rate, to more than 79 percent, nearly matching the white rate. The percentage of blacks over 25 with a college degree quadrupled from 3 to 12 percent over the same period.

He then discusses median household income:

> [It] grew, in inflation-adjusted dollars, from $22,974 in 1967 to $30,439, a 32.5 percent increase, more than double the 14.2 percent increase for whites. Although black household income remained well below white levels in 2000—66.3 percent of the white median—it was

significantly better than it had been in 1967, when it was 57.1 percent of white median income.

Clearly, the impact of fully enfranchising blacks legislatively through the Second Reconstruction had a profound impact economically. Yet the white backlash began to be felt and things deteriorated once again, just as had happened after the First Reconstruction.

> While the economic downturns of the last decade-and-a-half have taken their toll on the median income of all races and ethnic groups, blacks have been the hardest hit. By 2012, black median household income had fallen to 58.3 percent of white income, almost back to where it was in 1967—7.9 points below its level in 1999.

Edsall continues:

> [F]rom 1965 to 2000, the poverty rate among blacks fell from 41.8 percent to 22.5 percent. Since then, it has risen to 27.2 percent. The white poverty rate also rose during this period, but by a more modest 3.2 points.

So, yes, Chief Justice Roberts, "things have changed." But the more they've changed, the more they stay the same under the tyranny of the racial majority as it functions in the Disfranchisement Era.

Section IV. The State of North Carolina

Finally, we turn to my native state of North Carolina for an analysis of what happens when the state is ceded the protection of the minority by the federal government. As we have noted after the First and Second Reconstructions when such retrenchment has taken place, blacks are the victims of whatever the state governments in the South decide to do. And as we say in the South, this means folks "just ain't whistling Dixie." Indeed, they're doing all they can to restore Dixie.

There was an historical election for Governor in North Carolina in 1960. Terry Sanford bested I. Beverly Lake, an arch conservative supported by Jesse Helms, and was chosen governor. Sanford launched major education improvement, established the North Carolina Fund in conjunction with foundations to address the poverty issue and generally moved North Carolina into a progressive position for a Southern state. The forces of reaction, always present and prominent, were held at bay. (In the 1960s, North Carolina had more KKK klaverns than the state of Alabama.)

As the century progressed and the new millennium was entered, the North Carolina Democratic Party saw many of its members flee to the Republican Party, as happened throughout the South. Although North Carolina voted for Barack Obama for President in 2008, by the time of the 2012 elections the Republicans had organized and launched a state wide attack. It was a success and a super majority of Republicans was elected in the legislature and a Republican governor was chosen. The revanchement of the Second Reconstruction was at hand on the state level. Although there are other examples that illustrate this retrenchment, we focus on the death penalty and voting rights.

As we have seen with *McCleskey v. Kemp*, despite uncontroverted proof of racial discrimination in the administration of the death penalty, the U.S. Supreme Court let it stand. However, in the wake of the *McCleskey* decision citizens in North Carolina determined to pass a Racial Justice Act in the legislature which would provide the protection such a study warranted. An initial study was completed that revealed the existence of discrimination and the effort began in the legislature to pass the Racial Justice Act. After years of work, the Racial Justice Act passed the legislature and was signed into law in 2009. This made North Carolina the only state in the South with such protection against racial discrimination in the administration of the death penalty and one of two states in nation to provide such protection.

The case of Marcus Raymond Robinson was the first case to be heard under the Racial Justice Act. On April 20, 2012, Judge Greg Weeks, the Senior Judge of Superior Court in Cumberland County, ruled a pattern of discrimination had occurred in the case against Robinson … "race was a materially, practically and statistically significant decision to exercise preemptory challenges during jury selection by prosecutors." The disparity was significant enough "as to support an inference of intentional discrimination." The research in this case revealed prosecutors peremptorily struck 50 percent of blacks eligible for the jury pool but only 14.8 percent of others.

Judge Weeks went on to note that this discrimination was not limited to this one case or Cumberland County (Fayetteville). A study conducted by the Michigan State College of Law professors Catherine Grosso and Barbara O'Brien revealed a pattern of discrimination by prosecutors across the state. The study covered cases from 1990–2010. Although such practices have been a reality since the reinstitution of the death penalty in 1976, not only in North Carolina but across the South, this was the first opportunity to obtain relief for a condemned prisoner under the Racial Justice Act. Subsequently to the *Robinson* case, Judge Weeks also granted relief to three other death sentenced prisoners after documenting prosecutorial discrimination in those cases as well. There are 150 cases filed under the Racial Justice Act in North Carolina. The North Carolina Supreme Court is deciding whether or not to uphold the Racial Justice Act.

The legislative response to the Racial Justice Act has been predictable. The initial effort came at the behest of prosecutors (nationally, 98 percent of lead prosecutors are white) and a repeal of the RJA was passed by the legislature. Governor Beverly Perdue vetoed it in 2011. In 2012 the repeal effort was renewed and a modified version of the act was introduced. This bill prohibited the use of statistics beyond the county involved in the case. Governor Perdue vetoed it again, but the legislature had the votes to override the veto. With the Republican super majority elected to the General Assembly in 2012, the attack on the RJA commenced again in 2013. Not satisfied with the modifications of the bill in the last legislative session, this effort would eliminate the RJA completely. The bill passed the General Assembly and the newly elected Republican Governor Pat McCrory signed it into law in the summer of 2013.

The scene shifted in the fall of 2013 to the North Carolina Supreme Court. The case is *North Carolina v. Robinson*, and the state of North Carolina challenged the Act as it was originally constituted in 2009. The state argued that Robinson, and others, should be deprived of the benefit of the legislation passed in good faith to prevent racial discrimination in capital trials. The state is not content that the Racial Justice Act has no future, since its repeal in 2013. Indeed, the state wishes to stomp out its short previous life as illegal and beyond the province of the legislature to grant. This would prevent those on death row now, who have already filed under the Racial Justice Act, from receiving relief if discrimination is discovered to have existed in their cases. If the North Carolina Supreme Court rules for the state, North Carolina's brief experiment with providing racial justice in death penalty cases would be rendered moot.

The Racial Justice Act reveals how difficult it is to obtain justice for minorities when the racial tyranny of the majority is in place. It is nothing short of astonishing that the North Carolina legislature became the only one in the South to enact this legislation. It is a major civil rights issue in an area left unaddressed by the Civil Rights Movement. And the response to it by the white majority has been vociferous and ultimately fatal for its short life. Now it rests with the North Carolina Supreme Court and one must recall that these judges are elected and subject to the whims of the white majority at the voting booth. Such a prospect does not augur well for the prospects of justice for the condemned in North Carolina.

As Chief Justice John Roberts suggested when he eviscerated the Voting Rights Act in June of 2013, send it back to the legislature because "we have changed." As if the Racial Justice Act is not example enough of what happens when relief for minorities is sought through a Southern legislature, let us turn to the North Carolina response to the Voting Rights Act that Chief Justice Roberts invited.

The North Carolina legislature and Governor McCrory have enacted one of the most draconian restrictions of voting rights in the country in the aftermath of Chief Justice John Roberts majority opinion in *Shelby v. Holder*. Before detailing the provisions of this act, a few facts are in order: 1. 23 percent of voters in the last election in N.C. were African-Americans 2. 30 percent of African Americans cast out of precinct ballots 3. 34 percent of African American voters are without state issued photo identification 4. 41 percent of African American voters registered on the same day they voted 5. 70 percent of African Americans voted early.

The foregoing facts provide a context for the numerous restrictions in the newly enacted Voting Rights law in North Carolina. The restrictive provisions are as follows:

- Each voter must have a state-issued photo ID.
- Early voting period shortened.
- Same-day registration on the day of voting eliminated.
- Pre-registration of 16- and 17-year-olds eliminated.
- Paid voter registration drives prohibited.
- Straight ticket voting eliminated.
- Provisional voting eliminated if voter shows up in the wrong precinct.
- Counties prohibited from extending voting times beyond one hour due to extraordinary circumstances, i.e. lengthy voting lines.
- Allowing registered voters to contest the eligibility of voters beyond the precinct in which the voter votes.
- Increase amount allowed in campaign contributions from $4,000 to $5,000.
- Lessen disclosure regulations in campaign ads paid for independent committees.
- Repeal the publicly funded election program for appellate judges.
- Repeal the requirement that candidates endorse ads run by their campaigns.

The scope of this attempt to disfranchise voters is remarkable but not surprising. Indeed, it is what Alexis de Tocqueville warned of in *Democracy in America* as he contemplated the relationship between the judiciary and the legislature:

> Tyranny may be exercised by the law itself . . . in the United States the omnipotence of the majority, which is favorable to the legal despotism of the legislature, likewise favors the arbitrary authority of the magistrate. The majority has absolute power to make the laws and to watch over their execution . . . (*Democracy in America*, volume I, XV, The Unlimited Power of The Majority in the United States and its Consequences).

As our examination of the state of North Carolina reveals, as well as considering other states and the federal government in this work, the racial tyranny of the majority that Tocqueville warned against is still at work in our midst. The astonishing incarceration rate in the United States that leads the world and how it has been achieved by manipulating the criminal justice system to incarcerate blacks disproportionately after the First and Second Reconstructions, the uncontroverted evidence of racial discrimination in the administration of the death penalty, the recent revanchement on voting rights, all of this and how it came about has been the subject of this work.

It leads to the conclusion that we have despotism in this country and it is not limited to the "legislative despotism" Thomas Jefferson cautioned against. Rather, until the citizens of this country fully grasp the manifestation of the tyranny of the majority in all three branches of government with its resultant oppression, the United States will remain in the hypocritical position of proclaiming concern for human rights abroad while systematically depriving the political and human rights of its own minority citizens. It leads one to the conclusion that Thomas Jefferson reached some two hundred years ago: "I tremble for my country when I reflect that God is just."

12. Joe Ingle leaving home to visit death row at R.M.S.I. Photo by Gigi Cohen.

INDEX